'Always take notes! Notebooks, diaries, fill them to the brim as you go. Jot down things that you think aren't important at the time, because it will help you in the future. Good writing lives or dies on context, in colour. What did someone say? What were they wearing? What was for dinner? It might not seem important at the time, but it can all help.' • *'Pretty much every time I write a novel, I fail about 50 pages in.'* • 'My advice is to get some form of speciality. It can be anything - anything you're interested in. Once you start, once you've got going, the stories will lead one to another, it becomes very organic, but you need somewhere to start.' • *'It's kind of like being an explorer. What you're doing is, you are casting yourself out to sea. You don't know where you're going to go, and you don't know how you're going to get there, but you know, eventually, you will reach land - you will find some sort of Galapagos of the imagination.'* • 'Don't let the quality of your wordsmithery obscure the true aim of writing - which is to say something.' • *'Do proper research. Spend as much time as [possible] researching. Fight off everybody who wants you to start. Don't start until you're ready.'* • 'Don't worry if it's no good. Just keep going.'

ALWAYS
take
NOTES

Advice from some of the world's greatest writers

Edited by
Simon Akam *and* **Rachel Lloyd**

ITHAKA

First published in the UK by Ithaka Press
An imprint of Black & White Publishing Group
A Bonnier Books UK company
4th Floor, Victoria House,
Bloomsbury Square,
London, WC1B 4DA

Owned by Bonnier Books
Sveavägen 56, Stockholm, Sweden

Hardback – 978-1-80418-318-2
Ebook – 978-1-80418-319-9

A CIP catalogue of this book is available from the British Library.

Typeset by IDSUK (Data Connection) Ltd
Printed and bound by Clays Ltd, Elcograf S.p.A

3 5 7 9 10 8 6 4 2

Every reasonable effort has been made to trace copyright holders of material
reproduced in this book, but if any have been inadvertently overlooked
the publishers would be glad to hear from them.

Ithaka Press is an imprint of Bonnier Books UK
www.bonnierbooks.co.uk

For Hyun
–Simon

For James, and my parents
–Rachel

CONTENTS

INTRODUCTION

'There is only one thing you should do. Go into yourself.
Find out the reason that commands you to write; see whether
it has spread its root into the very depths of your heart.'
                                        – Rainer Maria Rilke

Can anyone teach you how to write? Many would say no. True
art must come from within. When asked for advice by a teenage
fan, the celebrated poet Rainer Maria Rilke somewhat unhelp-
fully replied: 'Nobody can advise you and help you, nobody.
There is only one way. Go into yourself.' Happily, Rilke went
on to contradict himself by writing ten further letters of advice
to his admirer, offering instructions on how he might produce
great work. The resulting book, *Letters to a Young Poet*, has
inspired hundreds, if not thousands, of wordsmiths since publication in 1929.

   Nearly one hundred years later, the world is still full of people
who yearn to write and who are hungry for advice on how to do
so. However, today the odds of getting one of your literary heroes
to send you a letter full of handy tips have significantly lessened.
That's where we come in. For the last six years the *Always Take
Notes* podcast (@takenotesalways) has peered – usually politely,

but often rather nosily – into the lives and working habits of some of the world's most renowned writers. During more than 150 candid conversations, we have asked a wide range of authors about every aspect of how they do what they do. This book is a distillation of what we've learned.

Who are we? We're both working writers, but just as importantly, we are voracious readers with tastes that span fiction, history, screenwriting, investigative journalism, and many other genres. Simon (@simonakam) is a magazine journalist and author. He wrote *The Changing of the Guard*, a book about the evolution of the British Army since 9/11, and contributes to a range of publications in the US and the UK, including *The Economist*, the *New Yorker*, the *London Review of Books*, GQ, *The Guardian*, *Outside* and *Bloomberg Businessweek*. He's written about everything from warlords in West Africa to the weaponisation of musical nostalgia by easy listening radio and the gruelling process of becoming a French mountain guide.

Rachel (@rachelsllloyd) is the deputy culture editor at *The Economist*. There she commissions stories on film, television, music, literature, games, art, architecture, comedy and dance, as well as writing widely herself. She's examined feminist revenge drama in the age of #MeToo, probed the popularity of bedtime stories for adults and investigated how *The Crown* will shape Queen Elizabeth II's legacy. In 2021 Rachel was nominated a young journalist of the year by the Society of Editors.

Interviewing these authors has been an extraordinary experience for us. We've had a privileged insight into how other people have developed their craft and their careers, and sometimes even the chance to visit guests' homes (on one memorable occasion, a houseboat), microphones in hand. We've amassed a huge archive of frank advice and hard-won wisdom from some of the world's leading literary figures. It's guided and inspired us, and now we hope that it can do the same for you.

Simon Akam and Rachel Lloyd
Hosts, *Always Take Notes*

1

EARLY INFLUENCES

'From a very early age, perhaps the age of five or six, I knew that when I grew up I should be a writer. Between the ages of about seventeen and twenty-four I tried to abandon this idea, but I did so with the consciousness that I was outraging my true nature and that sooner or later I should have to settle down and write books.'

– George Orwell

In 'Why I Write', an essay from 1946, George Orwell traces the origins of his calling. After launching his literary career at age five by dictating a rip-off of William Blake's 'The Tyger' to his mother, he went on to try his hand at short stories and plays, as well as penning articles for the school magazine. He mentions all this, he says, because it is tricky to 'assess a writer's motives without knowing something of his early development'.

We agree. We ask almost every interviewee about when they were first drawn to storytelling and the answers are fascinating. Their influences are wide-ranging, spanning the full spectrum from comic books to classics. Many writers can recall partic-ular works that shaped their sensibilities – stories that acted as turning-points in their lives, or books that provoked light-bulb moments.

Many were around the same age as Orwell when they discovered the joys of reading and completed their own narrative experiments. Howard Jacobson had a poster of George Eliot on his bedroom wall as a youngster. Alexander McCall Smith submitted his first manuscript to a publisher at the age of eight (he's sent off over 100 more since then). With the benefit of hindsight, they seem destined to have become novelists.

Orwell's essay resonates with interviewees' experiences in other ways, too. 'I had the lonely child's habit of making up stories and holding conversations with imaginary persons,' he wrote, 'and I think from the very start my literary ambitions were mixed up with the feeling of being isolated and undervalued.' Tracy Chevalier, Louise Doughty and Ruth Ozeki also describe the succour and escapism that books provided in solitary forma-tive years.

For many interviewees, however, the bug bit only later on. Some alighted on writing after a chance encounter with a film or book. Others enjoyed penning short stories, poems or lyrics as a pastime, but did not consider it a career. Still others needed to find the right mode – journalism, perhaps, or a particular genre – to take up their place in the world of letters. These stories are a reminder that you do not need to have been a child prodigy, or to have published your first book at a young age, in order to become a writer. Some of our interviewees, quoted later in the book, only put pen to page in their 40s and went on to produce prizewinning work. It's never too late to get started.

Alexander McCall Smith, novelist

I probably always wanted to be a writer. I remember, as many people remember, writing when I was a child. I loved doing that and I wrote quite a lot when I was a little boy – I sent my first manuscript off to a publisher when I was eight. I wrote a story – I remember the title – it was called 'He's Gone'. Obviously tremendously melodramatic. It must have been just a page or two, and I sent it off to a publisher and the publisher, believe it or not, wrote back, which was really, really kind and said unfortunately they wouldn't be able to publish my book. I remember nothing about that manuscript. I don't remember who he was, where he went or why he went, but he did go.

Tracy Chevalier, novelist

The public library was near my school; it was within walking distance. (In those days kids could walk, age six, on [their] own, to the library and back, 15 minutes away.) I would go and get a stack of books. Mrs Carney would ask me: 'Tracy, so did you read *The Witch of Blackbird Pond*?' Or whatever it was she had given me the week before. 'What did you think?' And I would say, 'Oh, I like this bit. I really didn't like this bit.' We'd have a long discussion about the book and then she'd say, 'I've got something special for you. I think you're ready for this. I think you're grown-up enough.' She'd hand me another book, and I would read that, and then we'd discuss it. It was like a mini book club.

I was a bookish child. My mother got sick when I was three, and she died when I was eight. I spent a lot of time having to be quiet so that she could sleep, and I was a bit of a loner. My aunt said once that I said, 'I am never lonely when I'm in a book.' I think I used them as a form of escape, and they became an integral part of my life. In a way that, like, brushing your teeth is – you couldn't imagine going to bed without brushing your teeth, I can't imagine going to bed without reading. I couldn't imagine not having a book on the go. I'm always reading at least one.

I used to say that, when I grew up, I wanted to be either a writer or a librarian, because libraries were where I got my books from. I just thought it'd be great to be involved in them.

Howard Jacobson, novelist

I can't remember wanting to do anything else. I'm sure I lied when I said I had George Eliot on my wall aged four, but I had her on my bedroom wall at an age when people thought it was a very peculiar thing to be doing, and I should have had a footballer or a pop star or something.

I was an unhappy, soft, sulky child. The only nice part that I recall was just making words. This is all distorted memory – that comes from telling tales so often that you now don't know whether what you're remembering is what happened, or the last time you told the tale. But I remember the first time I shaped a sentence or told a joke that made my mother and her friends laugh, and I thought, 'This is good. This is a way into the heart of women, in particular, but grown-ups. I hope this is a good thing. And it looks like I can do that. I can make a sentence.'

Thereafter, there was no other thing. I saw no advantage in being able to kick a ball around or do any of those things. I just wanted to make sentences.

Louise Doughty, novelist

I would lie to my mum: I would say that I was going to play with the other kids on the estate and I would put a book – normally one of the *Narnia* books, or an Ursula Le Guin book, in the pocket of my anorak – and I would go and build a den and I would read.

I was quite a strange and lonely child, really, for reasons that are not entirely clear to me. Reading and making up stories formed a huge part of my childhood. I decided when I was 11 that I was going to write my first novel. My father used to watch a lot of those old black-and-white John Wayne movies, the really early ones, on Saturday afternoons, and [the novel] was also influenced by *Watership Down*, which was the big children's hit of its day. In fact a lot of adults read it, too.

So I wrote this novel, which was about horses, laughing, living and loving on the plains of the Midwest – which, seeing as I was terrified of animals and had never left the East Midlands, was a slightly odd choice. They talked; I believe they also wore hats. I took myself very seriously. I decided that I wanted it to be a hardback, so I made cardboard covers for my book. I still have it somewhere, tucked away. I should dig it out, really, and give everybody a good laugh.

Ruth Ozeki, novelist

I was a bookish kid. I was an only child. My parents were both professors, they were both scholars, and it was a very quiet house-hold. Each of us were in our own bookish solitudes. Books were my friends and, since I didn't have siblings, and I didn't have parents who would play with me, these were my companions.

I think I started out reading children's books. I remember, in particular, books like *The Once and Future King* or the *Narnia* series or Tolkien. *Charlotte's Web* – I remember that so clearly – and I reread that recently. Suddenly, rereading it, I realised that we think that's a book about a little girl who saves the life of a pig, who then makes friends with a spider. Right? But what I didn't realise until I reread it, is that the spider, Charlotte, is a writer. She's the one who saves the pig's life by writing words in her web. I think that was a theme: many of the books that I loved were about writers and, particularly, little girls who are writers – *Harriet the Spy*, that kind of thing.

Then, too, I think I was a fairly promiscuous reader. I remember in elementary school I was reading – and my friends were reading – Philip Roth and Norman Mailer and these tough-guy writers. Who knows what I was actually getting from those books at the age of 11 and 12? But I do remember reading them and feeling incredibly cool and really mature.

Patrick Kingsley, journalist and author

I remember when I was about six or seven, I was asking my mum all the time what the differences between all of the newspapers were. One day, she bought all the newspapers – or five or six – and we made a spreadsheet. I had to work out what the differences between all the newspapers were: right-wing, left-wing, tabloid, broadsheet. Even as a child, I was fascinated by journalism.

Rebecca Mead, journalist and author

My first published piece of writing was when I was a child, in *The Observer* magazine. The back pages of the magazine were for kids, and they had a thing that they did called the Young Reporters club – which you could join. They would send you a little badge, like a little press pass, that said Young Reporters club, and there were these assignments where the magazine would tell you to go interview this kind of person or that kind of person. The very first one of those I did was a profile of my teacher in the final year of primary school, so I was 11. Mr Arnold, I wrote a piece about him, and it was published, and I got paid £10. That was my first taste of the minor art of writing words on deadlines.

James Graham, playwright and screenwriter

For me, it was television drama that really had a huge impact. Growing up, I didn't really have much theatre apart from the local panto every Christmas and school plays. I remember there was a period of really incredible, often quite northern, working-class dramas in the 1990s, particularly from the output of Granada TV studios in Manchester – things like *Cracker* and *Prime Suspect* and *Band of Gold*. Jimmy McGovern, Sally Wainwright, Paul Abbott, Alan Bleasdale, Russell T. Davies and Steven Moffat: it just felt like dramas that were politically aware, that came from a socio-cultural movement, and could capture a community that I recognised as being my own.

So I would stay up far too late when I was eight, nine, ten years old with my mum watching adult dramas after nine o'clock. They absolutely captivated me. I was quite a private kid. I wasn't shy, but I preferred my own company, and I would sit in my room, writing prose, mainly – not scripted prose – and short stories, probably thinking maybe of being a novelist. But certainly the word 'playwright' I'd never contemplated or heard.

I'd never met anyone who would call themselves a writer. My mum bought me a typewriter when I was five years old. I wish I could say it was a *Billy Elliot* story where they tutted at me and rolled their eyes and wanted to send me down the mine, but actually, they were very encouraging. They were happy to read my bad short stories and let me go off and do school plays and things like that.

I had a really good drama teacher who encouraged shy kids like me, but also cool kids on the football team, to come and do plays. I immediately loved both the process of building a show with a group of people over a matter of weeks and then – without getting romantic and sentimental and clichéd – the electricity that happens in a live space, where you're sharing something in the moment with a community of people, which you don't get on screen. I completely fell in love with it.

My school, a comprehensive school in Nottingham, created A-Level drama for a group of people who wanted to carry on with that work. From that, I went to university and then started writing plays there and taking them to the Edinburgh Festival.

Ian McEwan, novelist

We were in Tripoli, Libya, at the time. The local library was an army library. My parents had left school at 14, they were never read to, so they did not read to me, nor did they have any idea of the prescribed children's classics – *The Railway Children* or *The Hobbit* or whatever. So when we went to the library, I was left to my own devices; there was no one to recommend books to me. I worked my way through the shelves and read indiscriminately.

When I got to my boarding school there were, at last, some people to tell me what I might read and I became a very early reader of [William] Golding, Iris Murdoch. I read *Under the Net* – I must have been about 13 – and I thought, 'I just cannot wait to be a grown-up.' I mean, just the life, the world that Iris Murdoch described, to me, seemed so enticing and exotic, sexually exotic, and rather brilliant. Everyone had names I'd never heard of – Caitlyn – this sort of North Oxford-ish world just really, really appealed to me. In fact, many years later, I ended up living in North Oxford for 17 years, maybe haunted by these Iris Murdoch characters.

My parents valued the education they didn't have them-selves. I was lucky in that respect. I was free in some ways: I didn't have anyone breathing down my neck. I remember when I was at university – I wrote about this in *Black Dogs* actually – making good friends with people from much more culturally laden and privileged homes, which they couldn't wait to get away from. Their houses were packed with harpsichords and books floor-to-ceiling. I know one or two of those friends couldn't wait to become rough-hewn tough guys who had tastes for Lambrettas. I [was] rather tempted to run into the base that they had deserted. I was very pleased when their parents invited me in to come and talk about literature and listen to their mum play a harpsichord.

That was my teenage rebellion, I'm afraid. It was very pathetic, in a way. I didn't do outrageous things, I just discovered all the things that I didn't have at home, in a big way: poetry, especially, classical music, jazz and rock and roll all came at me at once. My proper teenage rebellion was mainstream culture – Bach delighted me almost from the very start and that's remained all my life.

I did have that experience that many, many British writers have written about – of feeling very alienated from my home, by the time I was 18 or 19. I think I was insufferable at that point. I felt that anyone who couldn't recite 'The Waste Land' [by T.S. Eliot] wasn't really worth taking seriously. It was a terrible state of mind to be in. Thank god it didn't last very long.

Robert Douglas-Fairhurst, academic and author

The fact that I'm interested in Dickens is partly chance and partly town planning. The town-planning bit is Dickens Drive [on which one of his childhood homes was situated]. Pickwick Close was around the corner, Copperfield Way was also round the corner. So in some ways, it was fate. It was destiny that I would end up writing about Dickens.

Another reason why perhaps I became interested in Dickens is I won a prize [at school] and had the chance to spend £50 in a bookshop. I went to a bookshop that had lots of second-hand books, and pride of place was a metre of shiny Dickens in fake-leather binding, which was £50. I thought, 'Well, that's a nice way of taking up a metre of shelf space.' So I bought it and then ignored it for about the next six months. Then I was encouraged to read something at college, so I started reading some Dickens. Then one book led to another, which led to another, which led to another and it was like literary dominoes in the end.

Hollie McNish, poet

I reckon from about 12, I wrote quite a lot of poems. I just loved them. When I was at uni, my mum found a poem that I'd written aged seven, but I think a lot of kids write poems when they're little. It was a poem about how much I hated my family – so it wasn't the best one for her to find – it was very angry about not being allowed a cat, and I rhymed quite a lot of rude words with 'cat' to slag off my family. So my mum sent it to me at uni and said: 'Oh, this is nice.' I loved it. I found it really freeing compared to writing prose.

Toby Young, journalist and author

I remember being at my mother's book party (my mother wrote a couple of novels). When I was a teenager, I think she had the party for her second novel. There were various journalists there – she knew various journalists, and she also worked as a journalist herself – I remember one of the journalists there telling me that it was better than working for a living. I had this vision, I think, of being able to stand on a soapbox, as my mother had just done, and speak and have people listen. As a precocious, attention-seeking teenager, that was very attractive in its own right, but the idea of getting paid for doing that seemed very appealing.

I liked the company of journalists and I liked the fact that they seemed slightly unrespectable and had a kind of 'honour amongst thieves' spirit: ne'er-do-wells all hanging out together, throwing stones at the windows of more respectable people. All that very much appealed to me as a teenager. So I decided, I think, around then – when I was 14, 15 – that, if possible, I'd like to be a journalist.

Ferdinand Addis, historian

As quite a young teenager, I was a classics nerd, I think it's fair to say. I remember, over one summer holiday, reading the whole of Livy, which is a frightful thing to do, really (not in Latin, that would have been really unforgivable). It's a long book – it's not typically what you read on the beach.

For me, it had the appeal of fantasy, almost – it was like reading Tolkien, for example. A new world of heroes, myths, stories, that also counted as history. It had the additional frisson of being purportedly true. It was, of course, a lot less true than I thought at the time.

Mark Haddon, novelist

The writing took a long time to come – that desire to write. What I always felt, from very early on, was the need to find something bigger, something different, some kind of hole through which I could escape. I remember that very vividly. It was science which provided that first of all. I read almost no fiction as a child and had no real interest in it. But I wolfed down books about science. I had a book, which I still possess even now, which is a kind of talismanic text for me, called *Origins of the Universe* by Albert

Hinkelbein. I'm so attached that it actually has a minor role in *The Curious Incident of the Dog in the Night-Time*. In fact, the physical book actually appears on stage.

And in that book – alongside many scientific facts which are now untrue because it's so old – was a little Renaissance woodcut. It's of a man who had walked away from a little Alpine town, with the sun above it, and he had reached the edge of a field. He'd butted up against the very lowest of the celestial spheres – he's poked his head through a hole in the lowest celestial sphere. He can see the fire and the cloud and the wheels all behind it. I always thought that was me. I was always trying to get far away from this little town, find the celestial sphere and stick my head through it and see what was actually happening on the other side. Science provided me with that sense of escape and insight, a mixture of answers to problems which were bugging me, but also a sense of bigger problems and greater mysteries, which drew me on.

It wasn't until I was, I think, 14 or 15, that we were first given poetry to read at school – I think for my O-Level in English (as it was). I have a very vivid memory of being given two books: one was the selected poetry of R.S. Thomas, and the other one was a very ghoulish anthology called *Conflict and Compassion*. It was designed to put children in therapy for many years afterwards. It was a selection of poems, separated into sections, which dealt with horrific road accidents, the shallowness of the modern financial society, racism, illness, mental illness and mental handicap, and nuclear war. Some of the poems were profoundly upsetting.

I think it was Edwin Muir's 'The Horses' which, like the opening poem in the R.S. Thomas, which is called 'A Peasant', lit up something inside my head, which hadn't been lit up before.

I think, quite literally on that afternoon, my life started to change. I realised that something I'd been looking for in science was more easily accessible by literature.

Hadley Freeman, journalist and author

I was at university and I was working for the student paper and my mum came across an advert in the *Daily Telegraph* for young female journalists under 30. Because I'm an American kid, I would send my mother everything I did at university and she sent off two interviews I did. One was with Richard Whiteley, the late presenter of *Countdown*, and one was with Ian Hislop, the editor of *Private Eye*, and she sent them off. I didn't know anything about this.

A couple of weeks later, I got this call and someone at the *Daily Telegraph* is telling me to come down to London for a prize thing. I said, 'I'm sorry, I'm doing my finals. I don't know what this is about' – and hung up. My mum went off and got up and accepted my prize for me from Lord and Lady Longford, who I think were a bit bemused by this 50-year-old woman who had apparently just won this writing prize for 25-year-olds.

I was doing my finals and I was one of the first people to have a mobile phone, because my parents are very protective and they always wanted to be able to get hold of me. I walked out of my finals in June 1999 and my phone rang, and I answered. I said, 'Hello?' – it was only ever my parents – and they said, 'Hi, this is Ian Katz from *The Guardian* newspaper, can you come in for an interview?' I thought, 'Wow, this is easy! You just leave finals and you get a job interview? Wow! Everyone told me this would be hard!' Like an idiot, I didn't realise for ages what had happened – that my mother had won this prize for me. So that was the stupid story of how I got my job.

Ed Caesar, journalist and author

I'd written a lot. I wanted to be a screenwriter. I'd spent a very happy three months in LA, just before I went to university. In the week, I was working for a Republican think tank – they were really, really far-out right-wing, I disagreed with almost everything that they stood for, but was fascinated by the thought processes and the political science. So that was my life during the week.

... Then, at the weekends, I had a really good friend from home, who was kind of making it as a screenwriter in Hollywood. I would go to these fabulous parties where there were bars full of ice with champagne bottles in them. We talked to him about his life and everyone would be talking about hot scripts and they would talk about ideas and pitch stuff. It was all like *Swingers* – the movie *Swingers* [1996], with Vince Vaughn. It felt very much like that. It was so fun and enticing.

I'd always written; I'd written some fairly unreadable poetry as a teen, some stories. I had this idea that I wanted to write and I was very into American fiction. I thought, probably: 'Where this is all going to end up is I'm going to write a really brilliant novel.' But as soon as I entered a newsroom, for the first time, I thought, 'These are my people.'

Lionel Barber, journalist, editor and author

It took me about a year or so to get used to reporting, particularly in Scotland, because I was an English guy and they'd just had the referendum [of 1979 on Scottish devolution] – narrowly lost. The other graduate trainee [at the *Scotsman*] was Sally Magnusson, who is Magnus Magnusson's daughter (of *Mastermind* and 'I've started so I'll finish'), and she was the doyenne of young journalists in Scotland. I had to find my own way of establishing myself.

I got a big break when I decided to take up a chance of going to Poland in 1980. I went with my younger brother, who was a student at the time, and while I was there in Warsaw, the government fell and it was the first Solidarity triumph. They toppled the government in the beginnings of the end of communism and there was a crackdown afterwards. So I wrote two dispatches from Poland. My flat was raided by the secret police after I'd filed the second piece and I captured that. That was part of the offering for the Young Journalist of the Year at the British Press Awards.

I'd also covered a prison break in Barlinnie, which I'd actually got slightly wrong on how they'd actually escaped, but that was overlooked by the judges. Then I'd also covered Scotland's first pornography trial. So I had a rather esoteric, rather exotic, offering – and I got the award.

I remember at the time getting about 80 letters of congratulation, including from Winnie Ewing, who was the first Scottish Nationalist MP. She said – I've got this card – and it said, 'Dear Lionel, I'm so proud that a Scotsman has finally won the young journalist of the year in Britain.' I didn't have the heart to say 'Well, actually, I'm English.' Anyway, as a result of that, the *Sunday Times* gave me an offer to join them as a business reporter. So I joined in 1981 and came to London.

George Packer, journalist and author

I always wanted to write, really, from the age of about 12. But I wanted to write the kinds of books I loved to read. What I was reading throughout my teens was mostly fiction, so I went through a period of writing horrible imitations of [James] Joyce, horrible imitations of [William] Faulkner, even worse imitations of [Saul] Bellow. I never lost that idea that a writer is a novelist – that was the prejudice that was somehow worked into me, and it was a destructive prejudice. But it takes a long time for some writers to figure out what they should write, and how they should write.

My idea of being a writer took a turn with the period in Togo as a Peace Corps volunteer, which was a pretty rough and unhappy time of my life. When I left Togo, I was 23. On my way back to the States, I stopped in Barcelona, and happened to pick up a copy of *Homage to Catalonia* by [George] Orwell in an English-language bookshop. I read it on the plane home and, somehow, the first sentences of that book had a really powerful effect on me – something about the clear-eyed, straightforward, honest prose of Orwell that was not afraid to look at life and at himself. He didn't look at himself in a solipsistic way, but in order to get to the larger importance of his experience.

All of that gave me an idea: writing does not mean getting lost in yourself. Fiction often had that effect on me – of disappearing into my imagination or into my feelings and having no connection to the world. I realised that, in order to get through this rough experience, I needed to look at it clearly and connect myself to the world, to the experience I had. Orwell seemed to offer a way. Non-fiction offered a way.

I had not read non-fiction. I didn't know what it was. I knew what journalism was, I knew what history was, I did not know what literary non-fiction was: we didn't read it in high school when I was a kid. I knew about *Nineteen Eighty-Four* and *Animal Farm* – I didn't know about *Homage to Catalonia*. But that book, in some way, was much closer to me, to my spirit, than Orwell's most famous novels.

Geoff Dyer, novelist and non-fiction writer

Writing is something that's left for you when other options haven't worked out. So, really, it was the fact that there were so few jobs available in the early 1980s. Nothing else was available in a way that – in a different time – it might have been possible to get on in TV or something else, or even academia. Writing was something I kind of drifted into. The first thing I wrote was a book review and that grew very naturally from life at university where, of course, one is reading a lot.

It was a time in the 1980s – the exact opposite of what it's been for the last several years, where, every time you go to buy *The Guardian* now in the shops, it's gone up another 10p and it's lost another four pages. In the 1980s there were just more and more supplements. The newspapers were getting thicker and thicker with more and more cultural, leisure, or non-news supplements. There were more and more opportunities to write about lifestyle and culture and books. That coincided with deunionisation, so it was getting easier to write for newspapers and magazines without going down the straightforward 'cub reporter' route. On the employment aspect of things that's really important.

That coincided also with the fact that the safety net of the welfare state was in very robust condition. While it wasn't easy to earn a lot of money, you didn't need a lot of money because the rent could be paid by the state. London, at that point, was still so geared up for people living cheaply.

Patrick Radden Keefe, journalist and author

I always knew I wanted to be a writer; I just didn't know quite how to make it happen. When I was an undergrad, I would send off – not even pitches – but I would write these articles and send them off to magazines. This is the mid-1990s. I would print them out and send them off in Manila envelopes and collect rejection slips. I went to school for years, to grad school in the UK, and then I came back and I went to law school.

It was the second week of law school for me at Yale when the September 11th attacks happened. At that point, I had done some graduate work on signals intelligence and wiretapping by intelligence agencies. Suddenly, what had been a pretty obscure field of study that I knew a little bit about – I'd written a master's thesis, so it's not like I was an expert by any stretch – it was suddenly germane in a way that it hadn't been before. I did it all backwards. I had tried and failed to be a magazine writer; what I did instead was get a contract to write my first book. That was how I got up and running. That happened when I was at law school.

Nikesh Shukla, author

I spent a lot of my 20s as a really average rapper. I was convinced I was going to be the next big thing – I really thought I was going to be a big rapper. The thing that, at the time, I never realised was that I was quite average. Part of that was just a lack of attention to craft or I just didn't do it enough. The thing about being a rapper is you either have to be amazing – because so much of rap is about bravado, and ensuring that your lyrics are constantly reinforcing the fact that you're amazing – or you have to be a bit shit, but have a certain quirk.

But in the background, I was always writing. I was writing short stories and I was writing poetry. I went and lived in Kenya for a year and, during that time, I took the writing a lot more seriously. I realised that I got a lot more enjoyment from writing than from rapping or doing music stuff.

Alex Perry, journalist and author

In some ways, I'm a bit of a fraud, because I never really had a great burning desire to be a writer. That has happened almost by accident. I became a journalist because I saw the movie *Salvador*

[1986] and I thought, 'James Woods's character was great.' He's a photographer who goes to cover the civil war in Salvador, drinks an enormous amount of whisky, his best friend is shot trying to take a picture of an incoming air strike, he falls in love with a Salvadorian woman and manages to smuggle out some film. It's an Oliver Stone movie. He takes Jim Belushi along as a sort of rock-DJ companion. It just looked fantastic to me. I saw it at a moment when I was trying to decide what to do with my life – and that looked great.

2

FINDING INSPIRATION

'Invention, it must be humbly admitted, does not consist in creating out of void, but out of chaos; the materials must, in the first place, be afforded: it can give form to dark, shapeless substances, but cannot bring into being the substance itself.'
– Mary Shelley

In rare cases ideas for books appear to be born fully formed. Crime writer Ian Rankin was staring at the gas fire in his student accommodation when the image of a man being tormented by picture puzzles came into his mind: Inspector Rebus was born. But that does not seem to be typical, even for Rankin. Developing the idea for a book is usually a process. Sometimes its parts will have been assembling in a writer's mind for years, just waiting for the necessary bolt of electricity to jolt through them and bring them shuddering to life. Some writers even push back against the idea of 'inspiration' at all, believing it's too suggestive of exterior forces, too much of an excuse not to write if the 'forgetful muse' – as Shakespeare puts it – neglects to turn up.

Many authors talk of a convergence of different factors over a period of time. Aminatta Forna's novel *A Memory of Love* had its source in a chance conversation with a friend years earlier. Sometimes ideas appear in an orderly sequence; travel writer Colin Thubron finds that as one journey draws to a close, the destination for his next often seems to emerge naturally.

But for some writers, generating ideas is a deliberate process. As a young journalist on the hunt for stories in a pre-digital age, Jay Rayner would scour print magazines and the records of legal cases. A contemporary variation of this comes from magazine writer Samanth Subramanian, who works his way through Reddit forums and news websites to find small stories that could become big ones.

Sometimes a story proves *too* big. The young Rory Stewart appears to have taken Herman Melville's injunction that 'to produce a mighty book, you must choose a mighty theme' to heart when he set out to walk around the entire globe. He gave up part way through, but the resulting book about his journey through Afghanistan was a huge success.

Finally, we've also included an example, from Margaret Thatcher's biographer Charles Moore, of a project that a writer was directly commissioned to undertake, rather than thinking up themselves. Sometimes the project chooses you.

Ian Rankin, novelist

I remember it well. I was sitting in my student digs, staring at the gas fire. I just got the notion of this guy who was being tormented, teased by little messages that were being sent to him – picture puzzles, a rebus is a picture puzzle – that were being sent to him by someone from his past. I scribbled down that note straightaway and said, the main character may be a cop. I wrote about three pages of notes that first night and I thought, 'That's enough for a novel.' It felt to me like it could be – it actually wasn't a 250-page novel. I think it was about a 180-page novel. It turned out very short, as crime fiction was back then. But yeah, it just presented itself to me almost fully formed. It's always exciting when an idea comes to you like that. There's usually a theme I want to explore, a question I want to find an answer to. Some moral question or some question to do with politics, or social justice, or whatever it happens to be. Maybe there's been a true crime that I've read about in a newspaper or magazine. I use that as the starting point – then everything else is fiction. I start to make stuff up.

Jay Rayner, journalist and author

I had a habit, which I developed very early on, of going to a newsagents on Old Compton Street and buying up a stack of magazines. In those days, £30 would buy you 20, 25 titles, and I would go as random as I possibly could. I was on the hunt for small stories that everybody else had not seen – things from niche parts of the world.

Also a classic habit – I don't even know how you could do it now – I would go to the Royal Courts of Justice and ask for the writs book. This was a handwritten book into which details of writs had been written – civil cases or libel writs – and you had to have a really good instinct to try and work out what it was. If it looked interesting, you could ask them to pass you the writ, because even before they'd revealed it in the press, if celebrities were suing each other, they had to write it in the book. I'd do it once a month. I'd pop into the Royal Courts of Justice and ask to have a look at the book, and they had to show you.

Sebastian Junger, journalist, author and film-maker

I found this great job as a climber for tree companies. I was working with a chainsaw on a rope, 50, 100 feet up in the air, taking trees down from the top down. Dangerous work if you make a mistake, which I did, and I got hurt. But it gave me the idea of writing about dangerous jobs. So through my 20s I freelanced for local publications. I didn't come close to earning a living at that, it was very frustrating and depressing. I was trying to be a fiction writer, which was a complete catastrophe, and started doing tree work. I hit my leg with a chainsaw and took a while to recover from that. I just had this idea. Why don't I write about dangerous jobs? They don't get much consideration in this society.

This was back in the early 90s. I was living in a fishing town named Gloucester, Massachusetts, a long-time fishing town. I was there healing from my chainsaw wound when a Gloucester longline boat, swordfishing boat, went down off the Grand Banks, 1,000 miles out at sea in a huge, huge storm. I thought, 'Maybe I'll write about that.' I wrote a section about it and I sent it to a magazine and they picked it up. They said, 'Yeah, we'll publish it.' It was a national magazine – that was a first for me. That eventually got turned into my first book called *The Perfect Storm*.

Aminatta Forna, novelist and non-fiction writer

I'm usually never looking or, at least, I'm not consciously looking, in the sense that I'm a writer and so I'm always alert to things. My friend told me [a] story about her father in Argentina – which was essentially that she'd begun to suspect her father had been complicit with the regime [during the 'Dirty War' of 1976 – 1983], even though he was a professor at the university and not apparently directly linked – because of a couple of things that happened in her childhood, but mostly because he had had such a successful career. In Argentina, at that time, it was a remarkable achievement to have really skated through without any political involvement or repercussions. She began to wonder about him. I remember at one point, she said, 'How can it be so? How can it be so?' She was convinced, ultimately, by the time he died, that he'd been complicit with the regime.

Usually what happens is I come across something and then later on, I realise I'm still thinking about it. And then later on I realise I'm *still* thinking about it. Then later on I realise I'm *still* thinking about it. So that conversation with that friend took place around the year 2000. I know that because it came out of a conversation where I told her that I was working on *The Devil that Danced on the Water*. Now, I didn't start working on *A Memory of Love* until about 2006, 2007. So it percolated with me for all those years. [*A Memory of Love* also transposed the story to Sierra Leone in West Africa.]

Samanth Subramanian, journalist and author

A lot of [finding ideas] involves reading relatively brief things that appear daily in newspapers and magazines and on the internet, and wondering at the larger, bigger story behind them, or trying to think of larger themes out there in the world that might be addressed in interesting ways. Now it's gotten to the point where maybe 40 per cent of the pieces that I do are ideas that are given to me by my various editors, and then 60 per cent are self-generated. That tends to vary. Really the crux of it is that you read small, interesting things, whether it's in newsletters or in Reddit forums or on news websites, and you sense there may be something bigger there. So it's sort of an intuitive skill that you try to hone. It doesn't often work out: very often I'll do a lot of basic research on a story and then realise it's going nowhere. But it pays off often enough that you can make a living out of it.

Sophie Elmhirst, journalist

[A profile of] Tampax was my idea. Why did I want to do it? The [*Guardian*] Long Read has this thing that, every now and then, they like doing brand pieces – this thing that's in your cupboard or the supermarket that everyone goes to, or the beer that everyone drinks, and to unpick it and unravel it and tell the story of it a bit. I guess I was probably hunting around for ideas and opened my bathroom cupboard and was like, 'Hmm, Tampax? That would be good.'

At the time, when I pitched it, I just thought Tampax would be a good thing to write about and wasn't aware of this surge in new tampon brands, which then obviously became part of the story – or the main part of the story, in a way. I often have the same recurring thought process when I'm doing a piece like, 'Oh, that was lucky. That was lucky that that came out being like that.'

It's more that the lesson is, when you go deep enough into anything, you find a story and you find something really interesting that you become – I become – obsessed with for three months or whatever. You can turn a lot of things into good stories, I think, if you pay enough attention to them.

Kate Mosse, novelist

The first two novels were contemporary. That wasn't my voice. There wasn't really any research. I realised that there are many people who have brilliant things to say about our current world, and I really admire them. A lot of them are crime writers, I would say also state-of-the-nation novels, you get a real snapshot of the way people feel and things when you read crime, I think. But what

I discovered was that – it goes all the way back to Emily Brontë – my biggest inspiration is landscape and land, and history. The combination of those two things creates the story for me. So I write imagined characters against the backdrop of real history.

Oliver Bullough, journalist and author

My advice is to get some form of speciality. It can be anything – anything you're interested in . . . Once you start, once you've got going, [the stories will] just lead one to another, it becomes very organic, but you do need somewhere to start.

Tim Rice, lyricist

Joseph [and the Amazing Technicolor Dreamcoat] was written for children. I chose that story because it was my favourite story when I was a child from the Bible. [For *Jesus Christ] Superstar* the Bob Dylan line from 'With God on Our side' was definitely a major factor in making me continue to think about Judas Iscariot. I'd certainly thought about him and Pontius Pilate, years ago when I was at school, because I went to two or three schools in my time that were fairly religious schools. They weren't church schools, but they were schools that were based round chapel and things like that. I was always intrigued by the fact that Judas Iscariot was a key figure. Without him, you wouldn't have Christianity, you could argue that. He doesn't really get any lines in the Bible. He doesn't defend himself. He doesn't have any motives that you can really read about. He's a bit of a cardboard cut-out figure of evil . . .

I thought, 'Well, Pilate was probably not a very nice guy – but, at the same time, he just happened to be the bloke who was there at the time. It was perhaps bad luck on Pilate that he was the bloke who had to condemn Jesus, who he thought at the time was just another rabble-rouser.' That said, he was definitely affected and realised that he was something more than that. So the stories of Judas and also Pontius Pilate always intrigued me. I used to think – at least I think I thought – if ever I'm in a position to write something one day, or paint something, or whatever, not that I'm a painter, that would be a great topic: the idea of the story of Jesus told from the other angle.

Samira Shackle, journalist and author

The book [*Karachi Vice*, published in 2021] grew out of reporting that I'd been doing for several years. I actually started reporting on Karachi back in 2011. When I first went freelance, I left my job at the *New Statesman*. I moved to Pakistan, which is where I've got family, it's where my mum's from. I moved in with relatives in Karachi in 2012 and lived there for about six months and reported on the city, though Pakistan was in a terrible situation then, in terms of terrorist violence and various different issues in Karachi, including organised crime, and so on.

That was how I kick-started my freelance career. Then after about a year in Pakistan, so six months in Karachi, six months in Islamabad covering the election, I came back. But I was still really drawn to Karachi; it was just such a complicated and such a fascinating place with so many different things going on. I found myself constantly coming up with different story ideas and going back there over the years.

The book grew out of a couple of pieces that I did. The first was in 2015. It was my first piece for *The Guardian* Long Read. It was a profile of a crime reporter in Karachi, who ended up featuring in the book. Then about a year later, I did a piece which was originally for Mosaic, which was an online publication run by the Wellcome Trust, which had quite generous travel money, which was great. But it was also republished by *The Guardian*. That was quite a similar piece, I guess: it was profiling an ambulance driver in the city.

In the course of doing those two pieces, I noticed that these two people, although they didn't know each other at all, had experienced lots of the same big, seismic events in the city, and been through these big attacks and so on together. That made me think about the points of overlap and maybe expanding it into a book, which I then did with three other people alongside those two.

Jon Lee Anderson, journalist and author

I quit *Time* magazine after a couple of years, when I realised that I wasn't that happy – square peg, round hole. They were very conservative, spiked a lot of my stuff; I didn't realise it was like that. I didn't like being rewritten, either. I went off after two years with *Time* in Central America, with my brother, Scott, to write a book based on some of my reporting into death squads. We wrote a book about right-wing terror called *Inside the League*. We then were given a contract to write another book – again, very paltry advances, but enough for us, in our late 20s, to do it – called *War Zones*, which was an oral history of five different conflicts around the world. We shared that urge to see the world's conflicts at the time.

At the end of that book, he went off to write a novel and I carried on with another book, my first solo book, called *Guerrillas*, in which I went around the world – it was kind of an ad hoc anthropology, really, of insurgency. I chose five different guerrilla groups to live with and to use as my instrument to write about the world of insurgency. I'd become fascinated by this idea of a parallel reality in the world, in which there were over 40 insurgencies at the time, some of them three or four generations old, creating their own tribal groups and mythological codes.

That in turn led me to Che Guevara, who was the personification of that kind of person, and I realised that there was a whole world of people out there who venerated him, in the jungle of El Salvador, in the Hindu Kush of Afghanistan. He really exemplified that life. He was a universal paradigm. I then spent five years doing that book [*Che Guevara: A Revolutionary Life*].

I came out of this 10-year period of writing books which were journalistic and historical rather than straight-up journalism, I had lived hand-to-mouth at times. I'd had advances. I'd started my family in England with Erica [his wife]. We begged, borrowed and stole in order to stay alive. I always had my mission first – it was never about a career, it was about what I wanted to do next – and we somehow made it work.

Colin Thubron, travel writer and novelist

With the travel books, I usually find that towards the end of a journey some other destination is beginning to suggest itself. I would hate to have to look at an atlas and think, 'Where shall I go next?' It would be too artificial and too pressured. I like to think that there's a destination that says 'Yes, me! Me!' and that it's absolutely natural for me to go there. That's the travel books.

The novels, I wish I could answer why or how I move towards a certain subject. I think some of mine have been, you might say, about distress areas in my own life, which you explore or exploit in your writing. It sounds a little bit cathartic. But an unfortunate love affair, say, or the death of a loved one, these have cropped up in my own fiction, I know.

But I can't say quite how I select a subject, it never seems quite like that. I wouldn't be so crass as to say the subjects select me, because they don't. It's a sort of muddled process, in which I find ideas washing out in my head while writing fiction, and then eventually one will stick like something that doesn't go through the sieve. Then that begins to expand with some sort of thinking around it. From there, a novel may emerge, a plot that seems to express what you're trying to say. But it's much, much more elusive than I've made it seem.

Rory Stewart, author

I wanted to walk all the way around the world. I thought I'd begin with some of the harder countries. I thought places like Afghanistan would be tougher to walk across. So the idea was that I was going to walk across Asia. Then I was going to get a boat, and I was going to walk across Latin America. I was going to get a boat, and then I would walk from Portugal back to Turkey again, that would complete my perambulation. It was going to take me, I thought, four years. So [the choice of] those countries initially . . . [was driven by the] seasons, which all went wrong, but I had some sort of idea that the late autumn was the ideal time to cross Turkey. In fact, I got seasons almost exactly wrong. I tried to walk across Pakistan and India in midsummer. I walked across Afghanistan in midwinter.

. . . So what happened is that I couldn't get into Afghanistan, the Taliban wouldn't let me into Afghanistan. I crossed Iran, I then had to hop to Pakistan, did India and Nepal. Then 9/11 happened, the Taliban fell. Suddenly, I got an opportunity to walk across Afghanistan. So I returned west to Afghanistan, started walking towards the east. During the course of the journey across Afghanistan, I decided that I'd done enough. I'd done enough in two ways. I'd done enough because I felt, actually, that walk across Afghanistan was so extraordinary, and gave me so much that I'd been looking for in the walk in the first place, that I didn't feel I needed to do any more walking. Also, at the same time, a sense that I had taken so many risks walking across Afghanistan, that it wasn't really fair to my mother. So I made a bet with myself that if I got to Kabul, I'd come home and stop doing this.

Lucy Hughes-Hallett, author and biographer

For me, my book writing has always been where I followed up ideas that were wandering around in my own mind, whereas my journalism has been what I did to order. So the first book was about Cleopatra. But actually, that's not where the idea began. My first idea was to write a book about propaganda and the way that you can take a single set of events, documented facts, and make of them pretty much what you will – they can carry absolutely any ideological message. Rather than writing a theoretical essay on that, I thought what would be more fun would be to take a single story, a story based on fact, and see what had been done to it over the years.

It could have been anyone. I was toying with other possibilities. I mean, Napoleon would have been an obvious one because he's been written about so much. Jesus Christ would have been another interesting case. But then as soon as I thought of Cleopatra, it was obvious that she was perfect, because she's female – which means that, in looking at the way people have written about her or made films about her or painted pictures of her, one's talking about the representation of women. She's foreign, from the point of view of a Western reader or writer, so in writing about her I could explore attitudes to race, and there was a good long span – she lived over 2,000 years ago, so there was going to be a lot of material. There's really almost never been a time in those 2,000 years when people weren't writing, thinking or talking about Cleopatra.

I found myself staying tightly focused on one human being, Cleopatra, who did actually live, although we know very little about her, frankly. The documented facts are few . . .

Then the next book, *Heroes*, was the reverse, in a way, in that it was all about one concept, which was hero worship, but with different people. So I looked at eight different case studies there. I suppose *Cleopatra* is my book about women and *Heroes* is my book about masculinity.

[*The Pike*, her prize-winning biography of Gabriele d'Annunzio] came very easily out of *Heroes*, the previous book, which was a boon, because, after *Cleopatra*, suddenly I had two babies to look after. I wasn't immediately available for book writing. But then once the girls were at school, I was thinking what to do next. It took me a while to find something I really wanted to get started on. I like having something I'm working on. All that time, I was doing lots of reviewing and other work. But having a big book-length project is very satisfying; it's nice to have that going as well.

Jeffrey Archer, novelist

My problem when I was travelling around the world, meeting people, was they were telling me amazing stories they thought would make novels, and nine times out of ten, they wouldn't make novels. They were incidents in their lives that were amazing. I thought when they told me, 'If I weave that in a certain way, I can make it into a short story. But there was no novel there.' I would go back to them and say, 'Look, I'm going to write this thing you told me very kindly. But you may not even recognise it when I've finished with it.'

For example, in [one] set of short stories, there's one called 'Who Killed the Mayor?'. My housekeeper in Majorca said, "in a Spanish paper this morning there's a story", and she read it to me. It was only four or five lines, saying that in a village in Spain, when the mayor was murdered, every single person who was interviewed said they'd done it. They told the police 'I did it', so they couldn't catch the real person. I thought that would make a wonderful short story. So she told me what it said in Spanish. I put it in an Italian village on the top of a mountain where they made truffles and wine and oil, and turned it into 'Who Killed the Mayor'. So the germ of an idea sometimes is enough for me. One sentence sometimes. But nine times out of ten what the person says, 'I've got the best story you've ever heard', it's been done 100 times.

Lennie Goodings, publisher and author

The story is called 'The Whirlpool [Rapids]' and it's in her collection called *Bluebeard's Egg*. It's the story that I told her [Margaret Atwood] once when we were on a long train journey. It was in the days when the train from London to Glasgow – we were going up there for book readings – took eight hours. There was a long time to have lots of conversation.

I told her the story, which is: when I was in university, some friends of mine were involved in a raft ride in the whirlpool rapids below Niagara Falls. Again, this is me as devoted to seeing my life through books – one of my favourite books as a child was *Daredevils of Niagara* [*Falls*], and I grew up near Niagara Falls. You could go under the falls, you could do Maid of the Mist, all sorts of things. We'd all been fascinated by that and [Charles] Blondin went across on a tightrope.

My friend said that they were working for this travel company, and there was a new ride, which was going to go on a rubber raft, a 40-foot-long rubber raft, and ride through the whirlpool rapids. So there's the falls, and then there's a bit of river and then there's this pool, called the whirlpool rapids. If you look down on it, it looks like a boiling pot of water. So we got on this raft, 40 of us, and took off. And, unbeknownst to us, the river is also part of the way we get power and they control the water. That day, not knowing that this raft ride was being trialled, they had opened the gate, so more water came out than normal.

We were riding the rafts and it was exciting. Then, suddenly, we looked up, and there was a 30-foot wave in front of us. We rode the raft, rode up the wave and then, of course, it couldn't go any further, so it just flipped over. The woman behind me drowned, and two other people drowned. I got to the edge, as did my friends, which was extraordinary. I did think I was going to drown in the middle of that rapid's whirlpool.

I told all of that to Margaret Atwood and, at the end – we're on this train ride – she said, 'Can I have that story? You don't often get urban disasters.' And I said, 'Yeah, you can have that.' About a year later, I read the story. What was extraordinary: she took no notes, and we were on that train for at least another four hours. Everything I had said, all my dialogue – obviously how I felt, she could pick that up – but actually what I had said I had thought while I was going to drown was all there. For a Canadian, to be in her story is pretty good.

Charles Moore, journalist and author

I don't know that the phrase 'authorised' necessarily tells you one single thing, but what it meant in my case was Mrs Thatcher had decided that it would be a good idea to let someone write her biography. When I say 'let', what I mean is allow that person to see all her papers, so that they would be accurately informed, and to get on with the work before the papers were released to the public, which they couldn't be immediately because of what was then the 30-year-rule, now a 20-year-rule, about government papers. So the sense in which she authorised me was she said, 'Would you like to do this? If you would, I will authorise you to see all my papers, and I will ask the cabinet secretary to let you see all the government papers, and I will authorise all the people who work for me to talk to you, and my family and so on. I won't pay you, it's up to you to get a contract with a publisher. Also, I won't control you. I, Margaret Thatcher, will not be allowed to read what you write, and it can't appear in my lifetime.' Because otherwise people would have thought this is just her talking through a proxy, like Diana, and of course, that would have been useless history. So she was very wise to make that suggestion and it made it much easier for me to accept. So that was the sense in which it was authorised. She had no relationship to the text, whatever.

3

PLOTTING VS PLUNGING

'A book, in my opinion, should not be planned out before-hand, but as one writes it will form itself, subject, as I say, to the constant emotional promptings of one's personality.'

– James Joyce

A question we frequently put to novelists is: are you a plotter or a plunger? If you're a plotter, you plan out your books before you start writing. You might have the arc of the story drafted in a lengthy document or worked out in colourful Post-it notes on the wall. You know what the major turning-points will be and when characters will come and go. You have the sense of an ending.

Working in this way has several benefits, its proponents tell us. One is that it is a bulwark against producing 'large, loose, baggy monsters', as Henry James once called 19th-century novels. As you have carefully thought about the plot, you are unlikely to write unnecessary scenes which weigh down the book and may end up getting chopped out later.

Plotting can also help to keep you motivated on those sluggish, uninspired days. If you don't fancy writing a love scene in the first third of the book, you can write the great betrayal in the second and fill in the gap later. And, if you have spent lots of time devising a story and all its twists and turns, you are more likely to have confidence in it. William Boyd, a dyed-in-the-wool plotter, says he has never abandoned a novel because of his method. As Antoine de Saint-Exupéry, the author of *The Little Prince*, reportedly once said: 'A goal without a plan is just a wish.'

If you're a plunger, however, you dive straight in. You eschew the outlines and the stickers – you may actively abhor them. Once you have the kernel of an idea, you start writing and, as you do, the characters and the story reveal themselves to you. It is a more instinctive approach, one that allows for surprise and serendipity, and the hope is that those sensations are then evoked in the reader, too. Writers have told us that the process of writing this way can be deeply pleasurable, as they themselves are embarking on a journey of discovery.

Many famous writers have fallen into the plunger camp. It is probably unsurprising that James Joyce, the great proponent of the stream-of-consciousness style, is among them. But so was Beatrix Potter, who said that 'there is something delicious about writing the first words of a story. You never quite know where they'll take you.' Maxwell Perkins, the renowned editor of F. Scott Fitzgerald and Ernest Hemingway, felt that you could tell if a novel had been plotted beforehand as it felt stilted and awkward. As he put it, 'A deft man may toss his hat across the office and hang it on a hook if he just naturally does it, but he will always miss if he does it consciously.'

We have interviewed both die-hard plotters like Kit de Waal, and plungers like Jeffrey Archer. Many interviewees, however, land somewhere in the middle – 'a plonger', as David Mitchell wryly puts it, or 'a platter'. For those writers, it is necessary to have a perception of the story in their mind before they sit down at their desk – but it is also necessary to allow themselves a bit of creative freedom.

William Boyd, novelist and screenwriter

It doesn't work for everybody, but the method I have – and I've employed it since *A Good Man in Africa* – is to spend maybe twice as long figuring out, researching, pondering the novel, taking notes, making notes, making rough plans, rough schematic plans of the novel, buying books that will be helpful, maybe travelling if required. I often use photographs as a research tool. I borrow the terms from Iris Murdoch, in fact: she talked about a period of inspiration and then a period of composition. That very much applies to me. It's two years of inspiration, one year of composition, roughly speaking.

It works for me. It's not for everybody. I have a great friend who is an extremely well-known novelist, who comes up with an incident, and then spirals out, as it were, from that incident to create his novel. There are other novelists who just start and wait for the muse to descend on a daily basis, but I think that's highly risky. That's how novels get abandoned: the 40-page novel, the 100-page novel.

I have never abandoned a novel precisely because of my method. I have figured the whole thing out. I won't start writing until I know exactly how it ends, almost to being able to write the last paragraph of the final page. And then I write with confidence, not particularly quickly but with confidence, because I have the whole scheme of the novel written down in front of me. So if I'm not feeling like writing in the middle of chapter 13, I can just look at the notes for chapter 13. I know exactly what I have to write. I spur myself on. I'm not waiting to think 'What happens next?'

It's how I plan screenplays. I plan short stories in the same way. Get the ending right: that's my general piece of advice. I give it to all young writers who say, 'I've got this brilliant idea for a novel.' They tell me about it and I say, 'How does it end?' And they say, 'I haven't quite figured that out yet.' I say, 'Well, don't start until you've figured it out, and you can work back from your ending.' A good ending will save a mediocre novel, and a bad ending will sink a good novel.

Tessa Hadley, novelist and short-story writer

I would so hate to just plunge into writing without knowing what I was going to do with it. In fact, I remember that as being part of a breakthrough when I started to write the right sentences. Part of what I discovered was how much I needed to know what came next, that I couldn't just write into the dark. I think when I was writing those bad [early] novels, I was writing like a reader thinking, 'I wonder what happens next. I wonder what happens to these people now.' I'd write another sentence to see if I could find out, which is not how you do it – you are the authority.

You do need to know what's coming next, absolutely not in a horrible kind of Post-its stuck on the wall and diagram way. It's intuitive and organic, and it can change and grow. You'll only ever have a sketchy map and a map is nothing like the land when you're on it and in it, otherwise fulfilling the map would just be tedious. But I do need to know where I'm going and I need to have a story.

Kit de Waal, novelist and short-story writer

It's much worse than index cards: it's a spreadsheet. I will think and think and think and daydream – I love daydreaming, it's the best thing in the world – and I won't do anything for months, maybe six months. There's a lot of thinking to be done before the spreadsheet stage.

Then, when I think I know what I want to write, I do a spreadsheet. It's got columns, it's got a timeline, it's got little symbols, it's a work of beauty. Then, once I've done the spreadsheet, which will probably be about 12 pages, looks great, colour-coordinated, I will not look at that again. I'll be able to write without ever looking at it. I have to know it's there if I wanted to look at it, but I won't look at it, I'll know it so well. I have to go through that process.

Candice Carty-Williams, novelist

I can't plot anything. It's just not something that I do. [For *Queenie*] I had a lot of thoughts and feelings and experiences of me and friends and family. I had to get them out somehow, had to do that then shape it into a narrative as it was going along, but I knew what I wanted to say and I knew the themes I wanted to explore. They happened to come out and I had to knock them into order.

There's a lot of family stuff in it and my family aren't like the family in the novel, my family are very different. I guess the friends stuff is just snaps of things I've heard, things I've heard on the bus and things I've heard girls talking about. This is the stuff that we need to hear and the stuff that we need to know. Sadly, she [Queenie] is not me, because I'd have a hell of a lot more fun.

Jeffrey Archer, novelist

If you're the sort of novelist who knows exactly where you're going, you'll sit there thinking 'he's making this up' – but I'll prove it. There's a character in *The Clifton Chronicles* called Lady

Virginia, who's a right piece of work. Book Three, I've decided to get rid of her. I decided that day I was going to get rid of her. How? Well, I'll have my heroine, Emma, sue her. And, of course, Emma will win – because Emma is the heroine, and my evil Lady Virginia will be knocked on the nose.

So I got up that morning and I wrote the first sentence with the barrister saying to her 'X, Y and Z' and out came 'A, B, C'. I thought, 'Wait a minute, she just stuffed the barrister.' So the barrister asks another question, and she stuffs him again. The barrister asks another question – and it's just coming off the end of the pen – until she won the case.

Now could I – should I – have gone back and said: 'No, no, the whole purpose of this is she loses the case'? No, her winning the case, for me, was thrilling and fun. I ran with it and went with it, but it was exactly opposite to what I had planned when I got out of bed that morning.

Howard Jacobson, novelist

I plot nothing. I plot absolutely nothing. For me a plot would be death. I have stories, because if two people sit and talk at a table over a coffee and a biscuit, it's a story. Henry James said that's a story. But I don't have plot. I don't have policemen. I don't have guns. I don't have secrets. I'm not interested.

I don't read books that are like that. I don't read thrillers. I don't read mysteries. I don't read science fiction. I don't read any of that. I'd rather read *Pride and Prejudice* again. That's what you want to read about: love, jealousy, despair.

I go to my desk not knowing anything. I'll just sit at the desk and see what happens. You must write with light hands, I believe. If you know what you want your characters to do, they won't do it. There's a cricket phrase, isn't there, they talk about a batsman against a certain kind of bowler having 'soft hands': he must know how to let the bat take the ball, rather than to strike the ball – to keep control of it. I think a novelist should write with soft hands and let the characters do it all. I absolutely hold to that.

Linda Grant, novelist and non-fiction writer

Many years ago, I met Yann Martel [the author of *Life of Pi*], and he told me that he doesn't start to write until he has detailed notes for each chapter. I am the exact opposite. I haven't a clue what I'm going to write about until I start writing. I don't even know what the book's about. I have some ideas in my mind and I test them out and see: does this work? Is there a story here? Very often, a novel that I write changes direction, changes tack, turns out to be not about who I thought it was going to be, or what the story was going to be. I'm trying to tell a story and it would bore me to tears if I knew what the story was – I wouldn't want to write it. I start writing to find out what happens.

Alexander McCall Smith, novelist

I stand in admiration of people who have closely worked-out plots and people who have the Post-it notes. I'm most impressed with that, but I tend not to do it. I have a very general idea of what the main feature of a book will be – I suppose the main plot is there in my mind, but that may be just one subject, one matter. And, of course, there may be all sorts of subplots, many of which I haven't anticipated before I start the novel.

I think that fiction comes to a very great extent from the subconscious mind. The human mind is always interrogating the world and wondering about what would happen 'if' – those sort of 'what if' questions are very, very much part of the process of creating a narrative. So I will be surprised sometimes by developments in the book. I could be writing about something and then, lo and behold, something happens, which takes me completely by surprise. This is something that obviously has been dreamed up by my subconscious mind and has surfaced.

So I find that the process of writing, in my particular case, is one of getting in touch with the subconscious mind, this mind that's creating stories. I don't hear a voice, I hear a rhythm. I hear a sort of beat in my mind, and the words just come from that. I don't really have to sit and think 'what is going to happen next?' – it just comes.

David Mitchell, novelist

I'm probably somewhere between – a plonger, or a platter – in the middle somewhere. You've got to get in at some point, otherwise you'll never get started. So plunge in an ungainly fashion, and end up with your face in the mud. But only when you're there can you really see the lie of the land – at least, that's how it is for me.

My metaphor is actually going on a road journey through the alphabet. You know what C is, there's that great scene with what's-his-face, he's going to say that. You know what F is – that's the thing you wrote 15 years ago, that gorgeous bit of dialogue you've always been looking for a home for. You know what O is, it's something based on that brilliant piece in the *New Statesman* you read six months ago, and you don't know why, but that's going to go into a novel at some point, etc., etc.

There's these points, but you don't know how to get from A to C. Then, once you're at C, you're not quite sure how you're going to get from D to G. But until you're at C, you can't see the view from C, so you don't know what the alternatives are.

I suppose also, a handful of occasions where, for whatever reason, I just can't write the scene yet ... there's no harm in leapfrogging it then. If you can't write scene O, then go to scene P and, pretty much always, you'll work out scene O backwards.

David Nicholls, novelist and screenwriter

When I started writing *Starter for 10*, I gave my publisher a 15-page chapter-by-chapter breakdown, which is what I would do for an episode of *Cold Feet*. I had never really seen a document like this before. But, for me, it was a way of giving me confidence: you know that even if you can't write the fourth chapter, you may be able to write the seventh chapter, that there'll be something further along that you're going to enjoy writing. And that if you put all of these things together, even though some elements will be better than others, you will tell a whole arc, a complete story.

The first three novels were quite carefully plotted in a way that was pretty close to how I would approach an hour of original television, with an A story, a B story, points at which they intertwine, character bibles.

I've moved away from that. *Us* had a definite structure before I started, but I didn't plot it out quite so precisely. With my last book, *Sweet Sorrow*, that was prepared for, but preparation for that was much looser – it was much more about a mood. It sounds a bit pretentious, but there was a kind of mood board for it, a sense of summer fading into autumn, certain pieces of music, certain landscapes. I wrote about 70,000 words over the course of about 18 months, but none of it you would really call a novel. It was a lot of sketches, a lot of improvised dialogue.

So often when people talk about preparing for a novel, you think of storylines and plots. Actually, for me, preparation is as much about mood, characters and their backgrounds, voice, point of view, the tense in which you're going to write it, the tone in which you're going to write it, whether it's first person or third person – all of that stuff I do need to know, even if I don't need to know the exact location where X meets Y, or what Z says to B. I can improvise within a framework, but I need to know what I want to achieve with the book as a whole.

So I do prepare; every time I've tried to improvise something, I've always ended up throwing it away. But the preparation is often quite abstract – a mood, rather than bare-bone story elements.

Colum McCann, novelist

I feel it's kind of like being an explorer. What you're doing is, you are casting yourself out to sea. You don't know where you're going to go, and you don't know how you're going to get there, but you know, eventually, you will reach land – you will find some sort of Galapagos of the imagination. Then you will explore that territory and go and go and go, and plunge in deeper and deeper and deeper.

Now that's not to say that that's necessarily the way that someone should write. I know plenty of writers whom I admire enormously who plot things out, they put up Post-it notes and they make charts and pie charts and spider diagrams and do all those things. For me, I keep it all in my head. The rest of my life is a complete and utter mess, I have to tell you: if you saw my office, for instance, you would say 'How does that person even exist?' – books here and bills there and notes here and pens and all sorts of things scattered all over the place. But in my head, for whatever reason, I can hold these complicated things together all at once.

So I basically plunge into the story. I generally also write from beginning to end. I know that sounds simplistic, but what I mean by that is, when I finish a book, I will have finished the actual book. I don't go back in and start rearranging a whole lot. This is particularly true of *Apeirogon*, which is a very fractured, intentionally fractured, book. It's written in 1,001 different cantos, or sections, but the way it is presented now is, more or less, the way it unfolded in my crazy, messed-up head.

Ian McEwan, novelist

I place myself in the category of a stumbler. I stumble into my novels. I have a vague idea of what I want to do; it's often running in parallel with two or three things I want to do. By writing a few paragraphs, I hope to find the specifics of whatever it is that would carry me into the material. I have a vague idea, but I'm not a plotter.

Each new novel teaches you how to write it – and it won't help you with the next novel, it will only help you with this one. It will teach you to be an expert in writing this novel. As long as I have something specific, then various opportunities and what seem like offers of freedom will be delivered. It often happens that I look at something that I've just written – and it has to be in longhand, has to be black ink, it has to be in a green notebook – I look at a passage and think, 'I can't even tell why I feel so intrigued by this, or why it seems to be holding a secret that I've yet to unlock. But I know this is the one.'

That's how *Atonement* began. That's how *Lessons* began. It rarely diverges from that. Occasionally it does. Once I was sitting in Wigmore Hall waiting for a concert to begin, and my friend, who's an appeal-court judge, told me of a case about a Jehovah's Witness boy who was refusing a pint of blood. Even as he was telling it to me, I knew that I had the entire plot of a novella. Then the Juilliard Quartet came on and I didn't listen. I didn't hear a note of it. Already my mind was racing ahead. It's the only time I've had a whole novel in front of me and that became *The Children Act*.

Most often writing a novel is, for me, a journey of discovery – it's like going up a river with only a sketchy map on the back of an envelope. There are certain scenes I know it's going to take me a year to get to them. I'll make copious notes along the way. Often I can see my way ahead. There's also particular scenes, I know it'll take me a year to get to them, and I don't want to see any notes or have any thoughts about them. So [in *Lessons*] when Roland goes to see his piano teacher, Miriam Cornell, who sexually abused him and drew him into a relationship, I had no idea what was going to happen. I wanted to ring the doorbell with him, I wanted to go into the scene and find out what happens by writing it. Likewise, when he goes to see the woman who abandoned him and their child to become a famous novelist, she's now dying, she's had her foot amputated, they go and get drunk together, I had no idea. Again, I did not want to write any advanced notes.

So it's a mix of those two – of having a rough idea, but also knowing that a good morning's work will sometimes throw up a new opportunity, a new direction and surprise. That's the gift, the surprise. The other gift is something that I know is not confined even to writers, but times when you are so deeply immersed in the scene you are writing that you cease to exist – you hardly know you're there, you're not aware of time. We don't quite have a word for this, I know the word 'flow' has been used. It can happen in cooking a meal, or playing a game of tennis or doing a spot of gardening. But I think, actually, one of the summits of human happiness is to be so absorbed in a task.

Even more exciting, this is not for a novelist, even more exciting though if you're engaged with it, [is working] with others, collaborating in such a focus of attention. When I was researching *Saturday* and shadowed a neurosurgeon for almost two years, I sometimes had fits of envy for him and what he called his 'firm' –

his team, the surgical team – that would carry out these incredibly intricate operations that could so easily go wrong, how they collaborated often in just murmurs and grunts. I thought, 'Well, that's one pleasure novelists can never have.' You do all your murmuring and grunting on your own. But still, a four-hour operation, even for a witness, would go by, it seemed like, in half an hour.

Those writing moments of abandonment to the material – often, for me, late at night, or early in the morning, writing when the rest of the world appears to be asleep – those are peak pleasure moments. They often yield opportunities for the future, for new ways of doing things – a new opening, another way of approaching the stuff that lies ahead.

Marlon James, novelist

I plot and I plunge. I have books after books and notes after notes of plot. I do have the Post-its stuck on all over my walls. I do try to map out a story right to its very destination. Then I start writing and just dump all that shit. At some point, for me, the novel characters become people, and people do things you don't expect them to do. They're volatile, especially if they're my characters. They don't really listen. They make bad decisions and they surprise and they disappoint. Those are all things you can't necessarily plot. You can't plot a surprise: it's a surprise.

4

RESEARCH

'The greatest part of a writer's time is spent in reading, in order to write: a man will turn over half a library to make one book.'

– Samuel Johnson

You have a great idea for a book. What happens next? Most likely, you will search the internet to make sure someone hasn't had the same idea and written it up already. If they haven't, you might then start reading and gathering material.

For writers of non-fiction, this is often the most important stage: the work may involve visiting an archive, combing through official reports and old letters for details that will enliven the prose, or conducting interviews. Robert Douglas-Fairhurst, an academic and author, describes research as a process of accumulation, like collecting the pieces in a jigsaw.

Every researcher hopes to find a special piece that will help unlock the rest of the puzzle. Maggie Fergusson, biographer of the poet George Mackay Brown, discovered a box of his never-before-seen personal correspondence. Lucy Hughes-Hallett discovered that Gabriele d'Annunzio had been a compulsive diarist, making him the perfect subject for a biography. Orlando Figes, a historian of European and Russian history, infiltrated archives in the Soviet Union. Those breakthroughs make the long days and weeks poring over documents worthwhile.

We ask interviewees to explain exactly how they go about their research. Rebecca Mead, a journalist and author, says a stint as a fact-checker – a role, more common in American than British publications, which involves verifying every single assertion and description in an article – taught her the requisite rigour. We also like to know how they turn unwieldy reams of notes into something intelligible. William Dalrymple uses a paper index-card system while others have digital alternatives. Niall Ferguson hires a research assistant to help find the necessary material.

Knowing when to stop researching and when to start writing can be tricky. Hadley Freeman spent almost two decades conducting research for her family memoir and regrets not beginning the writing sooner. Charles Moore points out that unfortunately it is often only when you start writing that you realise how much more research you still need to do.

For writers of fiction, research is also often vital, helping them to create an authentic mood in their work and ensuring their plots and characters ring true. For stories set in the past, or in an unfamiliar setting, writers need to know how the characters would behave, dress, eat and speak. A bit of information-gathering – whether you do it before you start writing, or go back and add embellishment after the first draft – can save an author from snarky reviews pointing out errors later down the line. As Tracy Chevalier says: research can be 'a shortcut to writing better'.

William Dalrymple, historian and travel writer

I have three card indexes ... One is people, one is places and one is topics. So every time I come across an interesting anecdote about a person that may be in the book, that person gets a card and then two, three, four, five, six, seven – however many cards it is. Ditto whenever you come to a place that you're writing about that you will need a lovely description of, or a quote from someone who visited it. You put that down. Then topics: everything else, really.

That means that when you're writing it, and this is the crucial thing, that the key is to be able to write quickly. Spend years at your research – three, four years, whatever it takes, in the case of a big history book, four years, five years, if you can afford it – but then when it comes to writing, you must have all your materials around you. You must write in a white heat and have everything to hand. If you have all the quotes already diced up and cut into your dateline, and a series of cards, maybe 10, maybe 20, about every major character, and a small amount of detail about the minor characters, and have all descriptions of a place to hand when you want to describe Delhi in 1750, or Constantinople in the sixth century, or Beijing during the Tang Dynasty, or Chang'an during the Tang Dynasty – when you have that kind of thing, you can just reach for those cards, and then reach for the original sources, which will hopefully be in your library or photocopied or on your laptop or wherever. And you can do it quickly.

Niall Ferguson, historian

I really don't rely very heavily on assistants – and not at all for writing. There are academics who have research assistants do the writing for them: to me, that's completely unfathomable. I'm far too snobbish about prose and far too pedantic to let anybody else near the writing process.

So research assistants have been people who – and this goes back 20 years – have generally been my students who, as a part-time holiday gig, have helped me gather material. Where research assistants are very helpful is in going to archives when you're too busy teaching to go, going to libraries and delving into historiographies, making sure that you've got everything. When you're teaching, and I used to teach, at one time, 20 hours a week, you need somebody to be your person in the archives and somebody to be your person in the libraries, so that you cut out all that time of going and searching and digging.

You do that at the beginning of your career, but once you've done it for a few projects, you realise that it's not a skill unique to you. In fact, I've had researchers better than me at digging in archives. So for the last 30 years, I've tended, on any book project, to have one person who is very crucial to the gathering of material. For example, *Kissinger* volume 1, which was published [in 2015] – was possible because a man named Jason Rockett would go to every conceivable archive where there might be material relating to Kissinger's early life, while I was teaching at Harvard.

But when it comes to writing, I'll sit there with all the material that they've accumulated and plough through it and then write. There's just no way of delegating that process because you have to read the material and you have to process it – and you have to then translate it into coherent prose.

. . . Methodologically, a serious scholar of the past should always begin by reading what's been written before on any given subject. Once you've ploughed through that existing literature, whether it's on the First World War, or the Second World War, or the Cold War, you will know what the conventional wisdom is, you will know what the big debates are, you will know what the consensus view is. And if you agree with this, if you are satisfied with what you've read, then don't write another book about it – do something else. I'm never satisfied with the conventional wisdom. I'm always acutely conscious, by the time I've done my reading, that there are gaping holes in the consensus view, or that the debates have missed something vital.

Orlando Figes, historian

As foreigners [in archives in Moscow in the 1980s], we were put into a special room under the guard of the KGB, effectively, with the head of a reading room being a KGB person. We had no contact with the Soviets who were in the rest of this corpus of buildings with their own cafeteria, which we weren't allowed to use. But there was one flaw in the system, which was that, in that part of the building, there was only one male toilet and that's where you went to smoke. I did smoke, so I started offering my Marlboro cigarettes and chatting with archivists and historians, and managed to find one who became a good friend and who provided me with the numbers I needed.

I probably need to explain that we didn't have access to the catalogues. Can you imagine trying to work in an archive or a library without knowing what's in it? Well, that's what we had to do. The only way of getting documents was by citing the footnotes of historians who had been published in the Soviet Union. That was the Soviet system of control. If some Soviet historian had used this document, then it would be okay to give it to a graduate student from the West, so getting hold of those numbers was all-important.

Jonathan Beckman, journalist, editor and author

[A] specific time that I failed was when I was writing my book on 18th-century French history [*How to Ruin a Queen*]. I went to Paris to the National Archives, I ordered up my first box of documents, took out the document at the top, looked at it – and couldn't make head nor tail of the writing. All of the letters looked the same. I more or less had a breakdown. I was convinced that I would never be able to read any of them, that the whole project could be a ludicrously expensive failure, and that my dream of writing a book would never be realised. But you work through this. And eventually, I was able to read more or less everything that was written on these documents just by spending time with them.

James Ashton, journalist and author

I suppose this is the name of the game – always take notes! Note-books, diaries, fill them to the brim as you go. Jot down things that you think aren't important at the time, because it will help you in the future. For me, good writing lives or dies on context, in colour. This is the stuff that really fades in time. So what did someone say? What were they wearing? What was for dinner? It might not seem important at the time, but I think it can all help the story.

Maggie Fergusson, journalist and author

It was always agreed that I wouldn't write anything until after [George Mackay Brown] died. We had arranged that in May 1996, I was going to spend a month in Orkney and I was going to see him every evening and we would talk about his life. That was the plan. There was no reason to think he was going to die. Then, in April, he died very suddenly. I hadn't really done much work and I wasn't going to be able to talk to him about it. Part of me thought: 'Somebody really, really needs to tell his story.' And part of me thought: 'I just don't see how this is going to be done.'

I went up to Edinburgh in that month of May when I would have been in Orkney, and began to look through his manuscripts in the Edinburgh University Library. The librarian came over one day to my desk and he said, 'I think I have something you might be interested in.' He showed me a box and it had a rather cryptic message on the outside in George's handwriting, saying something like: 'Not to be read for the time being.'

The librarian agreed to open it, and out tumbled about 250 letters from George Mackay Brown to his great muse, Stella Cartwright. Those letters are so extraordinary that I thought, 'Even if I can only tell that part of his story, it has to be done.' That was what kicked it off.

Lucy Hughes-Hallett, author and biographer

I'd finished *Heroes* and I'd actually already started writing about [Gabriele] d'Annunzio. I'd had this crazy idea – it didn't make any sense – that I would fit a chapter on d'Annunzio into the *Heroes* book. I started writing it – I had written about 40,000 words before I realised that this was a monstrous excrescence on the book. [There are] eight biographical essays in that book and none of them is as long as that. It was a sort of cuckoo, a monster child, which had landed itself into this already-existing book.

I came to my senses, took d'Annunzio out of *Heroes*, put it aside and thought, 'That's next.' I finished *Heroes*. The whole book is about, to sum it up rather crudely, the dangers of hero worship and the irrational emotions that people project onto the people to whom they give political power – and the muddle we all get into as a result. The last section is about the way that people like [Friedrich] Nietzsche and [Thomas] Carlyle, talking about supermen in the 19th century, opened the way for the 20th-century dictators. D'Annunzio was very much part of that story because he certainly saw himself as a Nietzschean superman. He was one of the very few intellectuals, writers, thinkers, who took those ideas out of the library into the field of political action because, in 1919, he made himself dictator of Fiume [today Rijeka, in modern-day Croatia]. He started to live his theories.

He's a great subject. As soon as I started to read about him, thinking I'd just squeeze a few paragraphs on him into that final chapter of *Heroes*, I realised that the wealth of material was astonishing, because he wrote all the time. He had notebooks in his pocket and wrote in them non-stop. You sometimes think: 'How did he get time to live?' He would write down what he was eating, he would write down what he was reading, what he thought about what he was reading.

He described every woman he met. He would put in his notebook what he planned to do with her. You sometimes think, 'How did he ever manage to have sex? He was so busy writing about it!' It must have been rather annoying for the woman when he said, 'Hang on, I'll reach for my notebook.'

Sam Knight, journalist and author

The way that I report every story, which is a secret asset of people trying to do this kind of journalism, [involves] going to the library. It's all in the library. Everyone else is too rushed and ripping shit off the internet. Whatever story I'm doing, I go to the library. I was writing about dressage – go the library. You want to talk about snooker? Go to the library and read books about snooker, because some other person has done a lot of work on this already. If you read up on something – actually read up on it – you're able to have much more interesting conversations with people.

Rebecca Mead, journalist and author

A fact-checker is the poor young person who gets given the manuscript of the celebrated, well-known writer and has to go through it with a highlighter pen, highlighting all the facts, names, dates, but also whether it really was a cream colour sweater she was wearing, not a brown one. You have to call the person up and say 'Is it true to say that you were wearing this or doing that?' You'd have to paraphrase the quotes back to them – you wouldn't ever read the quotes back.

Then for things that were not verifiable, you'd have to double-source things. So the writer might have said that such and such thing happened on a date – but you can never just take the writer's or the source's word for it, you have to cross-reference to make sure that it's accurate. We used to spend a lot of time calling the information desk of the Brooklyn Public Library, who were like the internet of the pre-internet era. You'd just call up these people and they knew the answers to everything.

It was much too stressful to be dull. It's a really, really stressful job, if you take it seriously and if you have any kind of OCD tendencies, which I definitely do and did. It's such a responsibility because you're the person between the reader and the writer. If you mess it up, it's your fault, but if you don't mess it up – if you get it right – the writer gets all the glory.

It's a great way to learn how to be a reporter, because you see how a story gets put together and what you need to have and who you need to have talked to. I learned which departments of the government did what, and all kinds of things. That was my education, really, in the fact-checking department [of *New York Magazine*].

Giles Hattersley, journalist

You always read everything. That's the rule, isn't it? You find every interview, every long read. When I ask for cuttings from my team, I need every major interview [the subject has] done in the past – sometimes if it's a huge megastar, they've only done about four – but I need everything released in the last ten years. And then the pick of the last three months' of news cuttings. If they're at the stage where they've written an autobiography, you're into that, and now, thanks to YouTube, you can spend your life watching bizarre Australian chat shows and see what they had to say on that.

Jennifer Croft, translator

I usually am open to being in touch with my authors as I'm doing the translation, but I'm not constantly sending them instalments. I've never sent people instalments, actually, and I usually don't ask them questions, because I feel that there's so many steps before I would get to that point. It's so hard nowadays to find things that you really can't decipher via the internet. It almost never happens that there's a reference or something that I can't track down – if that does happen, then I ask other native speakers of the language, because I also think it's so important not to over-explain in a translation.

That happened, for instance, in the case of my translation of an Argentine novel called *August* by Romina Paula. There was a name that I couldn't figure out. No Argentine could figure it out, either. I finally went, at the urging of the Feminist Press here in New York, which published the book, to Romina. I said, 'I don't know what this is.' She explained that it was an autobiographical novel and this name was the name of her childhood dog. For a while I inserted 'dog' into the English translation. Then I took it out at the last minute, just before the book went into print, because I felt like Argentine readers don't know that either. It's not like it's a common name for a dog that people would instantly understand referred to an animal. I don't want to know more background information than the reader in Polish or Spanish would know.

Robert Douglas-Fairhurst, academic and author

If you're writing a biography, or in fact any work which involves research, you're a collector. You collect stray facts and interesting anecdotes and jokes and so on, and then you treat them like the pieces in a jigsaw puzzle, because you have to work out how they fit together. There might be some pieces you abandon that don't fit. You might need to add some new pieces that do fit, once you've seen what picture seems to be emerging. Then you have to fill in the details of that picture to make it more lifelike, little narrative details here and there, little character sketches. And then you have to make it move, so that it captures what life is like rather than a kind of snapshot of it on the page.

In some ways, I suppose it's not that different, perhaps, to writing a novel. Although when you're writing a biography, you have to keep one eye on history, or at least the bits of it that survive, and one eye on the story which you're telling. You have to try and make those two things work alongside each other or keep them in dialogue with each other. That's tricky.

Ian Rankin, novelist

I'll tell you what makes [writing] a quicker process: I do the research after the first draft. When I was young, I would do all the research before I started writing the book. I could spend weeks researching haemophilia for a character and, in fact, when I started writing the book, I needed two sentences. So I'd 'wasted' quite a lot of time. Now I wait until the first draft is written, then I do the research. By then I know what I need to know, not what I might need to know. That speeds up the research process miraculously.

I've got a small cadre of professionals that I can go to for advice. I don't hang out with the cops. I don't want the books to become PR exercises for the police. I go to them when I've got a specific question. I mean, I do hang out a bit with retired cops – they're quite fun – but nobody is going to really give me a lot of information that's going to be useful to me with the books now.

Jeremy Gavron, novelist and non-fiction writer

Not knowing my mother at all, I'd had to construct her story [in A Woman on the Edge of Time] out of the fragments of memories. I spoke to about 70 people who'd known her, and we were talking about a period 50, 60, 70 years earlier, so they didn't remember much. Each person would tell me maybe one thing: one small story, or one fragment or one piece of information. I'd also found documents, as well, that had small pieces of information – because most of her papers have been thrown away. I found one batch of letters, but mostly I was finding a line in other people's letters, or a few mentions of her in other people's diaries that they dug up or shared with me. So I constructed that story out of fragments, a multiplicity of voices, the fragments of a multiplicity of voices, and it felt a very truthful way of constructing a story of someone you didn't know – you don't know.

Cal Flyn, journalist and author

[For Thicker Than Water] I went out to Australia three times for periods of four to six weeks in length. What I wanted to do was to reconstruct the life of [Angus] McMillan, and of Gippsland and the Gunaikurnai people at that time. A lot of it was going into libraries just to find the right books. I also really needed to get in touch with the Aboriginal group who were there, and I didn't know exactly how to go about doing that. I knew that the initial conversations with people would be difficult: I'd be like, 'Hi, I'm a relative of someone who's killed many of your ancestors, let's chat.' It's a weird conversation starter to have with anyone.

I didn't really know how that was going to work. I was quite lucky – I got in touch with a woman called Jeannie, who'd written a play about McMillan, and she put me in touch with a young photographer and his friend, Steaphan Paton, who's a Gunaikurnai artist maybe one year older than me. So we were 27, 28, and we all went on a road trip together of all these cultural sites.

That became a big chunk of the book – the conversations we had in the car, the places that we went to, trying to superimpose these historical accounts of massacres onto actual places. Just falling in with Steaphan also meant that I met his family, who were all really notable in the Gunaikurnai land-rights movement. Coming in that way, less cold calling, meant that they were much more likely to respond and take my questions seriously and have these big discussions about intergenerational guilt, which is what I wanted to discuss.

That's difficult to do with a stranger. But coming in as a sort of a friend of a friend who's interested – and has got an obvious reason to be interested, because I was looking into this family line – that made a big difference.

Geoff Dyer, novelist and non-fiction writer

I went to New York. I got an advance from a publisher in Britain to do this book about jazz [*But Beautiful*] and I suppose you could say that one of the things I was doing there was researching it. I went to the Institute of Jazz Studies, but it never felt like research at all. It just felt like following up on this great enthusiasm. There was never any of the drudgery that I associate with research and there was never any systematic approach. When you're pursuing a hobby, it never feels like any kind of work.

It was 1989 when I went to do this, so jazz was thriving still in New York and it was possible to see, to feel, to perceive such a direct connection between the people I was going to see play every night and the people that they had played with in the past, who I was writing about – figures like Charles Mingus and so forth. I was learning about it and writing about it.

I was absolutely the beneficiary of this really important technological breakthrough: the Walkman. We all take it for granted now, but it was so weird back then, the experience of walking around with headphones on and this music in your head. It was so different. It meant for somebody like me that, if I was writing about Thelonious Monk, I could walk up to the neighbourhood where Monk lived and see everything that he had been seeing, with this music absolutely in my head, which was so conducive to a kind of synaesthesia, whereby the music expressed itself in terms of what I was seeing and smelling, and what I was seeing and smelling was bleeding all the time into the music. That was absolutely important, that way of doing things. It made life very, very easy and open. It had been possible technologically only a few years before that, I think.

Tracy Chevalier, novelist

It's a shortcut to writing better. When I was writing *Girl with a Pearl Earring*, I knew I'd be describing a Vermeer painting. I thought, 'Well, I don't really know how to paint. I don't know how you hold a paintbrush, or how you mix colours, or what layers you put on a painting. How do you start it? How does it feel? How does it smell?' And so I thought, 'Maybe I'll just take a painting class.' That really helped. It helped make it easier for me to write what Vermeer was doing.

Subsequently, in other books, like *Remarkable Creatures*, which is about the fossil hunter Mary Anning, I went out on the beach and looked for fossils, because that's what she spends a lot of the book doing. It's much easier for me to describe it if I've done it. Similarly, *A Single Thread* is about a group of women who embroider cushions and kneelers for Winchester Cathedral. Once I started making a couple of things that my heroine makes in the book, I could feel what it felt like to make it, so when it came to describing it, it feels accurate and authentic. In a way it's as simple as that.

Kate Mosse, novelist

I write historical adventure – that's how I define it – rather than historical fiction. Consequently, an enormous amount about what makes it work is about momentum and jeopardy and adrenaline on the page. Which means that if I'm writing a chase scene, where one of my lead characters, Piet, who's married to Minou, for example, is running away from the soldiers, everything about making that scene work for the reader on the page is about the breathlessness and the charging forward and is he going to escape or not?

If I have to stop to check what shoes he's got on, or whether he would have a cape, or how long his sword is, then everything about the excitement of writing is just like dust in my hands. For me, I need to know that world backwards before I can put people in it. Of course, I will go back and double-check things, but when I'm actually writing that first draft, I just need to be a storyteller. Nothing else.

So it's little things like, why does it matter that I know what my lead character is wearing? What Minou is wearing? Well it matters because, if she has to climb out of a window, can she actually do that? We know the 16th century, we've seen all the pictures of Henry VIII and his wives, and Elizabeth is coming and all of these sorts of things. But of course, that was court dress. That wasn't what ordinary people in Carcassonne were wearing every day, but they were wearing quite hefty things. Nobody had heels on their shoes, and very few people had buckles. So everything about how I write that scene depends on me knowing those details. It's not research for research's sake, it's research in order to fuel the story to make it the best it could possibly be.

Jed Mercurio, screenwriter and novelist

I was working as a house officer in the NHS, although I was still in the Air Force. Once I'd finished my medical degree, I could have done medical practice in the air force, but they encourage you to do your house jobs in the NHS because it was better training. So I was doing that and there was an advert in the back of the *British Medical Journal* seeking advisors for a new medical drama [*Cardiac Arrest*] in development that a production company was working on.

I suppose what chimed with me about that was that I'd watched a lot of medical drama on TV – and possibly there was even an argument that I'd been influenced towards a medical career by what I'd seen portrayed in medical dramas. It looked like a very exciting and rewarding job, and it is both of those things. But there's another side of medicine that isn't portrayed in medical dramas and certainly wasn't being portrayed when I was working in the NHS, and that is the darker side of the pressures on medical staff and the pressures that really were severely burdening junior hospital doctors at that time.

So my agenda with responding to the advert – if you could even call it an agenda – was just to give them an insight into how the medical dramas that were on TV at that time were completely missing the authenticity of what frontline hospital life was like.

I kept throwing in anecdotes to illustrate points and giving examples of what I meant in terms of how things were in the hospital that I was working in. I guess, as part of that, I was trying to sell what those things would say about characters or the world that they were attempting to portray. As experienced programme-makers, they must have recognised that what I was really doing was pitching stories. They came back to me and asked if I would storyline an episode, which I was happy to do. That went sufficiently well that, after some thought, they asked if I would consider drafting a script. I'd never even written a script, so they had to show me the layout of a script and give me pointers about the absolute basics. But I kind of knew the story I wanted to tell, and that was helpful, and I knew the world I was attempting to portray, which was also very helpful.

. . . There's an idea that you have to write about what you know, but if you've done one particular kind of job and had a very particular kind of experience of a specific institution, often there will be similarities with parallel institutions – so you can exploit that knowledge. Having worked in the NHS and the military, I felt I had an instinct about how things might work in the police, so then it was a case of doing the most basic research about how things might happen that would make the story plausible.

The idea of an anti-corruption unit, the way in which they go about their work, and so on – that was the most superficial kind of research. Once I got to the point of realising that that would be a plausible social-realist drama, then it was more a case of researching any specifics as we continued the process.

We did meet with some police officers [for *Line of Duty*], but that ended up being shut down fairly quickly. We met a couple of retired officers, who were prepared to give us a very sketchy insight; they were very cautious about what they would tell us. We met with a serving anti-corruption officer in the Met[ropolitan Police], who was very keen to help us and then was ordered not to.

Then we did online research, read books that were written anonymously by police officers, blogs that were written anonymously by police officers. So that was Season One. Then, once the show went out, we got some serving officers to be advisors – they reached out and agreed to help us anonymously. That then allowed us to really open the show out and to deal in much more detail with the world of anti-corruption policing.

Peter Moffat, playwright and screenwriter

I wrote a series called *Silk*, which is about barristers. I've had a few writers who have written for that. I had one instance where a writer wrote a draft of a script in which a judge bangs his gavel, which tells me one thing: that that writer has never been inside a courtroom in his life and didn't go into a courtroom when he knew he was writing an episode of *Silk*, because he would know that judges don't have gavels. I can't believe it. It makes me really worried and upset about television – because I think it probably can be a lazier writer's medium than others.

[Do] proper research. Spend as much time as television can give you researching. Fight off everybody who wants you to start. Don't start until you're ready. Make sure that you have all the material ready to go. There's that kind of tipping point, isn't there? I think most writers feel it when they are ready to go and stop researching.

Charles Moore, journalist and author

I didn't have a very clear or good method [for his biographies of Margaret Thatcher]. I simply followed the advice of Simon Heffer, an experienced writer, who says there does come a point when you have to start writing – meaning, don't just pile up, pile up, pile up research, eventually start writing. I think it's only when you're writing that you realise what more research it is you need to do. You have to answer certain questions when you're writing. When you are writing, they confront you. You suddenly realise, 'I don't know about this' or, 'I haven't asked Nigel Lawson about this' or, 'I need this document.' The writing helps direct your research, though obviously you need to do a lot of research before you do write.

The relationship between oral history and the written papers is that the written papers are overwhelmingly more important in explaining, particularly in government, what actually happened and how she did govern. They're very telling because she writes so much all over the papers, you can see what she's doing all the time. But the papers don't tell you much about who thought what about whom, and all that sort of thing. They don't really tell you the surrounding stuff about how many other things were going on at the same time, so that, maybe on the day that you're doing the budget, there's also an IRA bomb and a by-election and a state visit by the Emir of Qatar. A prime minister has to deal with all those things.

Oral history is phenomenally inaccurate. All memory is inaccurate – politicians' particularly so, because they're always so busy at the time that they can only remember what they were doing. They can't really take an overview. But it's very valuable because it shows what they felt and what they minded about and what they didn't notice. So you compare one witness against another almost like in a court case. It's atmospheric as well.

You need this great collection of voices: about 600 people interviewed for the books, as well as the absolutely enormous collection of papers. The other thing about papers is that, of course, a lot of them turn up later, because as well as the government papers and her papers, people suddenly find they've got private papers, or they tell you that they didn't tell you before that they kept a diary, often very valuable. Or in the case of Mrs Thatcher herself, all these letters she wrote to her sister when she was very young – an absolute treasure trove of the private life that nobody knew about, in the first volume. All these bits compose the whole and I think to get the tone right, you do need all those different strands.

Hadley Freeman, journalist and author

A smart person would have done [research and writing] at the same time. A dumb person, like me, would have done 18 years of research and then suddenly decided one January morning, 'I should write this up.' Embarrassingly, as I was writing it up, I realised I'd researched some things three times and just forgotten. I'd found out about something in 2004, and then again in 2009, and then again in 2014. It was very disorganised and a lot of that is because I never actually really expected to write the book [*House of Glass*, a family memoir]. I thought this was this ridiculous long-term project that I was working on, that was basically like Casaubon in *Middlemarch* and *The Key to All Mythologies* and it would never actually get written.

Compared with research, writing is a breeze for me. I always enjoy writing. It really was the research I found hard because it meant having to ask questions to my dad and my uncle about their mother, which was the part I found the hardest. Their mother, my grandmother, was a very sad woman – that was what started me wanting to write this book, I wanted to write about her sadness. I knew that they, as her sons, found her sadness very overwhelming, very guilt-inducing, and that I found really difficult. I would be a terrible therapist. I hate asking people questions that are painful about their emotional lives.

5

GENRE, AUDIENCE, STYLE AND VOICE

'I could no more write a Romance than an Epic Poem. I could not sit seriously down to write a serious Romance under any other motive than to save my life.'

– Jane Austen

Literary taxonomy can be a minefield. What's the difference between a police procedural, a crime thriller and a murder mystery? Why are some books classed as 'literary fiction' whilst others attract labels like 'uplit', 'book group reading' or 'romantasy'? Much of this division of books into established genres is driven by publishers, who want to be able to market their products more effectively. Perhaps inevitably, though, the genre game involves value judgement. This is changing – as shown, for instance, by the increased acceptance of crime writing as a literary form. But for many people 'genre' fiction is still seen as having less merit than other kinds of literature.

Louise Doughty saw how the success of *Bridget Jones's Diary* in the 90s led to her early novels being marketed as chick lit, despite the fact that they discussed themes such as murder, mental illness and terrorism. But Doughty also acknowledged that, ultimately, 'your publisher is a commercial organisation. I don't blame them for it – they have to sell your book to people who are buying books already of a certain type.' Elsewhere, Jeffrey Archer, who has shifted industrial quantities of 'genre' novels, told us how a long-sceptical literary establishment has begun, tentatively, to take his writing more seriously in recent years. Besides, as he put it: 'Would I rather have sold 275 million books or have the Nobel Prize?' You can guess his answer.

Genre is bound up with the question of audience. Professional writers usually have a clear sense of who they are writing for, and this might inform both the genre that they are working in and the tone and style that they use. Playwright and screenwriter James Graham has the chance to literally see audiences respond to his work in real time, and he wants them to feel drawn in by story and plot, not alienated by Brechtian dramatic techniques. Merve Emre works as both an academic and a critic, but believes there is a binary difference between her academic writing, aimed at a niche audience of experts, and the work she produces for a general readership.

In the most successful writing, genre, style and subject matter all align to create a voice that feels authentic and true. 'I have some kind of faith in the idea or theory that pieces often end up – even if it's not the intention – in some way reflecting or being on the same terms as their subject,' journalist Sophie Elmhirst told us. And yet sometimes the voice of the writer also needs to be at odds with its subject – Giles Hattersley recalls how interviews at the *Sunday Times* were often withering takedowns of their subject, though he reflects that with time and the move to working at *Vogue*, his tone has mellowed. 'I think the world's got kinder and I think I've got kinder.'

Ultimately, the only way to find your voice as a writer is to allow yourself to make mistakes. As Ben Judah points out, experimenting stylistically is key to developing your writing. Find the approach that feels right to you. Questions of how to categorise your work can come later.

George Packer, journalist and author

Find out what you want to write and then work on that, pursue that. Don't be too mindful of what others are telling you you should be doing. If you're doing it out of that, you're not going to learn to write and you're not going to write well: it has to come from within. Then you try to make the world want it, rather than the other way around.

Joanne Harris, novelist

I think there are people who have liked certain things that I've done better than others, but I've got a very broad readership, actually. I'm aware when I go to readings, and when I see readers, it's clear that there are some people who will read anything that I write, whatever it is, and obviously will have their favourites, but whatever the next thing is, they'll read it because they want to try. Then there are some people who will only read the thrillers, and some people who will only read the books set in France, and some people who will only read the fantasy novels. But that's okay too. I'm not there to tell them what to read.

I'm very happy that there's this fairly broad spectrum of different people who all like different things. I mean, as far as I'm concerned, I don't feel that I really change direction at all. I think what I do is I move in a kind of elliptical orbit around a number of different areas of writing. There's a separation of four or five years between each time I visit any particular kind of little satellite. So I'll write a thriller every four or five years. I'll write a fantasy book every four or five years. And then there are some other things, some odd little isolated projects that I just do, because they feel like fun. I'll just do them because I'm trying something new.

Jay Rayner, journalist and author

I get endless emails from people saying, 'I like food, and therefore I'd like your job.'

I am absolutely intent on the fact that there is no such thing as food writing – there is only writing that happens to be about food. There is nothing specific to writing journalism which has a food content. It is the same as any other journalism; exactly the same rules apply. If you start thinking about it in a different way, you're going to start using words like 'mouth-watering' and 'sumptuous', and then where will you be?

I say it in a comic way, but the first thing I try to say to people is, 'It's not about the food. It's about the writing.' If you're coming at this thinking, 'Ooh, I like my dinner', and you fancy yourself peering over a plate of food, like I sometimes do on *MasterChef* with a furrowed brow, and adjectives are coming to mind and you have the searing instincts of Anton Ego in *Ratatouille*, it's all going to end badly.

Giles Hattersley, journalist

I think you do shift [your tone] slightly as to where you're writing for. I also think some really interesting things happened between, say, that interview with wonderful Plum Sykes, which I guess must have been about 2016, probably, or 2017, [and] now. I think the world's got kinder and I think I've got kinder.

You can look back at some *Vogue* interviews, as I often do: a favourite thing to do here is to pluck a random 1998 copy of *Vogue* off [a shelf] and see what they were up to. Some of the interviews are savage, because that was the time. It was the era of Lynn Barber reigning over everything and people were savagely on the attack.

I read my old *Sunday Times* interviews sometimes. My starting point always seems to be like, 'But who the hell do you think you are?' I think that was true of a lot of the media land-scape. So having arrived at *Vogue*, obviously there's always a tonal shift in which outlet you're writing for, but the more interesting shift is something that's happened across media.

Ben Judah, journalist and author

I've been experimenting with a different sort of writing style. When I was writing *This is London* I was experimenting. It's very experimental, actually. I decided, there's no point doing this unless you take risks. There's no point being conservative about your writing style, especially when you're young. This is the time you should make mistakes. It alternates between bits that are actu-ally written in prose poetry, and bits that are written in a kind of direct reporting style, or bits that morph into these people's ways of looking at the world.

When I came out of that, the chapters are written quite differently in ways I thought best reflected these people and their experiences. Some in which I was maybe more inspired by [Henry] Mayhew, some where maybe I was more inspired by longer sentences, like [Martin] Amis, some where I was more inspired by doing it like Jack London. But by the time I came out of that,

I had realised that a very, very sparse, lapidary style was best, almost very skeletal. I wrote this script for *Newsnight*, which I was very proud of actually, which I felt captured the emotions of these people. Then, after that, I've done a lot more experiments with that style.

Merve Emre, author, academic and literary critic

[Academic writing and criticism are] completely different. I do think of them as two different professions, and they are two different careers. Being an academic and writing for an academic audience has its own set of protocols, and its own set of procedures. The most important one I would flag is that academic articles, academic books need to go through a process of peer review. Part of the function of peer review is yes, of course, to make your argument stronger or sounder or more rigorous, or to point out what you could be doing differently that you're not doing. But another large part of its purpose is to make sure that you are cleaving to a certain set of essentially bureaucratised norms for what academic writing is supposed to do and who academic writing is supposed to speak to. Academic writing is supposed to speak to other academics. It is a highly institutionalised and highly specific and specialised form of writing.

Ruth Padel, poet

Poetry is a spectrum. It's a house with many, many chambers. There's poetry that I'm not very interested in, and there's poetry which I am interested in, and I'm interested in writing some sorts of poems. I like performing. I've noticed for a long time that the poems that perform best – if you have 200 people, you can stun them with a poem, but it's not often the best poem in the book. Some poems just read better than others, and the poems that are best on the page are poems which are not dependent on the personality and physical presence of the poet on the stage.

Poetry is very reactive. It takes a long time to write a novel. So there aren't very many great novels about climate change. There are a lot of very important poems that have been coming up about addressing the ecological disasters of our time.

I haven't really focused on them [so-called Instagram poets] very much, because I don't find their poems, as poems, very interesting. I don't find their language very interesting. I find the tone of voice rather repetitive. But it works for a lot of people. It excites a lot of people.

It's to do with tone. It's to do with, probably, craft. There are a lot of very wonderful, interesting poems being written and published at the moment, which don't always get reviewed in the papers these days. They would have done, ten years ago, but it's changed. And I suppose I'm interested in writing, I'm interested in poems that get me going – that take me to somewhere new.

I think a knowledge of the craft is very, very useful. But it's also the sense of pressure and the sense of the white space that we have on the page. It's a physical, visual manifestation of the pressure of concentration. Sylvia Plath said you have to go so far, in such a short time, you have to burn away all the extremities. I think it's that sense of concentration which is the first thing. You have to have an ear for how cadences go, how words relate to each other. Metre is helpful, so you know how many beats there are in your line, what you're doing, how the lines relate to each other.

Fraser Nelson, journalist and editor

Some people are born naturally gifted writers. Charles Moore has probably never written a bad sentence – the same is true, weirdly, with Rod Liddle. He was a broadcaster, but you should see how fast he turns around copy, incredibly gifted. Douglas Murray, the same as that. Now, I am not like that, but you don't have to be to be an effective journalist. To be an effective journalist, you can try to come up with information, talk to people, find out new things, find out what's being said behind the scenes, the investigative aspect to it, the research aspect to it. That's something which I think I'm comparatively good at. So when it comes to me as a writer, I would love to think that one day somebody will make a book out of my columns. But I don't particularly think so.

You do find books of columnists – Danny Finkelstein's done one as well – and those are people whose words, whose writing is of such high quality that it's incredibly beautiful to read years after the event. I've got I don't know how many books at home of those sorts of columnists. My journalism is rather less lofty. I simply try to tell people what's happening behind closed doors. I try to make an original point that might help them to see things in a different way. I like to think that my own writing is useful to people as they try to make sense of the world around them.

So, as a writer, I would say that I'm more of a journalist than writer, if that makes sense. Everybody has got a mixture. I've always hero-worshipped writers and one of the things with my job is I meet lots of famous people, as you would do if you're a journalist. None of that particularly excites me, but to meet a good writer – that's when I go weak at the knees.

I've tried to abuse my position sometimes and just try to meet hero writers and quite often ask them how they do it, as if there's some great secret they could pass on to me that I could somehow replicate and digest and improve my own writing. But the funny thing is, when I've spoken to great writers, the bottom line is they're born with it, in my view. You can improve, of course – anybody can improve. But I would say that I'm a constructed rather than a natural writer, more noted for my enthusiasm than my ability.

Aminatta Forna, novelist and non-fiction writer

When I think of non-fiction – there are various different kinds, of course, an essay could be ruminative, it could be argumentative – but I tend to think of creative non-fiction as a found story.

Think about Picasso's work – I sometimes use this when I'm teaching a class – think about Picasso's bulls, which he painted and produced in so many different ways, a painting of a bull or a line drawing of a bull. But then there's another bull, which is a bicycle seat and handlebars. He just put the handlebars above the bicycle seat, and depicted, in that way, a bull. I think of non-fiction, creative non-fiction, as a found story. You've got most of the elements already there: you've got a character, you've got a setting, you've got a story with an arc, emotional, but also in terms of an essay probably something else that you might wish to contemplate more deeply. And so actually, you're using much of the same craft mechanisms: you're going to use dialogue, you're going to use description, you're going to use characterisation, and you're going to follow that arc.

Now, not every essay in the collection [*The Window Seat*], or indeed, every essay written by an author does that. But broadly speaking, if you're telling a non-fiction story, that's what you're doing. I mean, if your essay is a polemic, it's going to be different again. But if you're telling a non-fiction story, you're pretty much using most of the elements of fiction.

Colin Thubron, travel writer and novelist

First I was interested in the works of Patrick Leigh Fermor, Freya Stark – those two – and [Jan] Morris, [she] was James then. Those three. They didn't seem particularly to form a canon to me exactly – and travel writing wasn't really established as a literary genre in itself quite as much then as it became in the late 70s, 80s, when, it was almost as if publishers had discovered it as a literary genre of some respectability or stature. People like, indeed, Bruce Chatwin, Paul Theroux, Jonathan Raban, Redmond O'Hanlon, and I suppose I joined them in the 80s.

Now, of course, they're looked at askance. That whole tradition of the lone Western traveller going off with superior knowledge and probably a privileged education, to look at countries that are much poorer. It seems like since Edward Said and Mary Louise Pratt – they're strong critics of this sort of travelling in which somebody who has power – I suppose you would say, knowledge is power, and you're travelling to people that don't have that power, if you're travelling in poor countries, as I was, largely or a great deal poorer than my own. It seems an act of presumption and injustice to some people that you are pronouncing, if you like, on these countries, from your neo-colonialist perspective.

I can see the logic of that, though I think for a practising travel writer, it doesn't have to be that way. You can travel certainly not for any other purpose than for understanding, even possibly out of respect and a desire to learn from another culture, rather than imposing your own. It's a very difficult balance. But I think if we regard all travelling of this kind as an exercise in some way of power, then we wouldn't travel at all. There would be no effort to meet, to communicate, to understand, because we'd be banned by the inequality of our status. And I think that that would quite obviously, in a world that understands itself too little, be foolish.

Sophie Elmhirst, journalist

This might sound either really pretentious or just wrong, but I have some kind of faith in the idea or theory that pieces often end up – even if it's not the intention – in some way reflecting or being on the same terms as their subject. Or maybe it's a ventriloquism thing, where you end up slightly mimicking the tone.

I do really like writing in really different styles and tones. I like writing seriously. I like writing very unseriously. I'm drawn to really, really different kinds of subjects.

Ann Goldstein, translator

[Elena] Ferrante doesn't really write in dialect, when you read in English, 'he said in dialect' or 'she said in dialect', in Italian, it says *disse in dialetto*. And then she goes on to write in standard Italian. There's various speculations about why. I mean, I think a lot of Italians wouldn't understand Neapolitan. And she has, I'm sure you've probably read in interviews, often said she wanted to be read. Also, I think another reason might be that Neapolitan is sort of private. There is a literature but it's very much a spoken language . . . I don't know Neapolitan.

Louise Doughty, novelist

Interestingly, it [*Crazy Paving*, Louise Doughty's first novel] wasn't marketed that way when it was first published, because it was first published pre-*Bridget Jones*. So when it was first published, it was just viewed as literary fiction. It was reviewed by people like Jonathan Coe and Jason Cowley. Pre-*Bridget Jones*, I think there was not the same sense that any young woman writer who wrote about other young women, or who wrote about relationships, must somehow be writing in what we can loosely call the 'chick lit' genre. But what happened later on, after the whole *Bridget Jones* explosion, is that my books were retrospectively recast that way, because I was a young woman writing about other young women, and therefore, that's what I must be.

The paperbacks were reissued. I mean, *Dance with Me*, which is a book about sexual betrayal and mental illness, was reissued with a girl in a summer dress with her head cut off, running through an orchard. That's the way the books were published, because that was what was selling. *Honeydew*, which was also printed very much the same way, that's about a girl who murders her parents. When my fourth novel, *Fires in the Dark*, came out, a review in *The Guardian* said, 'Oh, Louise Doughty, previously the author of cheery chick lit, has now published this very serious book set during the Second World War.' I thought, 'Have you actually read my first three novels? There's a girl who murders her parents, there's mental illness in *Dance with Me*, and *Crazy Paving* is about chaos theory and IRA terrorism.' It's a book that was set during a 1990s IRA bombing campaign. But, all people had seen were these covers with women in summer dresses running through orchards and that was it. I think it was simple and outright sexism. It was irksome at the time, I have to say, and it still is.

It does make me laugh when you think that, for instance, if *Dance with Me*, which has ghosts and mental illness, was published now, it would be called 'domestic noir'. It would have a black cover and coloured lettering. I think you have to accept as a novelist, however irked you are, that the way in which you are marketed is to do with what is selling at the time at which you're published, what are the mores of the time. Your publisher is a commercial organisation, I don't blame them for it – they have to sell your book to people who are buying books already of a certain type. But that process should always be seen as completely distinct from the quality of your prose. I think if you get too irked by this, you will spend your whole life worrying about how you're marketed and not enough time worrying about the really important issue, which is: what are the words on the page?

Terri White, journalist and author

There are a couple of parts to it, one of which is definitely the gender aspect [to writing], which is: men write essays and women write confessional pieces. There is a great history of men writing incredible first-person narratives, and they're not considered in the same way. But, at the same time, I do worry for young female journalists and writers who may feel that the way that they can develop a reputation for their writing is to have to write those stories.

I didn't write those stories for the first couple of decades of my career. When I did write them, I was very, very, very specific about where they were published, about what I was willing to write. The first first-person piece I actually wrote was for *The Pool*, which was the website started by Sam Baker of *Red* magazine, and Lauren Laverne. They did brilliant, brilliant, women-centered journalism, and I trusted them implicitly. I wrote about our time spent in a refuge, mainly because I was furious about government cuts. I wrote this piece and I was very, very careful about writing it, about what I said, about what I included about my family – because their stories are their stories, not mine.

I've always said to young female journalists that I know, 'Please be sure that you want to write about that – because it is out there forever, and it will be out there forever.' The number of dates I've been on and I'll meet a man and he'll say, 'Oh, I googled you, and this came up about you.' You have to be prepared that people know stuff about you before they even have met you. I wouldn't want young women journalists to think that is the way that they need to get published, or if they want to write a book that they have to write a confessional memoir.

I do think there's a snobbery around memoir. There's a shame about women selling trauma – that this awful thing's happened to you and, because of late-stage capitalism, you go out and try and flog it to the highest bidder. That's never how I've seen it. I feel like memoir is an incredibly powerful form, but the way it's considered – especially at the moment – can be incredibly reductive.

I think I spent a long time thinking and writing before I put this book [*Coming Undone*] out there. I don't know if I'll ever write non-fiction again; I'm actually writing fiction at the moment. But it was a book I felt compelled to write. When my book came out, I could sense a little bit of snobbery around the form, which I found frustrating. The writing in *Coming Undone* was as important to me as the story. That is, the craft of the writing was as important to me as the story. It isn't enough to have a shocking, upsetting, raw story. For me, your job as a writer is to tell a compelling story as artfully as possible.

There are multiple parts to that [topic of writing, genre and trauma]. Multiple parts of it infuriate me. But, as I say, I don't want women to think that is their only option.

James Graham, playwright and screenwriter

I think because I am a narrative writer, I'm driven by story, which is not necessarily the case across British theatre, and certainly not across European theatre. You'll have heard people speaking of post-drama, post-dramatic plays. We were meant, with [Bertolt] Brecht, to have left story and narrative behind. The purpose of theatre, particularly political theatre, was to provoke or experiment in different ways. It's all about form, it's about style. It's about what your intention is for the audience and what the audience should leave with.

Whereas I myself write stories. Brecht's argument against dramatic theatre – narratives with a beginning, a middle and an end – is that that was bourgeois and that was self-serving. Middle-class people would go to the theatre and they'd be satisfied and the point of theatre was not to satisfy you, it was to anger you, to provoke you, to unplug you from the matrix rather than plug you into the matrix. I would now strongly disagree with that. I think sometimes experimental theatre that indulges itself in an attempt to shake up theatre and break a form; as much as I love that, as a playwright, I worry that that's become the new bourgeois elitist theatre. That excludes a whole audience who, in the age of Netflix, engages with difficult ideas through stories and narratives.

Jeffrey Archer, novelist

To begin with, they [the literary establishment] were snooty, because I was selling too many copies. Recently, they've been very generous indeed. I mean, now *The Times* has subsequently described *Cain and Abel* as a classic. Someone as tough as [Alan] Massie has come out saying, 'there's a hell of a lot of writers who wish they wrote as well as Jeffrey does', which is very kind. I'm very touched by that. But if you're asking the more cruel question – would I rather have sold 275 million books or have the Nobel Prize? Thanks. I'd rather have sold 275 million books. And, by the way, just in case you didn't notice, with all that research of yours, [Alexandre] Dumas still survives today. Even in his day he wasn't thought of as a great writer.

6

FINDING AN AGENT AND GETTING PUBLISHED

'A person who publishes a book wilfully appears before the populace with his pants down.'

– Edna St. Vincent Millay

Unless you have decided to go down the self-publishing route, acquiring representation by a literary agent is usually a necessary step on the road to publishing a book. The days when major publishing houses would look directly at unsolicited manuscripts – rather than those sent to them by agents – are largely over. A lack of professional representation also leaves an aspirant author vulnerable to signing a contract on unfavourable terms.

There are some exceptions. Irvine Welsh, drawing from his experience with contracts from his time working in local government, has always represented himself. 'All you do with these things, you just ask for more money every time until they say no, basically,' he told us bluntly. Likewise, Ruth Padel explained how for poets – operating in an environment in which there is much less money – the usual route towards first publication is just to start sending your work to poetry magazines. But in general, if you want to write books, you need a literary agent.

One key takeaway from our conversations on this topic is that the way in which aspiring writers are often encouraged to acquire an agent – sending a query letter and a sample of their work out to a range of agents – often doesn't work. If you do this, your work can end up on what is generally termed 'the slush pile', being read by a young and inexperienced intern, if anyone at all. Acquisitions from the slush pile are rare, (though there are a few famous stories – *Harry Potter* was picked up by an office manager leafing through the submissions).

But more useful than just bemoaning what doesn't work is to know what has succeeded for other writers in the past. Look for agents who take an interest in similar writing to what you're working on. A number of authors told us about finding their agent by looking in the acknowledgements section of a book that they felt was similar to their own – many authors thank their agents in the acknowledgements. While personal introductions and other connections can also be useful, several writers additionally told us that entering writing competitions made a big difference. Leaf Arbuthnot won a prize for an 'edgy' novel with 'an embarrassingly grandiose title'. That never found a publisher, but it blazed the trail for the later acceptance of her first published novel *Looking for Eliza*. Likewise for journalist Andrew Hankinson, recognition from the Northern Writers' Awards helped him secure representation by a London literary agent.

However, even once you've secured representation, relations between early career writers and their agents aren't always straightforward. As the following stories reveal, manuscripts can go missing, publishers can turn down agents' pitches, and writers can be unceremoniously fired by their agents. Some authors admit to being less than completely honest with their publishers at times; both Irvine Welsh and William Boyd, having secured interest in their work via short stories, then promised they had novels ready. When publishers asked to see them, they had to hastily write these largely non-existent books. In both cases that worked out fine, but it's a high-stakes approach.

Perhaps the most pragmatic story we heard about how to get an agent came from Simon Scarrow. When he was starting his career writing historical fiction he wisely eschewed the recommended scattershot submission route. Instead, he researched which agents were representing similar books and spent an afternoon calling them up to sound out their interest. In an age of email and instant messaging this may seem an archaic approach, but it meant that, for those who had asked to see the manuscript, 'there would be a sympathetic pair of eyes looking at it, the moment it fell through the letterbox'. Scarrow swiftly acquired an agent. A publishing deal followed. Sometimes the old tricks are still the best ones.

Aminatta Forna, novelist and non-fiction writer

The one piece of advice I wish I'd had at the beginning of my writing career was: get an agent. It's a piece of advice I give people – get an agent as soon as you can.

Max Hastings, journalist and author

When I was 21 and I wrote my first book, the American book [*America 1968: The Fire this Time*], I was taken out for lunch by the then-dean of London agents, who was my first agent, a guy called Graham Watson. Graham offered me two pieces of magisterial advice. He said, 'First, if you're going to be a career writer, don't think it's clever to write one book on the history of the American Civil War and another one on old-fashioned roses. Try and build up a reputation for creating a certain kind of book, so that somebody who buys a book with your name on knows what they're going to get. Secondly,' he said, 'if you're going to write just one book, about rowing the Atlantic backwards, screw the publishers for every penny you can get in advances and run laughing to the bank. But if you want to make a living as a writer, then the best reputation you can have is your books add up.' I've stuck with that.

Nikesh Shukla, author

Don't let anyone ever question whether there is a market for your story or not, because they don't know that. I think the best thing you can do – as well as the thing that you're working on – is try and write other things and build up a name for yourself.

Get yourself into a writing group. Make sure someone who knows something about writing gives you feedback about it before you send it out to agents. When you send it out to an agent, you've only got one shot with that agent, because agents' inboxes are really, really busy. So if they get to your novel extract you have to make sure it's good enough for them to ask for the full manuscript – and that when they get the full manuscript, it is amazing and it's the best possible thing. So simple things like: don't have a spelling mistake on the first page. Format it properly. Even though you love that particular font, put it in Arial 12-point double space, because agents read all their submissions on Kindles and Kindles do funny things to Word files that are a bit odd.

Make sure it's the right agent, don't just send it to everyone. Don't just cut-and-paste your approach letter, tailor your approach letter. Find the personal connection with the agent – maybe it's because they loved a book that you love, or they represent a writer that means something to you, but just make them at least feel that you've chosen them for a reason. A 'no' is the easiest thing to get in the publishing industry when you're trying to get your work published. You only need one 'yes'.

Kiran Millwood Hargrave, poet and novelist

Don't do what I did. I will share my experience first. So the first thing I did was I wrote three chapters of this children's book off the back of an assignment that we were set as part of one of our first-year courses [on the creative writing masters at Oxford]. You had to write a page in a genre you've never written before, so I wrote a page about a girl running away. I thought, 'Oh, there's a story in this.' I started writing it, wrote three chapters, and then sent it to an agent. Don't do that – you're meant to finish the novel first. The agent wrote back and said, 'I'd love to read the rest of it.' I said, 'Give me time to finesse it.'

I wrote it in about three months, which was very stressful, sent it back. They said, 'This needs work, but we're willing to work on it with you.' We took it from there, developed a bit of a relationship. But after about two months of working on it, about two drafts, they still hadn't offered me representation. Now I know an agent will never work on a book unless they're going to offer you representation, they're very busy people, they're not going to waste their time. I didn't know that at the time. So I took my three chapters and my full novel at that stage, sent it out to a wider net of agents, and that's how I found my agent Hellie

Ogden. So I didn't actually end up working with the [first] agent – who is an excellent, very reputable agent.

Amanda Craig, novelist

I wrote a first version of what became *Foreign Bodies* and met a very distinguished editor, publisher. We got on and he said, 'You seem to be very interested in reading and are you writing?' I said, 'Yes.' He said, 'Well, do send it to me.' I did. This novel was accepted. I couldn't believe it, first-time lucky, this is fantastic. Then one of these putsches that regularly happen in publishing happened, and he was sacked; someone more powerful than him didn't want him there anymore. So I lost my first editor, and with it the hope of having that published, which was awful, because at the time I was unemployed. I'd told a lot of people that I was going to have this book published, and then I couldn't understand what had happened.

Then, time went on. I became a journalist, mostly a freelance journalist. I won a couple of awards as a young journalist, in particular something called the Catherine Pakenham Award. I was rung up by an agent called Deborah Rogers. She said, 'Yes, yes, yes. Show me your first novel.' She was the most lovely woman, incredibly eminent, the agent of people like [Kazuo] Ishiguro and so on. The founder of Rogers, Coleridge and White. But anyone who knew her will not be surprised to know that she had an utterly chaotic office, and a rather chaotic mind. She lost it. She lost this first novel. I was so poor at the time, I hadn't thought or been able to afford to make a photocopy. So it was just gone.

I sat down and I rewrote this novel, that was *Foreign Bodies*. That was then about to be published by Hutchinson, with a new agent who I'd found. I think it was the month of publication. I got this letter from her [Deborah Rogers] saying, 'I've just found your first novel. I think it's rather good.' She was very chaotic. So I was able to tell her, 'Thank you very much, but it's about to be published. And I do now have an agent.' So it was a very, very, up and down, not even beginning.

Andrew Hankinson, journalist and author

I started writing in 2010. At one point when I was writing the book [*You Could Do Something Amazing with Your Life*], I thought, 'There's no way I can do this,' because I was so worried [for legal reasons] about what I had, being able to use it, whether I *could* use it. I started writing a book called *Not Writing a Book about Raoul Moat*. I got a few thousand words into that.

Then what I did was submit about 5,000 words of it to this thing called the Northern Writers' Awards, which is an awards scheme for northern writers where they give you time-to-write money. I won one of those prizes – I won £5,000, which was just amazing. Also, they introduce you to agents.

So I'd spent about two years on it, and I'd kind of given up on it for a bit. Then, once that happened, I was like, 'Okay, that's going to get me to agents, and I've got some money, so I can do a bit more writing.' So then I met some agents – came down to London, they take you for a night out in London, and you meet all these agents. It's a networking thing. I got an agent from Greene & Heaton and she was so brilliant. She was a really great, great agent.

But she wanted a different book to the one I was trying to write. So when I was sending her the proposal, she wanted it to be like *The Suspicions of Mr Whicher*. She wanted it to be like this other true-crime book. I was like, 'That's not really what I want to do. I want to do this second-person, I want to do it like that.' So she dropped me. While I was in New York doing an assignment, I got the email. I was like, 'Oh my god.'

I had such good stuff, I thought. I knew it would work as a book the way I wanted to do it. I thought if I did it that way, it would get to the market quicker and it might have been commercial and things. But the whole point of writing this book was to try and establish myself as a particular kind of writer and to demonstrate – because I'd felt so frustrated with having all these [journalism] features out with my name on that I hated – I thought, 'This will be the thing that I can say, "this is how I write, this is the kind of thing I can write." And I'll look after every single word in it and it's mine.' So to then do something that somebody else wanted me to do – it would have just defeated the whole point.

So then I went back to this organisation in the north-east called New Writing North who run the Northern Writers' Awards. I said to them, 'Look, I haven't got an agent. Have you got any suggestions?' They suggested another agent, who was a good guy as well. I'd worked on the proposal in the meantime, I sent it to him, which was the proposal as it ended up – and he liked it and he was really great. He sent it to the big publishers.

. . . Then I just never heard anything back. I waited a couple of months. I emailed my agent. I was like, 'Did anything happen with that?' I think he didn't respond. Then I waited another few months. I think I called and he didn't respond. I left a voicemail message at the office and there was just no response. Then, it turns out, he was quitting the industry to go and do something else. I think he was becoming an estate agent in America or something.

He was really great, but I was frustrated. It was like, 'You kind of got a good reaction from those [publishers], but maybe we can try the lower-down ones now?' I said to him, 'Look, just send me a list of where you sent it.' So he got in touch in the end and I said, 'Send me a list of the ones that you sent it to and let's just call it quits.' He did that and then I just started sending it out to publishers myself.

Ruth Padel, poet

That route [to being published as a poet] is really the same now, even though the methods of communication are slightly different. You start sending them [your poems] to magazines. There are lots of poetry magazines – thousands. I always tell people, the best way is go to a place like the wonderful poetry library in the Southbank, or the Poetry Society.

You go look at the magazines, see what sorts of things they have. Every editor has a different taste, and then see how your own poems match up and send about six to them. Then you wait, and you send out others. The good, the great, poetry editors, they read the magazines, they see who's coming up, who's interested. They keep an eye on them, who's coming up, who keeps sending poems. And you get poems in *Poetry Review* or the *PN Review* or something like that.

Candice Carty-Williams, novelist

So I had admired her [Jo Unwin] for a really, really long time, because she used to do this thing – maybe three years ago – she had this little blog and she said, 'I'm an agent, and I walk my dog on Brockwell Park [in south London] at nine o'clock on a Friday morning. If you want to come, and you want to chat to me, and you want to get advice, do.' I just thought, that's amazing. You're putting yourself out there physically and saying to people, 'If you need my help, I'm here for your help.'

Her dog is very lovely. It's a nice dog, it would protect her from any harm. I just thought that was amazing. As an agent, that's such an amazing thing to do. So I followed her, but I followed her for years, then I tweeted that I'd finished my manuscript, and she slid into my DMs. She said, 'I'm very interested.' I was like, 'Oh my god.' I'd never met her. I'd just admired her continually for many years. I said, 'Is this a joke?' She was like, 'No, can you just get on with it and send it to me?' Then that was it. Basically, I sent it to her. I sent it to her on Thursday, and Friday she said, 'Can you come into the office on Monday?' I went to the office, and before I sat down, she was like, 'I want to represent you.'

Kit de Waal, novelist and short-story writer

For my first two novels, I did have an agent, a good agent, and she sacked me. There's not many people that get sacked by their agents, but I did get sacked by my agent, so that's a badge of honour. She said that she was going on maternity leave. When she couldn't sell the second novel, she said, 'I'm going on maternity leave, don't wait for me.' So I didn't. But she did say, 'Look, there's another agent who's just starting off, and she might be interested.' So I tried the other agent and, again, I didn't have any expectations. It proved to be Jo Unwin, who's fantastic, and she took the book to auction.

Samira Shackle, journalist and author

I actually did this in quite an unusual way. So I had had this idea for the book for about a year and was half doing the proposal. I found it quite difficult to motivate myself because there's just an extraordinary amount of work that needs to go into a proposal, and you don't necessarily have a guarantee of anything at the end of it. I had it half done and wasn't quite finishing it, basically. Then Granta, or their then non-fiction arm Portobello, which has now been folded into Granta, launched a competition for non-fiction proposals for first-time authors. I thought I'd enter it so that I would have a deadline, basically, because I think years of being a journalist has kind of broken my brain for doing anything without a deadline. So I entered that, thinking it would just be a good reason to get my proposal finished, and then won it. So that meant I got the deal with Granta and the agent I'm now represented by as a result of that, and then after that point, it progressed like a normal book negotiation, although there was the understanding that Granta was going to publish it.

Leaf Arbuthnot, journalist and novelist

I wrote this novella called *An Unnamed Man*, an embarrassingly grandiose title, maybe when I was about 23. I entered it into this now-extinct writing competition and the prize was £1,000 and an agent. I won the award, got the £1,000 and spent it on a flight for me and my friend to India. So the money didn't last long: it lasted maybe, like, an hour. My agent, Laura Macdougall, was working at a different agency, but then she moved over to United [Agents], and she's been really at the heart of my success, limited though it is, as a writer.

It was funny. When I won that prize, I've rarely felt more elation: I just felt like I'd made it. I was like, 'Oh, I'm on my way to becoming a published novelist. Wow.' I was so excited. Then we tried to sell the book to maybe six publishers – or maybe it was fewer, maybe four, five – anyway, the big ones. They were all like 'no', 'no', 'no'. Orion was kind of nice about it. They were like: 'We really like Leaf's writing but, you know . . .'

It was trying to be quite edgy. It was set over 12 hours and it was about a man, a very cut-off man. It was kind of Larkinian in its attempts. It was about this man who wakes up in Woking and decides to go to London and kind of meanders around the city and eventually meets his estranged family. The only scene of worth, I think, is when he's reunited with his wife in London, on Clapham Road.

So Orion said, 'We like Leaf's writing, but can you give this a bit more plot and structure?' So then there were these quite tortuous few months where I was trying to basically syringe in plot and drive and eventually the whole thing collapsed. They said, 'Well, it's not going to work, but does Leaf have another idea?' And I did have another idea, which was the idea for *Looking for Eliza*. I wrote the first chunk, maybe 5,000 words, and the synopsis, and then they bought it off that.

The manuscript prize was absolutely essential to me getting my first book – or maybe my only book, who knows – published. But it was a long journey from me getting that and I was certainly schooled in being so enthusiastic and happy about the prize, because it wasn't the end of the road.

Irvine Welsh, novelist and screenwriter

I've never had an agent. I've just done it all myself, basically. I was fortunate because there was a guy at [Jonathan] Cape at the time who was Robin Robertson, and he was the managing editor there. He was Scottish and he had a massive interest in Scottish fiction, particularly this new wave of Scottish fiction that was coming out; people like Duncan McLean and Barry Graham, and then later Alan Warner and Kevin Williamson. So there was a bit of a movement there, in a sense, and I got to know these people. It was basically through Duncan that I got in touch with Robin. Robin got in touch with me, basically, and I'd published a couple of short stories. He said, 'These are great stories, have you got anything else?' I said, 'I've got a novel,' which was a lie, basically. I never really had a novel at the time. But he said, 'I'd love to see it.' I said, 'I'm still working on it, I'll be ready in a couple of months.' I thought, I'd better batter all this stuff into some kind of shape. It incentivised me to do it, to finish the novel that I was working on.

I've kind of knocked them [literary agents] all back. I thought, 'I'll just do it myself', because, again, luckily, [when I worked in] local government, I was involved in the competitive tendering, so I was used to looking at contracts, and I was also doing an MBA at the time. I had quite a decent business head on me. All you do with these things, you just ask for more money every time until they say no, basically. Then you go back and you hope that they'll reconsider and all that. I mean, I think I probably would have been quite a decent agent, actually, if I'd been an agent myself.

We're going back 30 years to different times. I think now it'd be quite difficult to operate without an agent. If I was a new writer starting out now, I'd be looking for a decent agent probably. But back then you could get away with it. I've kind of gotten away with it since then. I think maybe I should get somebody, but I think the fewer people you have to deal with, the better. I've got agents for film and TV in America and in the UK, and they're great. You need it in these environments, because it is so corporate and so factored in. Publishing, you probably do need it now as well. But I've got by without it, so I've stuck to that since.

Monica Ali, novelist

I had worked in publishing and I had a friend from that time who was a copy editor, a desk editor. She happened to be doing a maternity cover, again, as a copy editor at Transworld. I was looking for a bit of friendly feedback on my early chapters; I thought it was way too soon to be thinking about sending it out or investing in a *Writers' and Artists' Yearbook*, so I sent it to her. She then rang up and said, 'Would you mind if I showed it to an editor here?' I said, 'Go ahead', thinking nothing of it, really. Then I had a message to say, 'Do you have any more chapters?' I had another couple by that stage. Then they made me an offer.

She asked to have lunch, then she made me an offer there and then, which was astonishing. I had to excuse myself to go to the loo to jig up and down in front of the mirror. Of course, I wanted to say yes straightaway. She said, 'Come in for a meeting,' and I met some other members of the team. Actually, one of them said, 'You should really have an agent.' [That was probably] because I was happy to just sign anything because it seemed so extraordinary to me. It *was* extraordinary. But then, I took that advice and got an agent.

I couldn't really believe it was happening. It felt as though it might disappear if I took it around and shopped it elsewhere . . . the agent of course got the money increased and stuff like that. That's why you have an agent. They're more hard-headed and not so overwhelmed by the idea that anyone might want your book.

Simon Scarrow, novelist

There is a lot of bad advice you get when you're starting out. A lot of it comes in terms of books, which say 'How to become a published author and become immensely rich in ten easy steps.' There seems to be about three or four of these books that are published every season. You're thinking, 'Well, if they were any good, then there would only ever be one of those, wouldn't there?' It's basically that kind of self-help guide thing that is a minor little industry in itself.

I was reading a lot of those, and they were all saying, 'What you do is write a speculative letter then sample chapters and you send it off to the agent, you wait for it to come back and if they don't like it, you send it off to the next agent,' and so on. Anybody who has tried this approach [will probably agree], it's so dispiriting, and it takes so long. So what I did was I thought, 'If I'm writing Roman adventure fiction, who's writing that, Bernard

Cornwell-type novels, whatever?' I went through and made a list of the agents who are representing those kinds of authors. Basically, I phoned them up, spent an afternoon calling them all up, and if they weren't interested, I'd saved a huge amount of postage and time, crossed them off the list. Those who were interested and said, 'Yeah', we had a conversation about it, and they seemed keen. So I knew that when I sent it in, there would be a sympathetic pair of eyes looking at it, the moment it fell through the letterbox. Very, very quickly, I latched on to an agent called Wendy Suffield, who said, 'I really like it, love the first three chapters, can I see the rest of the book?' At that stage I had to say, 'Look, it's all in there [my head] still.' So I had to write the rest of the book really quickly.

William Boyd, novelist and screenwriter

One of the other unpublished novels I wrote, at Oxford in fact, was a very experimental novel about the Biafran war, the Nigerian Civil War, which I had lived through as a late teenager. I was in Nigeria in the late 60s, when the war was underway, and it had a profound effect on me. I wrote this novel called *Against the Day* and by then I'd published a few short stories. I had a kind of mentor figure in this wonderful man called Alan Ross, who had a magazine called *London Magazine*. Alan was a poet and a cricket correspondent and a memoirist. He knew everybody, he knew Graham Greene, he knew Evelyn Waugh, etc., etc. Alan liked this novel I'd written and he sent it to an agent who took me on, but she couldn't get it published. After a year or so, we decided to call it a day.

So my first success, if you like, was with a short-story collection, which I sent into the slush pile of two publishing houses, Jonathan Cape and Hamish Hamilton. I wrote a letter to the managing director of each one saying, 'Here is a collection of short stories. Nine of them have been published in various places.' So I had kind of proved myself. 'And, by the way, I've written a novel featuring a character who appears in two of these short stories, a drunken, overweight British diplomat called Morgan Leafy.' The managing director of Jonathan Cape, Tom Maschler, who recently died – he denied this to his dying day – never replied to me. But the managing director of Hamish Hamilton, Christopher Sinclair-Stevenson, who became my first editor, replied and said, 'We love the stories, but we'd actually like to publish the novel first.' That's when I told my lie. I said, having said I'd written it, 'The manuscript's in a terrible state, I have to revise this and retype it.'

I wrote *A Good Man in Africa* in a white heat of dynamism. It was all there waiting to come out. I delivered it to him – I remember this vividly – in September of 1979. He really liked it, but he said, 'I'm not going to publish it until January 1981.' So I had a whole year and a bit to wait. I had a novel accepted, it's going to come out, but for me 1980 is one of those bad, black hole years. It seemed to take ages to pass by. Then *A Good Man in Africa* was published and then six months later, my short-story collection *On the Yankee Station* was published. So I had two books out in one year, which was amazing. Eventually I confessed to Christopher that I had lied to him, that the novel hadn't been written and I'd written it at this incredible high-speed energetic burst, and he's forgiven me.

7

FEEDBACK AND EDITING

'Drop 30 per cent of your Latinisms . . . mow down every old cliché, uproot all the dragging circumlocutions, compress, diversify, clarify, vivify, & you'll make a book that will be read & talked of . . . '

– Edith Wharton

In 1998 D.T. Max, an American journalist, travelled to Indiana University to examine the manuscripts of celebrated short-story writer Raymond Carver. He was trying to get to the bottom of a literary rumour. Max had heard that Carver's long-time editor, Gordon Lish, had 'been quietly telling friends that . . . he had changed some of the stories so much that they were more his than Carver's'. In Indiana Max found ample evidence that this was true, discovering that Lish had made endless cuts and additions to Carver's work, at times inserting entire paragraphs. 'Lish's black felt-tip markings', he observed, 'sometimes obliterate the original text.'

Before his death in 1988 Carver had written to Lish saying: 'If I have any standing or reputation or credibility in the world, I owe it to you.' But Max's revelations about the true extent of Lish's role provoked heated reactions. Some came to the editor's defence; seeing one early draft 'has not done Carver any favours,' wrote one critic. 'Rather, it has inadvertently pointed up the editorial genius of Gordon Lish.' Others disagreed. Stephen King summarised the relationship as 'difficult and ultimately poisonous'.

The carving-up of Carver's work was unusual, but being edited remains central to working as a writer. Which is not to say it's easy – Simon found it tough seeing his work modified when he first began to be published in magazines. But eventually, like most writers, he came to appreciate it.

When editor and writer are clear they are on the same team, working towards a common objective, the process can be deeply fulfilling. And many people will find themselves occupying both roles at times; Rachel, an editor herself as well as a writer, has served on both sides of the fence.

Yet there are some writers, including successful ones, who just really hate to be edited. Vladimir Nabokov referred to editors who dared to suggest making changes to his text as 'pompous avuncular brutes'. In 2008, restaurant critic Giles Coren fired off a 1,000+ word memo to sub-editors at *The Times* bemoaning the change of a single word. (A rival newspaper gleefully published the screed.) In return, some writers almost seem to enjoy challenging their editors. 'I made their lives difficult, and intensely rewarding, I like to think,' Geoff Dyer told us. One perpetual point of tension between writers and their editors can be deadlines, as Charles Moore's story of working with then-journalist Boris Johnson demonstrates.

Fractious editorial relationships are suboptimal, though. An ability to take on feedback, ideally with good grace, is a crucial part of manufacturing prose. William Dalrymple goes as far as to state that it's the willingness to listen to others, rather than some ethereal notion of inborn talent, that truly accounts for the difference between good and great writing.

Just because you don't have a formal editor – as is usually the case at the start of any literary career – doesn't mean you can't profit from feedback. 'Take a deep breath and show the work, if you can,' novelist and screenwriter David Nicholls told us. Ask friends, peers or mentors. You may not agree with everything they say, but regardless of where it comes from, an external response is a learning opportunity.

David Nicholls, novelist and screenwriter

I think a constant problem for writers at the beginning of their careers is a sense that they have a right to be writers. It is very hard to overcome that hesitancy, that sense that you're taking up someone's time by showing them your work and that there are other people saying this and they're doing it better than you are and you're wasting your time. I got to a point where a friend of mine said, 'If I could give you anything, it would be the gift of confidence' – which was a line that I used in *One Day*. I wish I'd had that gift of confidence a little earlier.

Take a deep breath and show the work, if you can. Often that's harder than you think – it's hard to find people who will read what you've written, even if you're intensely confident and proud of it. The battle to get people to read things seems sometimes insurmountable. But I think don't be afraid, would be the advice. No one has a right that you don't have to be a writer, so don't be intimidated.

Joanne Harris, novelist

With my editors, inevitably there's had to be a reasonably close relationship. I think you have to have an editor who believes in you and who knows what you're doing, and who likes it, and an editor that you can trust, because I think if you're going to rely on somebody to edit your work, you've got to feel that they have something worth saying and that they have insight that you can use, and that will help you. So I've had a few editors, and a few agents. In fact, I've not stayed with my first agent, who died. I then got another agent who has also died. Both of them were pretty old. It's not like there's a curse on me that kills agents. But I'm now with an agent who I knew when I was at college, who I get on very well with because I know what he's like, I've known him for years.

I think with agents – again, like with editors – you have to have confidence in them. You have to believe that they believe in you and that they're not just monetising something that they think is going to make a profit for them, that they actually see something in your work that's different and that's interesting and that's worth pushing. I think anybody choosing an agent, or anybody working with an editor, needs to actually look at that relationship and understand that it's going to be an important relationship in your life and to make sure that it's built on a reasonably secure grounding. I think I've been pretty lucky with mine. I'm very fond of my new editor at Orion, because I've changed publishing houses after having been at Transworld for some time. I had an editor at Transworld who was also very supportive. But I do know people who lose editors every six months, and it can be a very soul-destroying thing because you're losing, if that happens, your most supportive relationship in writing. That can be quite a traumatic thing.

Marlon James, novelist

One of the best gifts you could ever get is the rejecter who tells you why. More often than not, they don't, and a lot of times when the person takes the time to tell you why, they're turning you down. That doesn't mean they necessarily want to see it again. You don't need that either. The feedback they give can be really instrumental. I remember that.

I remember the agent who rejected *Book of Night Women* because he didn't feel for any of the characters. I remember, because he gave really, really good instructions, but he was such an asshole about it. I remember thinking, 'All right, just put your feelings to the side and ignore the manner in which he's speaking to you, and just take the instruction.' I did. I did take his advice and I rewrote the novel, almost to a tee to suggestions that he made. Then I sent it to a different agent, because fuck him. I managed to get it published through Riverhead, who remains my publisher. So there's something to be said for the person who turns you down and tells you why, even if they're not very nice about it.

William Dalrymple, historian and travel writer

One of the things I learn the longer I am in this business is that, as a student, you think there are writers who are geniuses and just produce wonderful books. Often, that's simply not the case. What happens is that the really great writers whose prose you really admire – such as, in my case, [Ernest] Hemingway, Robert Byron, Patrick Leigh Fermor, Robert MacFarlane, John Berendt – do not find it any easier than the rest of us to put a sentence down. But what they do do is they just rewrite, and rewrite, and rewrite, and polish, and polish, and polish, so that the adequate sentences they put down become good sentences, and then become very good sentences, and then become excellent sentences that are unforgettable.

That's what makes a difference. It's the rewriting, the polishing, the re-editing. It's like a sculptor with a block of stone. You start with a block of stone and you chip away at it, and it then begins to look like something and gradually looks like something beautiful. Then it becomes something polished and finished and ready to go out.

But that rewriting and self-criticism, and the ability to take criticism from editors and friends you trust, that in a sense is I think the thing that makes great writers rather than good writers. I've got some friends who are super talented, but who are quite touchy about editorial intervention by other people, and say, 'This is my work, publish it as it is, or not.' Almost inevitably, you just know that the stuff that they are publishing is just one stage off being very, very good, because they just can't take that criticism and won't rewrite and won't rework it and won't listen to other people's advice.

What I do with all my books is that I print them out and I show them to people. Often, particularly in the early days, you'd find that people would land on the same passages and say, 'This isn't working', or in another place, 'This is wonderful'. Both of those are important information, that you know the stuff that's really good and you know the stuff which is much, much less good and has to either be contracted or to disappear altogether.

I find that if you pass a chapter to five different people, and they pause on the same area as being problematic, or the same problem in general about the whole passage, then there's a problem, and you need to change it. I often show my books to my colleagues and peers who I respect, but also often just ordinary readers who like reading that kind of book. They're often just as useful – 'Just so you know, I got really bored in the second half', or, 'It starts really well, but that bit in the middle just totally lost me.' That's crucial advice for you. In a sense, as the writer, you cease to be able to look at your own work and think critically about it and are not always aware what are the good bits, or what are the no-good-at-all bits, until much later.

Geoff Dyer, novelist and non-fiction writer

For all sorts of reasons I said, 'Oh, well, I'll do a book about tennis.' I didn't need to do a proposal for this, for all sorts of reasons that we won't go into now. I very happily got the money for the novel that I'd finished and this new book. Then when it came to it, I had no desire to write it. To cut a long story short, 18 months later, I handed in the book about tennis, which had changed somewhat – it had become a book about [Russian film-maker] Andrei Tarkovsky. What I'd done is instead of writing the book about tennis, I'd summarised his film *Stalker*. This is something that I'd emphasise really, that writers are often bitching about publishers and about how publishers are always wanting them to be more commercial and all this kind of stuff. But actually, my experience of publishers, is that they've been really surprisingly tolerant, given that they could justifiably have said, 'This isn't the book that was contracted. And even if we like this book about Tarkovsky, the truth is that Tarkovsky is a lot less commercially viable than tennis.' But in both the UK, and America, they happily, well – they with some surprise – took delivery of and published this book about Tarkovsky. I mean, I'm grateful to them. But it's absolutely right, I make their lives more interesting. This is what publishers should be. Anyone can publish a blockbuster novel by anybody, but it's exciting for them to get this kind of crazy unpublishable book and find a way to publish it. So I make their lives difficult, and intensely rewarding, I like to think.

Charles Moore, journalist and author

Always late of course. That's the single most notable thing – that's unfair, the single most notable thing about his [Boris Johnson's] copy was it was extremely entertaining and original – but the second most notable thing was that it was always late. There was perhaps some relationship between the two things, because what he wanted to do was to have a sort of adrenaline going in his own system when he was writing. Also he didn't want to miss anything by being too early.

He wasn't terribly pernickety about whether it be changed or not. He wasn't a prima donna about it. But there wasn't any time to change it seriously by the time it arrived, because it was supposed to come in at – let's say 6:00 – and it would never, ever arrive before 7:30. Sometimes it didn't arrive till 8:30. Which really almost meant that you had to delay printing of the paper and it was just disgraceful. So it was a constant, constant problem. One time I did deliberately spike his copy though it did arrive. I had something waiting to put in its stead because I was determined to show him, and so it did. He got very angry but it was held out because it arrived too late. He behaved well for about a month.

Jed Mercurio, screenwriter and novelist

After I did *Cardiac Arrest*, I found myself being a full-time TV writer and I had to come up with the idea for my next show. I really didn't know where my strengths lay as a writer, and a lot of people wanted to give me opportunities that, maybe, I should have thought twice about. I ended up working on quite an ambitious science-fiction series. Although I was supposedly one of the producers of the series – so that I could have the level of influence over it that I'd had over *Cardiac Arrest* – it ended up being a series that had a lot of competing creative forces pulling in different directions. As a result, the series didn't turn out to be what I wanted it to be.

What I learned from that is that you have to stay true to your creative vision, that you have to keep talking to people and collaborating with people. If people take the work off in a direction you don't agree with unilaterally, and then they refuse to discuss it with you, then they're the kind of person that you really shouldn't be working with. One of the things I've learned over the years is that the best work comes from collaboration with people who may be challenging to work with, but who are prepared to discuss things and to listen. Often they really help me to achieve my best work.

Jonathan Shainin, journalist and editor

[On the editing process at *The Guardian* Long Read, which Jonathan helped launch in 2014.] If the outline stage has happened – sometimes we commission a piece before the outline, sometimes we commission a piece after the outline. Depending on who the writer is or what they're doing, often we'll have another meeting, or even two meetings, during the reporting, pre-writing phase. So, we don't do a lot of outlines, but Sam [Knight] will come in three or four times as he's reporting a piece and we'll talk through. 'Well, what do you think is the shape of it?' We talk it out.

The draft comes in. Often, I think, with writers we work with a lot, the best thing to do is just have a meeting then and say, 'Okay, let's sit down.' Ideally, two of us will read it. One person will be the primary editor. If I'm the primary editor, Clare [Longrigg] or David [Wolf] will give it a read and give me some feedback.

Then you sit down with the writer, and usually the first edit is the big one. You are saying, 'Okay, well, this beginning is all wrong. And we can't end here. And why is section three only 200 words and section four is 2,000 words? And I don't know what the timeline is here, or the chronology is all a mess' – whatever, whatever, whatever. The first edit tends to be the big edit.

One of the things I think is very different about working at a newspaper is that you have to put the thing out three times a week, and we're a really small staff. In a way, if the old American magazine model is polishing these things to like near-perfection, I think we do that more than anyone else in England, but I think we don't do it to the degree that an American magazine does it. So at a point, you're like, 'Are we close enough to the finish line that if I put it on the schedule for Thursday, Tuesday night and Wednesday we can go through the final things?'

Hollie McNish, poet

I think it's [an article critical of McNish's work published in the *PN Review* in 2018] because I was published by Picador. Really, I think that's the only reason. I think it was the fact that an established poetry press, with a lot of credibility in the poetry world, published a collection of poems by me. I don't think anyone really cared before then whether or not they thought my poems were good enough – whatever that means. I think it was because Picador published them, and Picador is picky about poetry. I think it was that. I think it annoyed, I guess. I'm guessing this just from reading the articles, mainly that article [in the *PN Review*] and a few others that have been written.

It annoys me though, because I have studied a lot of poetry and I have worked really hard on it. I read and read and read. I know that's not the same as a university PhD on poetry, but there's this snobbery. I think the reason that article annoyed me so much was because it made up a lot of stuff. The criticism was fine, but then if I responded to it, it was often deemed that I just didn't want my poetry to be criticised, which is the opposite. It's really helpful to be criticised, because I've never had that. I just really wanted feedback and having an editor and stuff was brilliant.

But it just made up quite a lot of ideas about what I found quite weak arguments. There was this idea, because I'd put poems on YouTube, that you're an attention-seeker that's desperate to be famous. There was this kind of view, which I think's amazing: the idea that if you're a poet and you're sending 20 poems a week to publishers and magazines that you don't want to be a famous writer. It's pretty similar, it's just different outlets for your writing. I think that that divide was quite stark.

Merve Emre, author, academic and literary critic

I really like the process of being edited. I like the conversation that takes place. I like the different rounds of editing. I like that Leo [Carey, a *New Yorker* editor] will give me different edits than the copy editor, who will give me different edits than the fact-checker – all of those things make me think differently about the work.

But I do think in order to undergo that, and to take a sense of pleasure from it, and to learn from it, which I think requires taking pleasure from it, you really have to be capable of taking your ego out of it. I really think you have to commit to a kind of mindset where you believe that what everyone wants at the end of the day is for this piece of writing to be the best piece of writing it can possibly be. I think that requires a certain toughness, a mental toughness on the part of the writer. I think it also requires a certain kind of compassion on the part of the editor, because I have worked with editors who I have felt were trying to be punitive or condescending. I don't think that that is good for anybody.

I don't know that students have that toughness. I don't say that in the sense that I think students are sensitive or anything like that. I simply think that because of the institutional position they're in, and the massive power differential between you as their educator and their role as your student, it is really hard for them to commit to that mindset. It's really hard for them to not feel like they're being judged. Or it's really hard for them to believe sometimes that your evaluation of them can go hand-in-hand with the desire simply to make their work better. So I think that there are just certain institutional reasons why marking and editing cannot be the same thing.

Andrew Hankinson, journalist and author

That *Observer* piece [a cover story he did] was great, because Ian Tucker [an *Observer* editor] gave me a PDF of the piece. That was the first time that had happened. He gave me a PDF of it and said, 'This is what it's going to look like when it's published. Are you happy with that?' I approved of every single word, and it was great. But then I was writing for some other magazines and they were changing stuff and I wouldn't know about it until I saw [the finished thing]. I didn't know to ask for PDFs at the time – I do now, I always get PDFs for everything – but I didn't know to do that.

So stuff would be published, and it had my byline on it, and there were just the most atrocious phrases in there. Clumsy writing. One place, they changed one of my quotes to kind of ramp up the piece. I was so furious. I stopped looking at stuff when it got published. When I was writing a whole feature that I'd spent a month on or something, and it would come out, I don't want to overblow it, but I felt very depressed for a month or so – really angry, frustrated at first and then just depression, because I just thought: 'I've put all that into that and then this has happened to it. It's something I can't now put on a website; I don't want to, I don't want anyone to see it. And I know people have seen it and read it and thought that I wrote that.' I was trying to establish my reputation as someone who could write decent stuff. Suddenly, there's this stuff that I'm embarrassed of, that I have to then tell people: 'I didn't really write that.'

Jon Lee Anderson, journalist and author

There's a lot of editing at the *New Yorker* – that's just the way it is. I feel that what's important to me is that the final piece has the integrity with which I wrote it and intended it – both in its creative sense and its philosophical sense. So the structure may change, and that will change through the editing or we may layer in new material, because the editor strongly believes that it needs that and I agree or come around to it – I have no choice but to agree.

I've had three editors in my 20 years at the *New Yorker*, each of them very different. And every piece is different. If I'm given more time on my own to write and produce the piece, I will produce a more polished, finished piece in the hopes that it will be ready for primetime. It never really is.

But if I'm really, really pressured – as sometimes I am because I am in places where there's a lot of breaking [news], wars or so on – I have less time to edit and I tend to write longer, which gives, of course, the editor the possibility of getting in there with their scalpel or their machete, as the case may be. So I have to leave it up to them to cut and to maybe suggest changes or structural changes.

Samanth Subramanian, journalist and author

Access [for a *New Yorker* piece on Arvind Kejriwal, an Indian politician and activist] wasn't difficult because, at the time, this was a small but rising political party and a well-known, but otherwise not-quite-powerful, politician. It was his very first election. He was just making the transition from an anti-corruption activist to a politician, so I wanted to catch him on that cusp and to explore this idea of whether activism has its limits and whether, as he seemed to think at the time, the only way to change the system was to be inside it as a politician. I thought that was quite interesting – and that was the premise on which I pitched the piece.

So access wasn't hard. I had enormous problems with writing and structuring the story, I remember. I did an entire draft and this was all very harrowing, I have to point out, because for that first piece, Remnick himself [David Remnick, the editor of the *New Yorker*] was my editor. I cannot tell you what that's like, knowing that if you fail, or if he wants to kill the piece, you will probably never write for the magazine again. So I had my heart in my mouth every time he sent me an email about the piece.

The first time I sent him a draft, he said, 'This doesn't work, you need to start with a guy' – the traditional *New Yorker* structure, which is to start with a man or a woman at a particular place on a particular day. 'Just stick with the template for now, it's your first story,' and so I did that. That's what the final version of the piece looks like.

The thing that I had a lot of problems with, which I'm articulating much better now than I was then, was to move past Kejriwal, the politician, to these deeper layers of these ideas about activism versus politics, the limitations of one, the dangers of the other, and this man who is making his transition from one to the other. I had to get coached extensively by David, as well as by another editor who I worked with, in bringing those ideas to light. It was a huge, intense learning experience, which I'll never forget.

Amanda Craig, *novelist*

Don't worry if it's no good. Just keep going. You must keep going until you get to the end. Because once you get to the end, you've got something that you can make better. But if you don't get to the end, you will never ever make it better, you will just be lost forever in the doldrums.

Alexander McCall Smith, *novelist*

I find that I have very light editing from my editors at the publishing houses, in that I will occasionally get a few suggestions about, perhaps, saying a little bit more about a particular instance in the novel, something of that sort. But often, none at all. That's not to say that they're not doing their job. They are: they're reading and they pay close attention to it. Of course, I get very good copy editing. I think copy editors are unsung heroes of the publishing industry. They will be the ones who will find inconsistencies; the editor at the publishing house may not be looking for [incon-sistencies] in quite the same way in which a copy editor looks for them. So I do find copy editors, particularly if you're in the hands of a copy editor who has edited a number of your books, can remember things that you forget yourself. So they'll say, 'Oh, excuse me, that character in the previous book was called something different.' That's a serious example – maybe less obvious errors will creep in.

Then as I say, I'm very fortunate in that I have very light editing, which is just as well, because often we have very little time between the completion of manuscript and the putting of the book into production. It's all done really quite quickly. They have a synopsis of the book at quite an early stage, because publishers will have their sales conferences and whatnot, and the editor will have to go and speak to people about the book. So they've got to have a general idea of what it's about. That, of course, can lead to embarrassment when the editor has gone and described the book in particular terms and then you produce a manuscript which has very little relation to what the editor has sold to colleagues, so to speak. They sometimes write the blurb in advance, and then you have to say to them, 'Well, I'm sorry that there isn't a horse in this story, as you've suggested', that sort of thing. Often before I've written the book, the cover's there and the title is there.

Ruth Ozeki, novelist

They were very, very low-budget, horrible films . . . But they were fun, it was fun to be a part of a film set and to learn to see things visually. I went on to work in television, I didn't stay in low-budget horror, that was just my entry. I went on to work in Japanese television and then started making independent films of my own. I realised early on, especially doing the documentary work that I did for Japanese television – I would take a crew out and we'd shoot and that was fun, I enjoyed that – that the programme itself was created in the editing room. So if I wanted to learn about storytelling, that's where I needed to be.

Now, at that time, I was working for Japanese television, so all of the editing was done in Japan. They were just using me to be out in the field in America to direct and produce things in the US. But finally, after pushing and pushing, they started asking me to come to Japan and do the editing. That's really where I learned how to tell a story. Up until that point I'd tried writing novels, but I could never move my characters through the arc of a plot in a quick, interesting and efficient way. I would always get stuck somehow. Even something as stupid-sounding as characters would enter a room, enter a location on one side, and the action was happening on the other side of the room, and I literally didn't know how to move my characters across the room to get to where the action was. I think I was just a very literal-minded person.

There were techniques to cut, to edit, to compress time, to manage time, and these were largely visual techniques, changing the camera angle, changing the frame size, doing reverse shots. There are all sorts of cutaways, all sorts of ways of doing that in film. I learned to do that in the editing room in Tokyo. After that, when I went back to writing again, and tried writing another novel, suddenly, I had the tools to do it, it was no longer a problem. The other thing too, of course, is that television is a very impatient medium and it's very expensive. So you can't mess around in TV, you have to cut to the chase really quickly, and grab your viewers and hang on to them. So techniques that I learned in editing helped me know how to do that, almost instinctively, when I went back to writing. It was wonderful, I remember feeling just like: 'Oh my god, this used to be so difficult and now it's not.' That was the big breakthrough.

Elif Shafak, novelist

Editing is a big, big part of this. Sometimes, when we talk about creative writing, we tend to think of it as adding a layer upon layer every day. People say: 'How many words have you written today?' But nobody asks: 'How many words have you deleted today, have you erased today?' But that, too, is part of the process. It's not like every day you add five pages, 20,000 words, whatever. There are moments when you stop, and you take out chunks of your writing, you let go.

I think that is the hardest bit about the creative writing process, letting go, because you've put [in] so much effort and faith and love – you believed in those pages – but now they don't work. So editing, destroying what you have written, not only constructing, but sometimes destroying, too, is part of the process. I have learned over the years that there are times when you feel anxious, lots of self-doubt, and there are times when you feel like 'Okay, this is working, this is going well.' That too, the highs and lows is, I think, part and parcel of the writing journey.

8

FAILURE AND REJECTION

'These manuscripts were perseveringly obtruded upon various publishers for the space of a year and a half; usually, their fate was an ignominious and abrupt dismissal.'

– Charlotte Brontë

Every writer has failed at some point in their career. The failure may have been small: bungling a scene or turning out a clumsy phrase. Or it may be something that feels a lot more consequential – maybe you sent your writing off to an agent or publisher and never received a response, or you find yourself with a bad case of writer's block.

A working day can feel like a failure if you haven't hit your word count or have spent more time answering emails than immersed in your project. Procrastination has long been a problem for many writers: even Charles Dickens found writing a constant exercise in restlessness and frustration. Producing *Little Dorrit* involved 'prowling about the rooms, sitting down, getting up, stirring the fire, looking out the window, teasing my hair, sitting down to write, writing nothing, writing something and tearing it up, going out, coming in, a Monster to my family, a dread Phenomenon to myself'.

Some failures can feel humiliating, as the quote from Brontë attests. A writer might spend long periods toiling away at their work, only for an editor or publisher to say that it is unsatisfactory and must be redone; worse, they may declare there is no market for it or that it is beyond salvation. It can be hard to maintain confidence in your work when faced with point-blank rejection.

If that all seems very depressing, it needn't: failure can be instructive. When we ask interviewees about a time they failed in their writing careers, we also ask them what they learned from it. Some realised that they were merely aping other writers and needed to find their own voice and style. Others found that only in identifying what didn't pass muster could they gain clarity on what did.

A few of our interviewees came to understand that they were expending effort in the wrong direction and that their literary talents would be better used in a different way. Simon Lancaster describes himself as a 'failed songwriter' – but a sense of rhythm and lyricism no doubt helps when he's writing speeches for clients. Patrick Radden Keefe did not make much progress as a screen-writer, but working with story beats and scenes helped him understand how to structure long-form journalism.

Sometimes writers will fail for reasons beyond their control – because an editor doesn't quite grasp what they are trying to do, for instance. The Brontës' experience sends a heartening message to dejected writers. Their manuscripts which were subjected to 'ignominious and abrupt dismissal' included *Wuthering Heights*. Charlotte wrote that Anne and Emily did not allow themselves 'for one moment to sink under want of encouragement' and they went on to find a path to publication. The rest is history.

Sara Baume, novelist

We were both on social welfare. During this period we adopted this one-eyed dog that was somewhat loopy. I was really struggling at the time, I think, to do anything, and felt like I failed at everything in life. At the same time, there was no sort of reasonable career path, either, because it was the recession. That was what wrote the novel [*Spill Simmer Falter Wither*], really – it was just having all of this time that I didn't know what to do with and writing novels was as meaningless as anything else I could do with it in a way.

It grew out of those experiences, because another part of it was sort of rediscovering the countryside in which I'd grown up. But for the past, or for the former, several years, I'd been living in Dublin, and being educated and sort of forgetting the names of wildflowers and trees, and the animals that live in rock pools and all these kinds of things. So it was walking the dog that sort of slowed me down and made me look at the world differently. Then gradually, the novel grew out of notebooks and observations.

Tessa Hadley, novelist and short-story writer

I do definitely have a sense of why [publishers] passed on [early books] – I think because they were awful. They were right. To flatter myself, I would like to think there's a funny kind of awful that happens when, one day, maybe you will be able to do it, but you're not halfway there. You're really catastrophically failing to do the thing that maybe, one day, you find a way of doing.

I think I was trying to write other people's books. I was still in a very submissive, admiring and worshipping phase as a reader. I was reading far too many classics and not enough contemporary fiction. If I was reading contemporaries, I was reading Nadine Gordimer and thinking, 'Well, I'll try and write a great novel, like her novels of the apartheid era in South Africa, but I'll set it in South Wales', where I was then living and do live again now. So there was some unspeakable novel about the miners' strike, which I'm glad is now rotted down in landfill. It wasn't me. I wasn't saying what I thought – I was saying what I thought someone else should write.

In the moments when I did finally start putting down the first sentences that were true, to some extent, it was in accepting that the terrain was small. It was what it was: it was my world, not my life, but my world. I can remember some of the first sentences I wrote that felt true – [they] were about a woman visiting Cardiff Museum with a child in a wheelchair. That was not directly connected to my life, but somehow, something in there clicked. I was fully me, utilising what I thought about things, what I had to say. I recognised the sound of myself. But that took a long time – there were about four awful, effortful, goody-good novels before that.

Simon Lancaster, speechwriter and author

Pretty much, I'm a failed songwriter. [Among speechwriters] failure is the only common trait. We've got failed poets, failed journalists, failed novelists, failed authors, but we're all happy doing what we do. I first started writing songs when I was 11. My first job, when I was 16 years old, was as a pianist in a restaurant off Leicester Square. I was sending demo tapes – never got anywhere – then I got into politics.

Jack Thorne, playwright and screenwriter

They [plays he wrote at university] were awful. One was an adaptation of a really lovely book called *The Wave* by Morton Rhue. One was a reinterpretation of *King Lear* – oh man, it was awful – called *You Have Been Loved*, named after a George Michael song. It was telling it from Edgar's and Edmund's perspective. It was dreadful. It was awful. It was one of the worst things ever. There was one called *Boy Meets Girl*. One called *Tender*.

I was working it out, you know? And people came, which was very nice. It was really good from that perspective – you learn a lot from sitting, watching an audience as they watch your thing. I was writing a lot of funny stuff, or trying to write funny stuff. A comedian, a stand-up, will say: 'You have to stand up on stage and you have to work out that what people might find funny in the room is very different from what people might find quite funny on stage.' So there was a lot of that. There was a lot of what people find truthful.

The big thing is: what stops the sweet wrappers and the coughing? That is the test, I think, for every dramatist. Those moments of stillness in a theatre, where suddenly everything goes quiet. Those moments, you can feel them. They are the most exciting moments you have as a writer. I definitely learned about those moments and there were a couple in those [early] plays. There were a lot of coughing moments beside them.

Patrick Radden Keefe, journalist and author

I have a really impressive record of unproduced screenplays. It's amazing to think that somebody could go as long as I have, writing things as paid gigs, and seeing them not get made.

I don't even remember when it was, but I think it was probably 2005. I had a friend who was a screenwriter who had a meeting with somebody at HBO and he brought me into the meeting and we pitched a show. That first thing we did was a story about the world of intelligence. So it was right after I'd written *Chatter* [about government eavesdropping] and it was a world

I knew about. We sold the show to HBO and wrote a pilot. They didn't make it, but they liked it, so they got us to write a different pilot about something else. They didn't make that. And at that point, I was kind of off to the races. But it's just been a thing I've done on the side for years.

The screenwriting has been really helpful for my journalism in terms of thinking about structure, in thinking about how you construct a scene and particularly how you transition from one scene to another. All my years as a failed screenwriter have at least hopefully paid dividends in that respect.

Gary Younge, journalist and author

I was way out of my depth [in his early years at *The Guardian*]. I do not mind admitting it. I'd been to City [University in London to do the postgraduate journalism course]. I knew not to make stuff up. I knew not to steal other people's work. But the craft of gathering and assembling I was learning on the job. It felt like quite a high-wire act, actually.

. . . I was the super junior Scrappy-Doo person in the office. Then one day someone said, 'Gary, you just do the news today.' It was all kind of kid gloves. Anyway, I still completely fucked it up. Just fucked it up. Because I didn't know what I was doing.

There were talks between Inkatha and ANC [political parties in South Africa] and the election board, something about participation or not-participation. Somehow I had figured out – I didn't make it up, it was on a [news] wire somewhere – that they had reached an eleventh-hour compromise. We ran with that. They had not reached an eleventh-hour compromise. The story the next morning was about how it had all crashed and burned, apart from in *The Guardian*. I think I was told, 'Oh, yeah, that news agency. They're not very good.' Anyway, I just didn't know. I would say for about the first three years, my heart was always in my mouth when a piece was coming out. What have I done? Where's this going to go? What mistake did I make? Not confident at all.

Alex Kay-Jelski, journalist and editor

When I was at *The Mail* sports desk – when I was really, really near the beginning of my career – I was put in charge of the cricket scoreboard. I completely screwed it up. My boss called me and I was like: 'How the hell am I going to get out of this?'

I over-apologised. I apologised so much – as if I had caused some harm to his family. I think he was completely taken aback and didn't know what to say. I learned that when you mess up, own it, because then people can't be angry with you.

George Packer, journalist and author

I spent ten years writing two novels, and they could be called failures. They're not terrible, although I don't look at them much anymore, but they never found many readers and what writers need, above all, are readers. That was a long – and I would say depressed and depressing – period of my life. Why I spent ten years, crucial years, doing that is a little hard to say other than that I just had it in my head that I was a novelist and therefore I had to write novels – which is not a very good reason to write novels, they should come out of some more organic impulse.

But what I did learn was to write narrative. That stood me in very good stead when I started getting journalism assignments from magazines like the *New Yorker*, because I already knew how to write a narrative, how to create characters, how to tell stories with scenes and dialogue. So they were not totally wasted years, but at the time, they were a rock bottom of my life as a writer.

Colum McCann, novelist

I was 21 years old, full of fire and vim, thinking that I was going to be like Jack Kerouac. I bought a big roll of paper and I put it into the typewriter and I started typing away. At the end of that summer, I had about a foot and a half of absolute gibberish. I had to look at myself and say: 'You do not know what you're doing.'

I had to question myself: 'What am I going to do? Am I gonna go back to Dublin and go back to the newspapers (which was an option) or am I going to do something a little bit more reckless?' [That] is kind of what I ended up doing. I got on a bicycle and took it across the United States for a year and a half. That was an incredible journey that really helped me out in extraordinary ways.

I entered what I now think of as that vast democracy of stories and storytelling. I would meet people, and they would tell me their stories, and I would carry them, I would chew them up and take them down inside me and carry them down the road. I didn't realise that until years later, but I was learning how to really, really, really listen to other people. In the end it was the most extraordinary thing for me to do. I think it made me into a writer.

Anne Enright, novelist

If you start working at eight o'clock at night and work through to four or five in the morning, you may not be entirely sane four months later. That was something I knew by the end [of her stint on the University of East Anglia's creative-writing course]. I also knew that putting little note cards all over your room would not invite the book in, even if they were in different colours; you might wake up and look at your wall and think, 'I don't know what any of this means.'

Those things, which are the kinds of things you might tell your children or your students – get a bit of fresh air, go for a walk, all of that – it was decades before I really properly learned those things, which is to stop working and organise your head.

But what did I learn? What did I learn? I used to like to say I learned about failure. I learned about ambition. I perhaps learned how to fill the gap between the two. At the end of the year, I dumped the book and all my imaginings, because it was untenable. It didn't exist, it wasn't in any way real.

Rosie Nixon, editor and novelist

With my third novel, I felt very pressured to hit a deadline given to me by my publisher. I love writing. I am so passionate about it. It's a hobby to me, and something that I feel I absolutely have to have in my life. When I felt that I was not going to hit this deadline, I was trying to stay up late and shoehorn it into any spare minute in the day, which was very challenging and making me feel quite stressed.

So I learned the power of saying 'no', and I actually was prepared to walk away from the book if they weren't able to extend the time for me, which obviously would have been quite a heartbreaking decision. But I managed to go back to them and say that I was struggling. I was honest about it and, actually, it was amazing. They listened to me and they extended the deadline. So actually, I managed to turn what felt like a failure into something that has made it a much better book.

Ferdinand Addis, historian

I started my career as a writer of trade non-fiction, with three quite short books of 30,000 words – the sorts of book that you'd pick up by the till, not super-serious. But it was very exciting for me. These were the first books that would have my name on. The first one, I put a lot into, a lot of effort, and the result was very good. It was a good book. It was successful. That gave me an amazing sense of confidence in myself as a writer. I really began to believe that this was something I could do, that this was a career that I could have.

I attributed a lot of that success to some sort of talent, to a facility with words, to a fluency in writing. So when it came time to start working on the second book, the second of these short books, I really felt as though I could just whip something up out of thin air just using dexterity and using style, using effect. It didn't work at all; it was a very bad failure. I rewrote it, so it was okay in the end. But the first draft didn't work at all and it was very humbling.

What I learned from that is that, as a writer, it's important not to get too excited about your power with words. The words are not the point, the words are the medium. There's a more general point here, which I think is really important. In the modern age of writing, which is overwhelmingly online, a lot of writers hone their craft on Twitter. But that online ecosystem is a world of style. It has a very distinct voice, a lot of in-jokes. People who want to be writers often have a good ear, they're able to pick up the voice, to perform in the style. That can be superficially funny or attractive.

But there's a terrible emptiness at the heart of a lot of online writing. There are a lot of people doing the style, doing the jokes, but without saying anything. I think that's a real pitfall to avoid. Don't let the quality of your wordsmithery obscure the true aim of writing – which is to say something.

Sebastian Junger, journalist, author and film-maker

Any writer, myself included, has failed in their career. In my 20s, I was enormously enamoured of fiction writing; fiction writing is very romanticised, I think. I was growing up as a writer in the 1980s, when the short story had been elevated as an art form. I had these crazy ideas like, 'Oh, I want to be a short-story writer.'

First of all, it just doesn't work financially. You wind up being a professor in a college, which is fine, but I didn't want to do that. Secondly, you're just not affecting the world. We all have a duty to make the world a little bit of a better place, and I'm not sure fiction does that – maybe a little bit.

But journalism – good, responsible, moral journalism – is an incredible tool for helping humanity. The truth is sacred, the truth is necessary, and that's what journalism should be about. Fiction is gorgeous. It's a beautiful medium, but it feels rather self-indulgent. I spent ten years trying to become a fiction writer, and it failed – thank god it failed. It was an important failure. That was probably the biggest setback of my career and I'm glad it happened.

Christina Patterson, journalist and author

I sent off a chunk of a book I'd been working on, or my agent sent it off to a publisher. I saw their response. [My agent], unfortunately, when he told me it had been rejected, forwarded me the email from the editor who had rejected it, whom I knew. It was A: socially excruciating and B: extremely upsetting, because he said, 'Christina Patterson is a first-class journalist, but I must admit I was disappointed by this.' I was really crushed by it.

Now, as it happens, I think what I sent him was a pile of shit, and thank god nobody published it. But it really did crush me. I allowed myself to be very scared for a long time before I tried again.

Oliver Franklin-Wallis, journalist and author

Being a writer is to have a tremendous sense of failure. In my experience, nothing I've ever done ends up as good as I imagined it in my mind. That can be tremendously challenging for your own mental health. Something that people should bear in mind, particularly at the start of their career, is that a lot of the time magazine stories, in particular, are a multi-person process.

You might have the idealised version of the story in your mind. But then you might have problems with access, which take it down a level, then you might have a couple of not-great interviews, or some people don't want to talk about things, or there's a scene that you can't get that might take you down a level. Then you file a first draft to an editor, and they don't like the way that you're taking things or this turn of phrase that you love, and you've got to kill your darlings. So, all of which is to say that, by the time it actually reaches the page, there's been a lot of compromises, and it's not the ideal version in your head. The challenge then is to pick yourself up and go for it next time and try and get closer and closer to where you want to be. Make every story as good as it can be.

David Mitchell, novelist

Pretty much every time I write a novel, I fail about 50 pages in. I thought this was going to be great; I had this image in my head about how this was going to be the best damn thing I've ever written. And oh my lord, look at this sorry, gobbling, vomity mess of a pile I've got here.

That feeling's good news. That's your ally. Most of it's right, but something's wrong. Often there's something in it that you don't want to give up – you're right, there's nothing wrong with it, it's a great idea. It just doesn't belong in this book and you've got to kiss it goodbye. You reboot at that point and you think, 'Okay, I've got to get rid of that. What bits do I really like now and, actually, who is this story about? Who is it really? I thought it was about this, but it's clearly not. So who and what is it about?' Give yourself that licence to go wrong, because I think you usually have to.

Linda Grant, novelist and non-fiction writer

I left it very late. I didn't become a novelist until I was in my early 40s. I think there's a number of reasons for it.

I was always writing and I was winning teenage literary competitions, so I always thought of myself as a writer. I wrote an enormous amount. I was always reading; I was an only child until I was eight. I was reading all the time and looking for books which were relevant to my personal experience. Well, if you're growing up in a Jewish immigrant household in Liverpool, there really were not any children's books which were relevant to my personal experience, there was absolutely nothing and I'm sure there is still nothing. So I was having to read books about people sculling on Lake Windermere, without understanding any of the vocabulary.

I think that because I was reading English literature and then American literature, I found it really quite hard to find a voice for myself. American literature is about the immigrant experience: Philip Roth said the Jews, like the Irish and the Catholics, made their contribution to the construction of the national identity, which didn't happen in Britain. It has started to, in the last ten years, but certainly not when I was growing up.

So what happened was, I felt that there was an English novel, which I admired enormously and still revere, but I didn't know how to write such a novel. I didn't understand how you wrote about class, for example; I felt too much of an outsider. But I didn't feel an outsider in the sense of having an identity anyone could easily understand, so everything seemed kind of second-hand. I was writing almost as an act of ventriloquism.

I gave up for a long time, and journalism suited me very well, because it allowed me to inveigle my way into the homes of complete strangers and ask them quite detailed personal questions, which suited me down to the ground because I was very curious.

May Jeong, journalist

I'm writing a book right now and, most of the time, I have no idea what I'm doing. I have this image of having been dropped in a box and brought into a vast house and I've been left in the hallway; the lid is open so I can peer out and look around, but that's all the visibility I have. I have no sense of what kind of a house I'm in. I have no idea what the attic looks like. I haven't been to the kitchen yet. I don't know what the drawing room looks like. That is a terrifying prospect.

But maybe one thing I've learned in my old age, is that there is a truth in a lot of the platitudes that people say – trust the process is one. It's deeply uncomfortable. It's human nature to want to categorise things and make sense of things that don't make sense. But perhaps, what rewards you is your ability to just sit with something that is quite formless.

9

MONEY

'When I was young I thought that money was the most important thing in life. Now that I am old, I know that it is.'

– Oscar Wilde

Money is the Voldemort of the literary world, the great unsaid, the thing that everyone, from authors to agents and publishers, is loath to talk about. Who would want to dwell on such a grubby matter when they could be discussing the finer points of storytelling and craft?

And yet, there are few things which obsess writers more. Look behind the façade of art-for-art's sake and you'll find that literature is itself full of wordsmith characters whose financial triumphs and woes mirror the hopes and fears of their creators. From plucky Jo in *Little Women*, supporting herself by her pen, to Jack Torrance in Stephen King's *The Shining*, a struggling writer who is driven insane, the economics of writing are everywhere.

We asked every writer we interviewed the same question: how has money interacted with their writing lives? No one was exempt, from first-book debutantes to global celebrities. We did this because we think it's important for aspiring writers to know the financial realities as they embark on literary careers. But there's an undeniable thrill too, in saying the unsayable, and listening to the responses. 'Be as candid or as guarded as you like,' we told our interviewees, in the obvious hope they would lean towards the former. Responses varied. Certainly not everyone wanted to venture into this territory, and we've had at least one very well-known writer ask us to subsequently delete this part of the conversation after the interview (we declined). But we've been pleasantly surprised at how often, and how openly, authors, including the really very famous, have deeply engaged with the question. It's as though they too are glad to bring this oft-shrouded subject out into the light. And successful writers can usually still remember being struggling ones.

Every top-selling author has experienced the life-changing moment the money first arrives, and they realise they have made it big – like when Ian Rankin read a royalty statement and thought someone had accidentally added too many zeroes. These kinds of anecdotes are dramatic, but they're also not typical. If you are a writer yourself, prosaic stories can be more useful; accounts of how writers kept body and soul together as they carved out time to write, from the common day jobs of teaching and journalism to a range of other occupations. Our interviews have also revealed moving accounts of real financial hardship.

The responses included in this chapter, as with so many of the themes covered in this book, represent only a fraction of the discussions we've had with our interviewees. We hope they're useful. But we're also aware that stories of people making substantial money from writing are overrepresented, as we mainly speak to highly successful authors.

The fact is that most writers in Britain are unable to support themselves without other work. The latest (2022) report commissioned by the UK Authors' Licensing and Collecting Society (ALCS) found that professional authors earn a median of just £7,000 a year, down from £10,497 in 2018 and £12,330 in 2007. Money, or a lack of it, and the way it is shared between authors, publishers and publications, is also central to the issues of literary diversity that have become prominent in recent years. We believe that having open, frank discussions about writing and money can be a first step to a more equitable world of words.

Ian Rankin, novelist

I was very lucky in the early days; my wife had a job and she was supporting me. She believed in me and she wanted me to be a full-time writer, so she was subsidising me for a while. But she also persuaded me we needed to get out of London at some point if I was going to be a full-time writer. We couldn't afford to live in London. We couldn't afford to take the hit by losing the salary. She said, 'Let's go and live in France'. So we went and lived in France in a ramshackle farmhouse with very little money.

Suddenly, I was getting a bit panicky. I was having to write two books a year just to make enough money to live on, because the books weren't selling very well. The publisher didn't want two Rebus novels a year. So I created this character, Jack Harvey, a pseudonym, and wrote thrillers under that name for a little while till I was making enough money from the Rebus books. It was kind of fraught. There were a lot of times when I thought I was going to be dumped, because it was midlist, as it's called, which means you're selling, you're ticking over, you've got fans, you're selling a few copies, you're making a little bit of money for the publisher. But they can't get excited about you. They don't know if you're ever going to break out from that midlist.

Then *Black and Blue* came along. I remember it vividly. It was towards the end of the year, there was a little teaser in *The Times* newspaper, and it said the best crime novel of next year is published next week. That was early January, and I thought, who the hell's written that? Then I bought the paper the following week. There was Marcel Berlins, the crime-fiction reviewer, saying *Black and Blue* is the best novel I'll read all year. That was the first week of January. Come November that year, it won the Gold Dagger, which persuaded my publishers I knew what I was doing, persuaded me that everything was going to be okay. That was Rebus novel number eight or nine, I think. It was a long way into the series.

I thought, okay, I know what I'm doing. They know that I know what I'm doing. And, although *Black and Blue* wasn't a best seller, it didn't hit the top ten, the next book, I think, did. It got one week in the top ten. The book after that, I think, got to number one.

Rebus novel number 11, 12, 13 maybe, I remember it well. I was in America on a book tour. It was hopeless. It was cold, and it was wet. I was in a motel and I think I was snowed in, almost, and I think my event had been cancelled that night. I phoned my wife back in Edinburgh. She said, 'Your six-monthly royalty statement's come in.' You get royalty statements twice a year for your backlist sales. I said, 'Yeah.' She said, 'It's six figures.' I went, 'Oh, that's a mistake.' I phoned my agent. I said, 'Look, it's been a mistake.' He said, 'No.' What it was, it was the critical mass. It was people who'd read the most recent book, had liked it, and gone back and bought everything. And everything was in print. So if you grab them at book eight and they go back and read the first seven, hallelujah. So my six-monthly royalty statement had gone from four figures to six figures. I thought, well, that is a substantial change in my fortunes.

Anne Enright, novelist

I've no problem talking about money, because I think that these various purities that we impose on writers, especially actually in the Irish setting – where a writer is far too elevated, or pure or poor, to talk about money – feed into a lot of mythologies about Irish poetics. Anyway, how did I do it? First of all, this is what I say to anyone who wants to leave a full-time job. And I had a good job by the standards of the day, although I was too young to realise what that was.

First of all, I say you build a bridge out of your workplace. So you don't go cold turkey. I worked at the weekends. And it took considerable effort, I have to say, in order to write a book of short stories, which was my first publication. I had been published, *The Portable Virgin* came out in [1991]. I was with Jonathan Cape, and that was a really fantastic first step. So I had that under my belt, before I decided to give up the day job.

I then started saving, and put a deposit on a flat. So we only had the mortgage. We had somewhere to sit cross-legged on the mattress in the corner . . . I had a place to live. After that, I starved, thanks for asking. There was an anxious decade, and I wasn't really doing anything great. It was full of anxiety and full of weird procrastinations and difficulties. I got a fax machine. This is how old I am, I got a fax machine from my husband, Martin, for some Christmas maybe. And I realised I could send little columns off to Radio Four. I did Radio Four columns, which turned in £80 sterling each, for the John Peel show. And so it took till very late in my writing life before

I stopped translating words written into a shirt on your back or a meal on the table. I had a freelancer's attitude to money, which is if I do this, then I can afford that. And this became really critical later, when I had kids.

When I had kids, I found money was a hugely stressful and useful motivator. When they were about a year old I had to afford childcare. In Ireland it's astonishingly expensive. So I would look at a job, say you could review for this paper or that paper. I'd say, 'Well, I'll get that amount of money – and I'm a slow writer – for a week's work. And that will pay literally a fifth of what I need to pay my childcare.'

I really worked to stay above the poverty line – there was a line, it was a really clear line. You earn that amount of money and you can keep writing. And I don't know how, when I think back on it, I put myself through it. All that I was buying, all of those years, was the luxury of writing time. I appreciate for people who have small children that it takes an astonishing amount of self-belief to say, 'Okay, this is how I'm going to work it.' But I had had at that stage a couple of other novels published, so I wasn't flying completely by the seat of my pants.

Maggie Fergusson, journalist and author

What I remember being paid by various publications in those days was not very much less than what you would be paid now. That's 25 years ago. So I think the money is much harder now – much harder.

I've never made loads of money, but I've never been desperately worried about money, either. It's funny, we were talking at lunch about how some of our friends, certainly the people I knew in the City, made absolutely squillions of pounds. Now you would think that it was just impossible to have a decent life on a journalist's salary. I mean, you earn 30, 40, 50 [thousand pounds] maximum, that kind of thing. But actually, you do [live a decent life].

We were very lucky that we were living in West London, we were surrounded by the most outstanding Catholic state schools. So our children went through those, so there was no question of having to raise school fees. But it's fine. I can't think of anything [I wanted but could not afford]. I suppose some people really, really want to have a second house and I can't think of anything I would less like to have than a second house. I know I would just spend my time on the motorway worrying that I'd left the brie in the fridge in the other house and that kind of thing. I just couldn't bear it. So I'm very happy not to be very rich.

Niall Ferguson, historian

I have never been interested in making money, but I've been forced into it by – how can I put this – dependants. Once you start asking the question – how the hell can I pay this tax bill? – you get creative. My way of solving what was a pretty intense financial problem (in the 90s when I had, by the end of the decade, three children, a large, mortgaged farmhouse in Oxfordshire, and all the attendant expenses) was to do journalism, and then do television. By doing television, I was able to increase the sales of my books by a factor of roughly ten, maybe more, and get myself the breathing space I needed.

I have been propelled by financial worries for the better part of 20 years. I always identify with 19th-century writers like Walter Scott, who was prolific partly because of intense financial anxieties. I can relate to that. I think Dr Johnson had it right when he said that a man is a blockhead who writes other than for money. When people started blogging, which goes back now to the early 2000s – people like my good friend, Andrew Sullivan – I told them they were insane, because you were writing for free. I refuse to do that. I don't write for free.

One has to recognise the tradition of Grub Street, the tradition that writing is a kind of trade. It's not something only open to wealthy men and women of letters with unearned incomes. It's also a trade you can ply as a commoner. And as long as you're prepared to work hard at it, and do your daily thousand words, you can make a living. It's getting harder, because there's so many people writing for free now that a career as a writer is becoming more and more difficult. But at least for my generation, who were graduating from university in the 1980s, it was possible to be a professional writer, writing books and articles and then television scripts – and to make a decent living.

Hollie McNish, poet

One piece of advice that I wish I had had at the beginning of my career is not to just do whatever anybody asks you to do. I did a lot of that – and a lot of feeling guilty about asking for money for gigs – and a lot of free work, a lot of actually losing money paying for trains to get to gigs, that people offered me a cup of tea to do. I didn't need to do that. But I genuinely did, because I felt guilty saying no. [My advice] would be to really think before you say yes to everything, and try to work out the balance of career development opportunities [that might come from] working for free.

Samira Shackle, journalist and author

I actually found the finances of book writing a total nightmare. I've been freelance now for nine years. It took a good few years of being freelance to feel comfortable financially and professionally and so on. I think, initially, you have this real fear that every bit of work you do is your last – or I did anyway, as a natural worrier. That lifted and at the point when I got the book deal, I was reasonably financially comfortable. I had a regular editing job at the *New Humanist*, which I still have, and was doing reasonably well-paid writing work, and so on. It all felt like it was sort of working.

Then with the book, it was just a lot harder to make it all work, because what I hadn't appreciated was that you don't get your whole book advance upfront. You get it generally in either three or four instalments – mine was in four. So that's a quarter of it when you sign the contract, a quarter of it when you submit the first draft, a quarter when the hardback is published and a quarter when the paperback is published. That means that my advance wasn't huge – it was fine, but it wasn't huge. Very quickly, smallish, but fine amounts of money become a miniscule amount of money when it's being broken down into these chunks. It ended up that I had basically a few thousand pounds effectively on signing the contract, which was very frustrating because you think, 'Well, I don't need it when I'm publishing the hardback and I'm doing all my other work or certainly not the paperback in three years or whatever. I need it now when I'm doing the research.'

So that was difficult, especially coupled with the fact that I needed to pare back on my other reporting. I think I had 15 months from signing the contract to submitting the first draft and I initially just carried on doing lots of freelance writing and my editing as well. After a point I had to really cut back on that. The other thing was that I needed to travel for the book; it was expensive to research, and paying for translation and all these different things. I had a few grants, which I think lots of people get when they're doing non-fiction. One was from the Society of Authors, which is amazing. They give grants out to help you with the research for a book, or you can even get them just to support you while you're writing. I also had a fellowship with Columbia University – a media fellowship. It was a cross-disciplinary programme that I'd done two years in a row, but I got it again that year, which involved a reporting grant as well as taking part in a conference. So I was able to put some of that towards doing book research as well.

I muddled through that, basically. Then, in terms of money to live on, I found that I was able to carry on with my editing job, which was two days a week – something about it just used a slightly different bit of the brain. The last six months or so, I was primarily just doing editing and working on my book with the odd bit of other freelance writing, but it basically meant that my income dipped for that year, and then bounced back after I submitted the first draft. But it's really challenging. I think, especially as a freelancer, your income depends on what work you're doing. You have this long stretch where it feels like you're working unpaid even though the money is coming later. It's tricky, for sure.

Jack Thorne, playwright and screenwriter

Film and TV are well-paid mediums. The difference between film and TV is in film, you're paid by the draft, whereas in TV, you're paid by the product at the end of it. So in film, you can do a draft of something, which pays a lot better than a year's work on TV. Theatre is weirder, because the amount you get paid upfront is less. If the show is successful, and has a future life, a commercial life, then you get the constant, ongoing income. Whereas with film and TV, there's a little bit of that after the event, but mainly it gets swallowed up in accounting.

So *Wonder*, a film I wrote, did very well for its budget, but I've never got more money for it. I knew that that would be the case; I'm totally comfortable with that. It just goes somewhere. Certainly if you get a film on streaming now, you're not going to get more money. I think they are negotiating that now. I don't quite know where it's at in terms of that – the amount of streams you get will change the money that you get as a result. But I certainly haven't seen any streaming money for anything that I've written.

Patrick Radden Keefe, journalist and author

During the whole time that I was freelancing, I had another job. I had a full-time job, I worked at a think tank pretty much the whole time. I say full-time job – that position didn't pay all that well either. But it did accommodate some of my writing. So I was able to support the writing and research in that way. And in some ways, it kind of subsidised the work that I was doing.

But I started doing work as a screenwriter. Certainly during those freelancing years, I probably made a lot more money writing unproduced screenplays than I did for magazine articles or books. So that aspect of it was tricky. But here I may differ from some other people you've spoken with. I never expected it to be otherwise, in the sense that I just thought, this is the greatest job imaginable. It kind of makes sense that it's not hugely remunerative and stable, and that you don't have to worry about sending your kids to college. To me the magic of the job itself was always enough that I took it for granted from the outset that it would be a hustle, and that it was a hustle that I had to work hard to maintain. That was always my attitude.

It was fine for me trying to find other ways to pay the bills along the way, because truly the magazine stuff, I was doing for pleasure. And I did eventually get put on staff at the *New Yorker*. That was a big change for me. It introduced a degree of stability, it allowed me to leave the think tank. So that was a good development for me, six years in.

Sara Baume, novelist

My attitude is very much any money that comes from it [writing], I just try to make it last for as long as I can. At the moment, I'm kind of living the dream in that I'm able to live off my writing, but then I couldn't live in London off my writing. It's circumstances. We live in the middle of nowhere and my boyfriend's an artist, so that's no help to me. I'm sure everyone says this, but a spouse with a salary would be probably the best form of advice – just some kind of regular income. But just trying to make it last. I mean, I know I've already made certain choices in life and will continue to. I'm never going to have kids, I'm probably never going to have a mortgage, I drive this clapped-out van. I just desperately want to be able to not get a real job, get a day job. That's about the height of my ambition, money-wise.

The people who really need them [grants and prizes] don't get them because you need to be already established and to be seen to be winning prizes and publishing. If you win the Booker one week, you're probably going to be eligible, you're probably going to get a grant the next week, which is kind of mad because you don't need it, because you won the Booker. But that's the way it works.

I'll definitely be pursuing as many of those opportunities as possible, but what I won't be doing is writing a book that I think will sell because the chips are low. I'm really not writing another book unless I feel desperately compelled to, unless something obsesses me, or unless it's a project that I could actually care about, and see to the end, because I think it's transparent if you don't. That's certainly not a good financial move, I'm sure.

Gary Younge, journalist and author

There's a reason why I stayed at *The Guardian* for 26 years, and then moved into academia. I would look at people who are free-lancing and I'm scared for them. My mum, when we were going to university – she didn't go to university, but she was a teacher, she had a teaching certificate. If there had been a degree in plumbing, she'd have said, 'Do that, you get a good job doing plumbing.' There's a reason why I was trained to be an interpreter, while my brother, who ended up running the Travel Channel in America, he studied mining geology. It was about security and jobs. If you didn't grow up with much money, one response to that is to want stability.

Moving from *The Guardian* to Manchester [University, which he joined as a professor of sociology in 2020] was about always having a pay cheque – even before I had kids – always having a pay cheque. Then that's combined with another thing, which is always wanting to be able to tell your boss to go fuck themselves, which is about having a sense of financial security – or being able to walk away from your security, actually.

I guess money was never not important. It's always been important. It's never driven me; it's never been the primary [motivator]. I genuinely don't have much of an interest in getting rich. I wouldn't mind being rich, I wouldn't mind getting rich, but I'm not very interested in the process of doing that. I would much rather be interested and engaged. But I need to know that there'll be a shirt on my back and a roof over my head and food in my stomach for as long as I can see. That's one way in which I'm deeply conservative.

Sian Meades-Williams, journalist and author

HMRC [the British tax authorities] told me I may have to declare bankruptcy. If we're talking about the biggest mistake I made when I was a young freelancer, that was it: not taking my finances seriously. And thinking that HMRC would have been incredibly impressed with my candour, as I called them up, and I was just like, 'Hello, I'd like to be on a payment plan, please.' And they were just like, 'No.'

I was like, 'Well what do I do if I can't pay this bill?' They were like, 'You will have to declare bankruptcy.' Even now, saying that out loud, makes my blood run cold. It's chilling to me. I had no idea and I don't think I had realised for years after that, just how much stress that put me under. The knock-on effect of that chain of events, which I am happy to talk about, it impacted my life for several years afterwards.

I was put on a payment plan. My payment plan was hundreds of pounds a month, which I could pay, but the problem with that is that I could then not save for my next year's tax bill. I could not save for my payment on account. I couldn't save for anything outside of paying my rent, which was a blessing because it was actually very cheap. That's probably the only thing that kept me in London.

I absolutely spiralled. I got into debt incredibly quickly. I think I started having panic attacks. I was diagnosed with a panic disorder before I was diagnosed with depression. Both of those led to agoraphobia. I was waking up bolt upright at four in the morning. It was an incredibly difficult time. I drank through most of it. I wrote a book I don't remember. I just have no memory of one year. I don't talk about that much in the book [*The Pyjama Myth: The Freelance Writer's Survival Guide*, published in 2022]. I think I mentioned it in passing. But I wrote a chapter of a guidebook for Frommer's London, and I have no recollection of that project at all.

It came to a head when I realised that I was going to make myself incredibly unwell. I went to the bank. I asked for help. They said no. And they said no, because in trying to fix everything, I'd borrowed too much in too short a time, I think without realising it.

This is one of the reasons that quite possibly led to me very much wanting to help freelancers, and very much wanting to write a book.

I don't in any way think that I am a stupid person. I made a series of very, very small judgement decisions, and it's so easy to do. There is this huge jump when you go freelance between when you start and when you actually have to pay your tax bill. When you throw in unpaid invoices and chasing clients and the wonderful joy that is payment on account, it's so easy to tumble out of having enough money in your savings account. Especially if you have moved from a staff job where you're very, very used to regular money. It's really easy for three, four, five small things to become a very, very big problem. It took me years to recover. I think it took me years to recover financially and mentally. The damage that I did to my mental health was ongoing. It's very, very strange to think about that time.

Peter Moffat, playwright and screenwriter

I wrote a couple of plays – two or three plays. One about lawyers at the Hampstead Theatre. The set producer of *Kavanagh QC* came and saw it, said, 'Do you want to come write an episode of *Kavanagh*?' I was tremendously snooty about it. I said, 'I don't want to do that. I want to be a playwright when I grow up.' My wife [Leonora] said to me, 'How much money do you get for an episode of *Kavanagh QC*?' I [told her], and she said, 'Well, you're going to go and write television then, aren't you?'

The really simple, big thing about television writing is you get a fee for writing each episode. If it's made, you get all of that money all over again. So on the first day of photography, you get 100 per cent of what you've been paid for writing it all over again. So it's a key difference getting things made; it matters financially. I'm a bit out of date now, because I haven't written a play for 12, 13 years.

But there's so much more money than in the theatre. It's a huge inducement, I think, for people to want to write television.

Luckily, I think, I've fallen into a time when television is really where it's at. Not that long ago [people were] thinking, 'Oh, my god, Nicole Kidman at the Almeida, isn't that amazing? She's only getting paid £200 to do something really kind of serious, and everything, and that's at the Almeida and it's terrific.' I think it's the other way now. I think all big actors, film actors, are desperate to do telly. Because you get 10 hours or 13 hours of storytelling with you, the actor, at the heart of it. That's not possible anywhere else.

Rory Stewart, author

I made a lot of money from the Afghan book [*The Places In Between*] It was a *New York Times* bestseller for 18 weeks, which meant that, I think, that book has sold many hundreds of thousands, maybe 600, 700,000 copies. I very foolishly bought a house in the United States in 2008, and then sold it at a fantastic loss. Almost all the money I'd saved up I managed to lose through my idiocy.

Helen Lewis, journalist and author

You have to train [when she started working at the *Daily Mail*] in a very small village called Howden, which is outside Hull, and that's the Press Association's training base. So I went and did that. But because I'd already got a flat in London, I was in a flatshare, I basically said that I just can't. Because the salary was then £15,000 a year – I'm not sure what it is now – this was in 2003 . . . a very difficult amount of money to live on at the time. I said, 'Look, I just can't afford to pay my rent in London and pay rent [elsewhere], even on somewhere that you find me.' So they let me off and I got to do my placement at the Metro, which was then in Canada Water. Then I turned up early to the *Daily Mail* and it was fine.

A couple of different things about working at the *Mail*. Okay, let's not beat around the bush. It is a tough working environment. You don't produce a paper like that by just everybody swanning around and having a lovely time and dropping in at 3 p.m. and doing a bit of work. It's incredibly demanding. What it did do, which I think is something that it doesn't get enough credit for, is it actually paid for you to be trained. So I'd already done a masters, nearly, but in terms of actually the craft of teaching you how to do stuff, they paid for that. That was a big investment that they made in you at the time.

I think it's less so now with training for people for online – I think they throw them more in at the deep end – so I think that that deserves some amount of credit. There's quite a lot of hatred towards *The Mail*, particularly from the left, which I consider myself to be on. But I think there are some very exploitative practices that happen at other places that consider themselves to be much better than *The Mail*, but really use up and spit out young writers and still want them to be writing the same – loads and loads of pieces a day. But because they don't have the reputation of *The Mail* they get away with it a bit more. It's not a friendly place to work. Certainly Paul Dacre [editor of the *Daily Mail* 1992–2018] is an editor of enormous power. I think he's one of the very last editors who will ever have that kind of incredible power over the newsroom, which makes for a very muscular paper. But then it also makes it a very, very tough working environment.

Fraser Nelson, journalist and editor

I am in quite a fortunate position. I've got a national column. I'm a newspaper editor. I am paid well. [The funny thing about] the *Spectator* is that we've only got three or four staff writers, and people who write for us occasionally. The *Spectator*'s never paid what you might regard as commercial rates. So people like Rod Liddle, Charles Moore – I don't know how much they get paid by the newspapers, probably £5,000 a column. I don't know: a lot of money. Obviously we can give them absolutely nowhere near that.

People write for the *Spectator* primarily not for financial reasons, but for uncommercial reasons, because they cherish the magazine's integrity. They love the project. Also, they know that we simply cannot afford Fleet Street rates. Now if I'm doing my job, the *Spectator* is the sort of magazine where people will feel proud to write for it. That's for people who write for us occasionally: we're talking about once or twice a year. Now, my colleagues. When I first became editor, I think there were seven or eight editorial staff – now there's 35.

There's a trait in writing, where people are rich enough to afford the low salary. That's a problem. So you get people whose family are helping them, sometimes topping up their monthly salary or helping them with accommodation, etc. That will mean that you can work in London for £20,000, £25,000 – these are tiny salaries. It had become quite difficult for me, even as an editor, to try to negotiate better salaries for my colleagues, if the market salaries are so low. You can go on the websites now and find out how much writers are paid. It's very, very little.

So it becomes difficult to make the case internally, as any editor has to, saying, 'Look, I know that the market value for this person is £30,000, but I think they should be paid £35,000, because they're so good and they're so productive.' It's difficult in any business to make that sort of argument. The way I like to think of it is, our writers at the *Spectator* are different because we're so multitasking. You can do a podcast, you can do sub-editing, you can do a whole bunch of things – there's production as well as writing.

Writing has never really paid that well as a career in this country, as any writer knows, with a handful of exceptions. But I do think that our industry, journalism, is making a big mistake. The problem with the low salaries is it is socially exclusionary. In other words, you end up with people rich enough to afford the low pay. It also means you lack diversity; journalism is a very white profession. When you look around, you can certainly see a lack of BAME [Black, Asian and minority-ethnic] representation.

I work with the Social Mobility Foundation. They deal with kids who are very bright, they go on free school meals so they're from poor families, but then they get great results. Very, very few of them want to be writers – understandably so. If you're [from] an immigrant family and your parents moved halfway around the world, you don't want to be messing about on about £25,000 writing. You want to be going for a career that can reasonably get you on the path to buying your own house.

Journalism is at risk of allowing itself to be dominated by a certain social class of people who come from comfortable backgrounds. But I also think that's changing as well. I think sub-editors are being more highly valued. I think newspapers are beginning to change – although for a long time, typically the model of a young journalist was somebody whose partner would be a lawyer or something, so they could bring in the money and the other person could live their dream. Over even my relatively short [career] – I say short, I've been 25 years in journalism – the salaries in the profession have gone down a lot in real terms. And it's not a good thing.

Ann Goldstein, *translator*

Translators make no money. It may be better in England than it is in America, but the pay is very small and you really basically have to have another job to support your habit.

The [Elena] Ferrante was an exception. I just had royalties written into my contracts. I don't know when I started doing that – not with the expectation that I would ever get any royalties, but just as a sign of respect or something. Just on principle, you want royalties in the contract. And they're very small. But with the Ferrante, there were some royalties. It was amazing, but I should emphasise that it's very unusual. It's very hard to make a living just as a translator.

10

WRITING ROUTINE

'Be regular and orderly in your life, so that you may be violent and original in your work.'

– Gustave Flaubert

The English Romantic poets Lord Byron and Percy Bysshe Shelley had rather different approaches to their work. Shelley, who felt that 'poets are the unacknowledged legislators of the world', proceeded in an industrious, orderly manner. A friend and biographer observed that he 'rose early in the morning, walked and read before breakfast, took that meal sparingly, wrote and studied the greater part of the morning, walked and read again'. He went to bed at ten o'clock.

Byron, meanwhile, lived up to his image as a rake. 'He was seldom out of his bed before noon,' another companion observed; the poet's day usually involved a ride and a visit to one of his lovers. Only late at night would he turn his attention to matters of the mind rather than the flesh. 'He sat reading or composing until two or three o'clock in the morning, and then to bed, often feverish, restless, and exhausted.'

We frequently ask our interviewees about their writing routine and their answers are fascinating. From peanut-butter sandwiches and strong lager to propulsive heavy-metal music, it's surprising what helps writers to get their words on the page.

Several fall into Shelley's camp, rising early in order to make the most of quiet, undisturbed hours. When William Dalrymple is in the writing phase for one of his history books, he aims to sit down with the previous day's pages by six o'clock in the morning. Peter Moffat decamps to a local coffee shop bright and early with his dog in tow. Others are more Byronic. Simon Scarrow confessed he sometimes only starts writing when he gets a phone call from his editor checking in on his progress.

Many interviewees simply fit in writing whenever they can. Candice Carty-Williams penned her hit novel *Queenie* at the weekend while working in publishing. Christina Lamb negotiated with her newspaper employers to allow allocated time each year to write books. For those with families, writing time is circumscribed by childcare. Sophie Elmhirst describes taking a newborn baby along to a celebrity interview. When working on a magazine feature that required travel, Ed Caesar had to negotiate a better fee in order to pay for some additional help.

As Shelley, Byron and the authors quoted here demonstrate, there's no single 'right' way to work. Find a method that works for you – whether it involves early mornings or the midnight oil.

William Dalrymple, historian and travel writer

The writing phase is like doing finals – it's no fun at all. It's the payback for all the fun you've had in the previous three years [of research]. You do get up very early. First of all, I have by my bed, the printout of the passages that I've just been writing, and I try and produce at least twice or three times a week, a whole chapter up to where you've got – so you have by your bed, maybe 20 pages of A4, on a folder or something that you can lean against. I get up, I go out to my terrace in my house in Delhi. I always write in India because my social life is less busy there, and there's less distraction, and I can really get focused into it.

You go to bed with the printout beside your bed, you make coffee every morning and you read it through with a pen and you correct everything that doesn't look right. That can take an hour or two hours, even, if it's towards the end of a chapter and you're printing out 40 pages. What inevitably happens is that, as you reach the end of a chapter, the early bits of the chapter begin to have come good and don't need much work and you'll spot odd infelicities that you correct. Then you get into the bit maybe ten pages in, where you're spotting more. And then you get into the recent work, from the last two, three days, where it's only been through one edit, or none. That is often full of horrors and misspellings and terrible sentences and sentences which are too long.

If you've got down to work by six, by half-past seven, you've got an annotated manuscript. I then often go for a run or a walk or have breakfast. Then the day begins, then I send some emails if it's anything urgent, though I try and put that off until the evening ideally – ditto social media which can absorb your whole day, if you let it. Then lock up the phone, turn off the internet. You start typing in the corrections that you put on your annotated manuscript – and by that stage, it's often 11 o'clock. So you've got up very early, but by 11 o'clock, you haven't written a new word, you've just been correcting.

Then often about 11, the writing begins. The key then is to put off lunch as long as possible. I find that if I can put off lunch until three o'clock – which drives my family mad – but if you can, you get four or five really prime writing hours of new material. Again, then a break, then more emails or chores or changing light bulbs or whatever needs to be done in the house, collecting children, doing whatever real life intervenes for a bit in all this mess and clobber. Then in the second session, by evening, maybe five till seven or five till eight, going over what you've done in the morning, first edit and planning the next day's work.

Patrick Kingsley, journalist and author

Both books [*How to be Danish* and *The New Odyssey*] I wrote in about a month. The Danish book I wrote in a month – I had three months off, maybe two months off. I did reporting in one month and the writing in one month. I treated it as a really intense period of reporting as I would for *The Guardian*. The book about migration, I think I wrote it in five weeks. Parts of it were already there, because I'd written versions of them for *The Guardian*. So it wasn't like I was writing 90,000 words in five weeks.

I'm used to working really intensely. I love being a journalist on a day-to-day basis, and I'm not ready, by any means, to be in a phase of my life where I'm just writing a book for a year or I'm doing a project for three or four years. I like working as a reporter, doing shorter pieces. If writing a book in a really intense and short period of time is the only way to balance those two desires, then so be it for the time being.

Jack Thorne, playwright and screenwriter

I loved working before I met Rachel, my wife. I was living alone in Luton, and very happily working seven days a week, 12 to 14 hours a day. I got a huge kick out of it. I think writing is the greatest thing in the world and I am absolutely psychologically dependent upon it. When I'm in a bad mood Rachel will send me off to write to make me better. I'm not someone who struggles with that thing of getting in front of a computer. I like it. I would do it all the time, if it weren't for the fact that I have a family and I love them, too.

Peter Moffat, playwright and screenwriter

I think there'd have to be an awful lot wrong in my life – an awful lot – for me not to go out of the house every morning and write. Caffè Nero opens at 6:30 in Kentish Town, which is great, and they play only classical music and nobody comes in there. The coffee is horrible, but the nice Italian franchise owner allows Italian Spinones, [so] my dog comes with me. We sit together and write. I mean, I do the writing – Django the Spinone doesn't do so much of that. Then he comes home and I go to the British Library. I love the British Library.

Giles Hattersley, journalist

We have average days at *Vogue*. I think the mystery of this office is always – and I'm sure I thought to myself before coming to work here – that it is this full *Devil Wears Prada* fantasy land. Some days you have to catch yourself and realise that a lot of it is. But, that said, some days you've got to be in at seven, because you've got 18 different pieces to try and progress, to edit, a writer to speak to and you've also got three meetings in the day. It's the normal chug of modern media life.

I would say that, in terms of the features director job here now, writing is the extra thing I do. I often go a month or two without a piece in the magazine. Partly because it shouldn't just be me writing everything and, partly, because of time. I think I thought when I came from weeklies to monthlies – even in the digital age, with the daily necessity to focus there too – I thought, even with that, the lunches would be quite long. I thought I'd mosey in mid-morning. But absolutely not.

Merve Emre, author, academic and literary critic

I try to stack all of my teaching at the beginning of the week – to do two days of teaching, so that I have three days left for writing. I try to alternate between works of criticism and works of scholarship. Usually, on days when I'm writing, I try to meet a quota of 1,000 words a day. Those don't have to be new – so sometimes revising something will meet that quota for me. But usually I try to make it new.

I usually do all of my reading at night after my kids go to sleep. My kids go to sleep around nine and I'll stay up until about midnight reading. That's how I divide my life. It's a slightly monkish style of living. I don't really watch any television, I don't watch streaming series, I don't really see movies, I don't listen to podcasts. That's the only way that I found it possible to do the various things that I do.

Robert Douglas-Fairhurst, academic and author

University terms take up about half of the year. During that time, I don't do anything much apart from teaching and admin and mopping tears: the everyday life of an academic. The holidays are when I sit and do my own writing. I might slip in a book review during term time, but nothing more than that, or I might correct some proofs. But the actual business of sitting down and researching something and writing it, you need a few days at least to build up a bit of a head of steam, to use one of Dickens's favourite metaphors. You can't really do that when you're grabbing half an hour here and 20 minutes there.

Candice Carty-Williams, novelist

I would do my work [in a publishing house] from Monday to Friday. I would leave work on a Friday, go to the shops, get my supplies in and then I would lock myself away. I would use my phone – that was allowed. I like to write to music, I like that as loud as possible. I like loads of distractions – music can be on, TV can be on, headphones on – I want everything going. I listen to a lot of grime when I write because the energy [helps me] bang loads of words out. Then on Monday morning, I'd go back to work. Then the same thing – rinse and repeat for a few months.

Gary Younge, journalist and author

With the first book [*No Place Like Home*], [I had] no kids. My then-girlfriend was working at the *Washington Post*; she'd go to work and I would sit down and write about 2,000 words a day. I got it done within four months – seven, if you count the travelling.

The second book [*Stranger in a Strange Land*], a baby arrived in the middle, and it really just threw me off actually. I didn't know how to do it, so [the book] was about a year and a half late. That's probably one of the reasons why it was so hard. By the fourth one [*The Speech*] I'd figured something out, which was: it's very, very rare that you're going to have the time to sit down and write 2,000 words uninterrupted. So look at your diary, figure out where the times are and gun it when you have the time.

Sophie Elmhirst, journalist

I'd wanted to go freelance for ages and never had the guts for lots of reasons – because it's a scary thing to do. It was almost like having a baby was my disguise for going freelance. That was my way I could slip out of the building unnoticed and not go back.

At the same time, and I want to make this point, it became really clear to me early on in motherhood, that I didn't want to go back to a full-time office job. I obviously do not judge anyone that runs back to an office job as quickly as they can after having a baby, but for whatever reason, I just thought: 'What if I can forge a career?' I didn't want to stop working for a second, but if I can forge a career that means I can be around a bit more, and at home a bit more, then I'd like to. That was very incentivising as well as being a good disguise.

What it also meant was that I got going really early. I remember when my first kid was six weeks old, I went to interview Keira Knightley in a stately home, with my mum in tow, and was breastfeeding either side of the interview. Actually Keira Knightley was really down with it and really cool about it, so she was a good person for such a weird experiment.

I've had a few things like that now over the years where the kids – one or other of them – has had to come along, or I've been doing phone interviews while taking someone to swimming. In a way there's an absurdity to it, but there's also an absolute gift and great fortune to it. I think being a freelance journalist is one of the things you can do while having kids. It's hard at times, really hard practically, but it's also possible. There are a lot of jobs [where] it's a bit more all or nothing: you can't have that middle ground. So I feel very grateful for that in lots of ways.

Ed Caesar, journalist and author

When I went on [Petrel, a research vessel, for a story for the *New York Times Magazine*], Chloe [his wife] was in a murder trial – she was defending someone who had been accused of attempted murder. That's a really serious thing. She was working really hard and barristers work really late as well. They come back and then they've got all this stuff to go through. She's a proper, super-accomplished, brilliant barrister.

The kids have to get to school and eat and it's quite nice to see them occasionally. In order for that to work, I had to kind of think, 'Well, okay, I've got to be on this ship for however long. We're just gonna have to get one more person to help us out.' And I built it into my deal with the *New York Times*. I was like, 'Right, you are gonna have to pay me more.' I didn't say it was because I needed childcare, but I said, 'You'll have to pay me more because it's a huge commitment of time.' I spent another £700, £800 or something on someone to come and help in the mornings and the evenings with the children.

It's not perfect, because you miss your children, but that's the kind of stuff that you have to think about all the time. It's like playing a game of three-dimensional chess. We have these diary meetings: it's just trying to work out like, 'Okay, I need to be in – I don't know – Kigali for two days to do something for work. But I can't do it then because this other thing's happening.' Most of the time, it's totally fine, because we're both reasonable people and we try and make it work.

Christina Lamb, *journalist and author*

Some years ago, when I was hired from the *Sunday Telegraph* to the *Sunday Times*, they offered me more money. I said, 'I don't want more money, I want more time.' They said, 'What do you mean?' At that point, I had a young child. 'I want to write books as well and so I need more time. I only want to work half the year.' They were a bit astonished, but ended up doing a deal, which I believe works very well for both sides – of working seven months of the year for the newspaper.

It would be better if I just did seven months for the paper and had five months off for the book, but that isn't how it works. I'll go off on a trip for three weeks somewhere, then I'll be back for two weeks, so those two weeks count as my time off. Then I'll go somewhere for a month. Sometimes that's difficult because, although I love doing both writing for the paper and the writing of books, it often takes me time to switch from one to the other.

Usually when I sit down to do the first chapter of a new book, after I've been doing lots of journalism, I'll write the chapter then realise it's only 2,000 words – when I thought I was going to be writing 10,000. Then, equally, I'm sure my editors get very frustrated: when I go back to writing for the paper after I've been writing books, I write way too much for the articles.

Sara Baume, novelist

I don't really have any difference between art and life. Working, for me, is reading and writing, or looking at art, or quietly observing the world, or feeling things: this is all work, in a way, to me. I don't go on holidays, I don't change my routine at the weekend, everything all feeds into it in some way. I'm always switched on. I think that's more important than word count – the way I work anyway, because so much of writing is smelling the roses.

I don't really get any decent material from sitting at my desk, trying to think of decent material. It all comes from other places, from moving around. You really have to pay attention. That's the most beneficial form of working – that's the only bit that really boils down to anything.

Kiran Millwood Hargrave, poet and novelist

One of my favourite poets, Lucie Brock-Broido, says that there are two types of writers: there are 'oxen' and there are 'cats'. The oxen get up, they plough the field, nine to five. Cats sleep most of the time and then they sort of attack the work – and that is who I am. That's very well facilitated by having deadlines, by having contracts that I can work to.

Some weeks, I won't write a word – I'll be thinking, but I won't write a word – I'll be doing school visits, I'll be seeing friends and family. I'm a very social person and when I'm in the grip of a deadline, I don't see anyone. I lock myself in my office and allow myself to be obsessed, to be consumed, by my book. That is the way that I work.

It's not the best way to work, I would argue; I think structure and routine is very important. If you can work like that, that is the better way to work, because it's more predictable – you have that glow of achievement every day. I can't work like that. I need a deadline; I need to be slightly up against it. I don't believe in inspiration being this mythical thing, but I do believe in letting ideas ferment. Thinking time is as important as writing time to me.

William Boyd, novelist and screenwriter

I look back at my younger self, when I was living in Oxford in the early 80s, and I wish I could tap into those energies now. I was writing this DPhil thesis, I was writing stories and a novel, I was writing a TV column for the *New Statesman* and writing reviews and teaching as well. I was teaching English literature to the undergraduates of St Hilda's College and sometimes teaching English as a foreign language to foreign students who'd come to Oxford to learn to speak English.

I think when you're that age – I was in my late 20s – you have boundless energy. While I was waiting for *A Good Man in Africa* to be published in 1980, I wrote a huge chunk of my second novel, *An Ice-Cream War*, at the same time as doing all these other things. So *An Ice-Cream War*, which was published in, I think, September 1982, had been delivered in January 1982.

I could write for five or six hours a day. The wonderful thing about having that sort of Oxford life was I had masses of time to do my own writing. There's no doubt I've slowed down – I can manage two to three hours a day now. But back then I could do a full nine-to-five writing fiction, no problem. I think it's just your own energies and your own enthusiasms that fire you up at that stage.

Jay Rayner, journalist and author

I've had TV companies say, 'We'd love to do a day in the life of Jay Rayner!' And I say, 'Well, that's very flattering, but you'll mostly see a sizeable man sitting on his sizeable arse, trying to read the whole of the internet as a distraction from doing the thing he's meant to do. And then maybe I go for lunch.'

Simon Scarrow, novelist

I'm afraid I have to admit that I'm not one of these disciplined people who gets up at six o'clock in the morning, writes 3,000 words, has lunch, another 2,000 words and so on. It tends to be the case that I'm enjoying the research so much that I only start writing when I get a call from my editor and she says something along the lines of: 'Simon, that book that you're going to be handing over in two months' time – how's it going?'

That's the point at which I settle down and get really carried away. I used to probably spend about three, three and a half months writing a book, fuelled by Tennent's Super and peanut-butter sandwiches. I discovered that Tennent's Super slowed down my thinking process to my typing speed. I don't know if you know them, [they are] these lovely 500ml cans of intensely strong lager. I found it worked really well for me, but now I just find that I'm old enough that coffee does the job.

Toby Young, journalist and author

I remember, at one stage, me and Matthew Norman were the most prolific columnists in Britain. I think we each had five columns per week. When you're doing a column a day, you get into the habit of writing them fairly quickly. I think in the past that may have been harder, because how would you go about fact-checking a column that you have to produce daily? But, with the internet, that obviously becomes a lot easier.

When I was at my column-writing peak, sometimes I was out and about, talking to people, going to see things, trying my hand at different kinds of crazy things like working as a greeter in Asda and whatnot. Often I had to write a column on the move. I remember being in a radio studio once and, in between interviews, dashing off a column in about 20 minutes.

But, generally speaking, now that I'm down to one or two columns a week, I usually spend about three and a half, four hours, writing a column, depending on how intellectually ambitious I'm being, how difficult the subject matter is, how little or how much I know about it, etc.

Dylan Jones, journalist, editor and author

I don't have hobbies. [I write] at night, in the morning, in cars, on aeroplanes. I write quite quickly. I write on a phone; I used to write on a BlackBerry. I wrote a 6,000-word feature on Tony Bennett, coming back from New York, having interviewed him, and I wrote it on a BlackBerry. It was a pretty good piece, frankly.

Henry Winter, journalist and author

It always fascinates me how fascinated people are with the match report. If I'm walking into a ground or coming out of a ground, they often say, 'Well, when do you write your match report?' It has to be filed by 85 minutes.

1999 was an amazing year in [Manchester United's] history. But for journalists in the press box at the Nou Camp for the Champions League final against Bayern Munich, when Manchester United were trailing 1–0 . . . I had already filed about 950 words on Alex Ferguson being tactically inept, the Germans having this control over England, the tactical naivety, what was Ferguson doing playing three wingers in a four-man midfield . . .

The glory of this game is: 'Football, bloody hell', to quote the great man Sir Alex Ferguson (Alex Ferguson as he was at the time.) The whole thing changed around [Manchester United scored two goals in injury time to win]. I was looking around the press box and I'm quite calm, but there were people screaming down their phones saying, 'You won't believe what's happened!' The deadlines are so tight. Back then – I was at *The Telegraph* at the time – the print run of *The Telegraph* was probably about 1.5 million. Every second costs hundreds of pounds, so you cannot delay.

So, the art of the match report is I write about two-thirds by 60 minutes. For me, the sports journalists I admire most – Paul Hayward and Matt Dickinson and Oliver Holt and Danny Taylor – these are the ones who file against the clock. Anyone can file a beautiful piece sitting in their ivory tower, stroking their beard. I've seen certain distinguished sports writers come in and try to do a 1,100, 1,200-word runner on a huge European night, against the clock, and absolutely melt because they just cannot cope with it, because they want to polish every word. You can't. You have to deliver; it's almost like delivering a radio commentary.

... It's that first edition, that instant impression, the first draft of history – and it's manic. I still think that we actually went [to press in 1999] at 1–1, because the edition was so tight. But then 30 seconds later, I updated that and it went at 2–1, one of the glorious moments. The final story on 1999 is that obviously the first edition was: 'In a dramatic late turnaround, Manchester United turn history and German supremacy on its head with two late goals', followed by about 1,000 words of me excoriating Ferguson's tactics. Obviously it was then better for the second edition.

Of course, what were the editions that got delivered to the Manchester United hotel in Barcelona? So Ferguson and all these coaches woke up – probably with slight hangovers, probably hadn't been to bed – to see the first edition, which was 'Well done Manchester United', followed by 950 words [of criticism]. The second edition was more balanced. At the first press conference at the start of the next season, Ferguson went: 'I saw your first edition.' So it is the test – it is for me, it's the adrenaline shot – doing that first-edition runner.

Elif Shafak, novelist

I've been a 'metal head' or heavy-metal fan since my early youth. People find it odd that a middle-aged Turkish mother might be listening to heavy metal [when writing], but I've always loved that type of music, especially subgenres of heavy metal like progressive, symphonic, folk, Viking, metalcore. I love its high energy, and I can listen to the same song on repeat 70, 80 times. That really, really helps me to concentrate.

I think there's no such thing as an exact, precise schedule. It's usually male authors of a certain age who are fond of a very precise schedule: they know every day when to start, when to go out for a walk and come back. For all the rest of us, it's juggling – as parents, as people who do many things, you try to carve out a zone, a time for yourself.

People like Toni Morrison, they have left a big impact on me. She was a single mum, she was an editor; as a novelist, as a public intellectual, she's someone I always respected a lot. In one of her essays, she describes how sometimes she writes during the day and during the night. I would say my process is very similar as well. What I do make sure of, however, is every day I read. It doesn't mean that every day I write, but every day I make sure I read, whether it's in the morning or during the afternoon, and I take notes.

Rosie Nixon, editor and novelist

I had very young children and needed to get out of the house to be able to concentrate. There was something like the umbilical pull of having your baby in the home that made it quite difficult to switch off and focus on creative writing. I'm a bit more able to do it now they're slightly more grown up and I hide myself away up in my room at the top of the house, and it's quite peaceful.

If I'm really on a deadline, and I need to get the words down, I'm a bit of a binge writer. I've often managed to convince my husband to allow me to go away for three days. I go to a hotel room and pretty much lock the door and stay in there until I get all the words down. That really is my happy place. I love it. I think there's something – like with a café – of not being in your own home, so not distracted by the noises and the things that you could be doing at home. It's all about getting the headspace, really. A hotel room for me is the ultimate because it's immaculate and it's peaceful, generally. And there are nice slippers.

Sian Meades-Williams, *journalist and author*

I really think pyjamas, if you're going to work in them, have to be clean ones. Staying in what you wore the night before and not showering – it's horrible. I don't think anyone does their best work like that. It doesn't stop me from doing it probably two days a week. One of the best things about being freelance is being comfortable where we work and in how we work. Perhaps the opportunity to work in your pyjamas isn't necessarily a definition of success, but the opportunity to have that freedom and autonomy in our own lives certainly is and to trust ourselves to do the best work.

Sometimes that means I am curled up on the sofa writing in a notebook with the cat. Sometimes that means working at four in the morning and I probably should have gone to bed. Comfort makes us all work better.

Samanth Subramanian, *journalist and author*

[Freelance journalism] is basically an endless hustle. It always involves working on a minimum of three pieces at once, at the same time, in various stages of publication, writing or editing. I'm going to come right out and say it: it's unsustainable. If I had to keep doing this, at this pace, I would just burn out in a couple of years. I have to clearly find ways to balance it out in a way that I don't do this many pieces.

. . . At some point in the summer [of 2020], my editor at *Bloomberg Businessweek* wrote to me to say that they were doing a special issue on vaccines and [ask] if I had any ideas. At this point, I was already working on three other pieces, but, because you're a freelancer, you never turn down the opportunity for a pitch. And so I sent him a couple of ideas, thinking that he would say, 'Well, this one works but the other one [doesn't].' He commissioned both of them, for the same issue. So suddenly I was working on five pieces at once. I didn't turn it down, obviously. I just said yes and went ahead and did all five at the same time.

. . . But, to go back to my original point, it's not sustainable. Freelancing is intensely hard. I don't know how people do it long-term. It's frightening to think that you have to hustle this hard and work this erratically and in bursts of such intensity for the rest of your life if you want to be a freelancer.

Niall Ferguson, historian

Work life – that implies that there's some other life that I lead, but I work all the time. I think about work all the time. That may be a kind of curse, but that's how I am.

11

STAYING MOTIVATED

'It is worth mentioning, for future reference, that the creative power which bubbles so pleasantly in beginning a new book quiets down after a time, and one goes on more steadily. Doubts creep in. Then one becomes resigned. Determination not to give in, and the sense of an impending shape keep one at it more than anything.'

– Virginia Woolf

Building a career as a writer requires fighting both internal and external battles. Just getting a first book published requires – in strict actuarial terms – overcoming some rather long odds. Published authors, even the most famous, have usually had to push on through numerous disappointments. Booker Prize winner Marlon James told us about the 78 'nos' he received en route to acceptance of his first novel, and, perhaps equally importantly, told us that he did not always have the strength to carry on.

For some writers, dealing with their own doubts and insecurities is as challenging as anything that the rest of the world can

175

throw at them. The 'terror of the blank page' – as Colum McCann describes it – is very real. And producing a book is a marathon not a sprint. As Virginia Woolf indicates above, you need motivation that will last, not just a first flush of enthusiasm.

Again, we found different approaches to this problem. Historian Ferdinand Addis finds it useful to break the challenge of completing a book down into the smallest chunks possible, right down to writing a single word. For others, their drive to start a project and then keep going was fuelled by seemingly negative emotions like rage or a need to prove themselves. Nikesh Shukla was so outraged by an anti-immigrant poster that it drove him on through an edit of one book. For Terri White, a deprived childhood and family instability fuelled a profound adult drive. 'My ambition was born out of desperation and panic,' she said.

Staying motivated is not just a challenge when it comes to writing books. We heard elsewhere about how writers had to struggle to make themselves fit into – or finally determine that they just do not fit into – various organised professional contexts. Sam Knight had a frustrating stint working for *The Times* before going freelance and building a career as a magazine journalist. 'I just don't know what to do with you,' he recalls the newspaper's editor telling him. Helen Lewis likewise felt great relief when she left the *Daily Mail* for the more harmonious environment of the *New Statesman*, but that was mixed with a sense that she'd also somehow failed in a challenge she'd set herself.

Resilience is of great value to any writer, and for Elif Shafak this is born out of cultivating an 'inner garden', an internal sanctuary that one can retreat to in the face of exterior difficulty. In the end, perhaps the greatest motivation comes from plain and simple self-belief. As E.B. White once said, 'Writing is an act of faith, not a trick of grammar.'

Colum McCann, novelist

I wrote two books before I published my first book [*Fishing the Sloe-Black River*]. They were both awful. Thank god they never got published; they're still in a drawer somewhere. But once I had the taste of it, I knew I would never give it up. I wallpapered a bathroom with the rejection slips. I could look up and think of them at various times. But I had the desire, I had the taste for it then. I knew that I wouldn't lose the taste for it.

It's one of the things that, when I look at my potential students, I look them in the eyes and say: 'Okay, do you have it? How much do you want it? Are you going to show me how much you actually really, truly want this thing?' I can pretty much assure you that those who have 100 percent of the desire and maybe only 90 per cent of the talent, will be much better than those that have 100 per cent of the talent and only 90 per cent of the desire. So much of it is about stamina, and almost being an athlete in relation to this. To sit on your arse for eight hours solid is not as easy as it seems – and to fight the terror of the blank page – it takes something peculiar to be able to do that sort of thing. The taste for it was with me fairly early on.

Ferdinand Addis, historian

I've always struggled with procrastination. I find blank pages very daunting – the blinking of the cursor. So something I've had to work on for a long time is developing strategies to overcome that initial aversion. The best strategy that I have found is to work in very, very tiny increments. Sometimes I'll set myself a goal: write a single word, or to sit on a chair and just think about what I'm going to write for five minutes. It sounds absurd, but these tiny little grains of sand do add up, over time, into whole endless books.

The great thing is just to begin – not to be too overcome with fear at the task that faces you, the scale of the challenge. None of us is equal to the projects we take on, but we have to approach it like ants, a little bit at a time. It's amazing what gets done in the end.

Monica Ali, novelist

I wish someone had told me to end each writing day at a point that you are not completely out of creative juice and you're pretty certain about what is going to happen next, because that makes it so much easier to pick it up the next morning. It's very tempting just to keep on writing until you run dry.

Marlon James, novelist

Man, I wish I could say I did keep going, I actually didn't. I didn't keep going. I remember, funnily enough, rejection number 78 for *John Crow's Devil* because I didn't know it was number 78. I would print out, send out six letters, and wait six weeks, a month, eight weeks, whatever. If I didn't hear from anybody, or if they said no, I just printed out another six. I kept doing that for around a year and a half, I think, not really paying attention because I had other things I was doing. I'm like, 'Okay, I didn't hear from them. It's the same damn letter, just put a different address and send it out.' When I got this card from a publisher who should remain nameless, meaning Soho Press, the card just said, 'Not for us,' which I thought was really rude. But it was the first time I stopped and I went, 'Hold on, how many of these have I gotten?'

That's when I finally counted it, and it came up to 78. I have no memory of what else I did that day, because I was just so shocked and stunned. I don't know if I had known all along that I'd have persevered to 78. I don't think I would. But I'm not sure being hit in the face with that revelation felt any better. Either way, I gave up. I gave up, I said 'No. These people aren't idiots. These people are some of the smartest people in their field. If 78 people think this is not good enough, it can't possibly be good.' So I gave up. I threw the book away.

Actually, I burned it. I did a whole ritual burning. It was great. It was very cathartic and I erased it from my computer. I remember – because I didn't have a printer so I'd always print these printout files at my friends' houses – and I'd go to their houses and go on their computers and find the file and delete it there ... Kaylie Jones came for a workshop, actually Kaylie Jones was a last-minute replacement. This is why I'm terrible on careers day because people go, 'What do you do?' I go: 'I don't know, get lucky, have dumb shit happen to you?' I'm horrible with careers day. Anyway, I was in a workshop which I only went to because I felt duty-bound to do it. She saw that I could write, and she made it clear she was not going to leave the country until I found a copy of the manuscript and gave it to her. Someone managed to find it in an outbox of an old computer and gave it to her, and she edited it for free. So she loved it. She found a publisher, which was her publisher at the time, an independent publisher, Akashic books. They published it. I would say that was that and that was the start of a great future, except that the second book was rejected by nearly every publisher too. It wasn't smooth sailing after.

I just realised, the publishing industry, they've come a long way. But, certainly when I started writing, they had a very narrow idea of what kind of books get published, and they had an even narrower idea of what kind of books get published by black people, or people of colour, or anybody that wasn't white, and usually male or female. They just had a very narrow idea of the stories that could be told, and I just didn't fit into their idea.

Sam Knight, journalist and author

I applied for the graduate training scheme, I applied for the *FT*. I applied for all of these jobs, but didn't get them. So in terms of gaining experience, I was just trying to earn a living vaguely in the field of journalism. It was kind of helpful that it was so far away from what I wanted to be doing. It was earning money, in order to be able to do other writing, more ambitious writing on the side.

I think if I'd got a really nifty job as a features writer, it might have shafted me a bit. Because you'd think – this is going to sound really rude – but you think you're doing interesting stuff, but you're just doing 800 words on a pop star or something like that. You're like, 'You're living the dream.' But actually, you look back over the course of the year, and you're like, 'Did I write anything good?'

[Robert] Thompson, the editor of *The Times* said, 'I just don't know what to do with you. I don't know what's going to happen if I put you on the business desk for two years.' He was kind of right. I'm sure I would have been terrible.

Really, I can't believe you embark on doing this kind of stuff with a particularly well-made plan for how it's going to go or where you're going to end up or which magazine that looks good now is still going to be good in five years' time? You could grow up dreaming of writing for *Newsweek*. I didn't have a clear plan and I think, as you get into it, you realise that places pay and places don't pay, and it's not always totally obvious what those are.

Occasionally people write to me, ask me these questions, especially people in their early 20s trying to do things now. I feel, maybe this is a really appalling thing to say, but I feel [you have to be] much more open. Maybe you have to do copywriting or some job like Kafka had during the day to enable you to do it. Likewise, you can make quite Faustian compromises to work at big, fancy-sounding publications. But actually, they're shit jobs and you don't get to write anything interesting.

David Mitchell, novelist

If you do have a career, then it behoves you to think about it as a career. As an artist, with a small or an uppercase A, how are you going to avoid repeating yourself? There are more people publishing books in their 20s, 30s, 40s than in their 60s, 70s and 80s. How come? I'll be able to give you a more informed answer when I'm there. I'm 52 now. I don't think it's because people forget how to write novels, it's likelier because the compost heaps that you take nutrients from, you take stuff from, locations, ideas, experiences that you put into your work – that's what you build up in your youth, in most cases. It's youthful experiences, especially if you do become a full-time writer.

If you're not doing something else, if you're not a doctor like [Anton] Chekhov or a chemist like Primo Levi or – other examples have flown from my mind – but you know what I mean? If you are a full-time writer, I think that compost heap gets smaller and smaller and a kind of diminishing-returns cycle can kick in, unless you take steps to replenish that compost heap with other experiences. Now, if you've got kids, you can't just do what I did when I was 26 and take the Trans-Siberian Express for the best part of a year, or however long. But in your choice of collaborations, or in your choice to collaborate, you can explore other narrative forms, like libretti or like film, and go into it with the mind of a student again. What do you know about narratives that I don't, you scriptwriters? The answers can be really instructive.

181

Well, they are really instructive, always. They might not be applicable, but even thinking about why they're not applicable, that's instructive; you can't lose.

So these [are] holidays that I've taken in other narrative forms. My home is still the novel, that's still my home art form. That will always be the case. I love the damn thing, it's a big, baggy, forgiving, cranky, ramshackle, 300-year-old, ever-evolving form. I love it. But little holidays in other, maybe slicker, maybe more glamorous narrative forms, I've continued to treasure these experiences, because of what I learn there.

Nikesh Shukla, author

I'd been doing all this thinking around immigration and immigrants and my family's story and all these stories that you never hear about, of these brilliant people who make up this country. Then Brexit happened and the week before Brexit there was that infamous – or some might say infamous, I say fucking racist – poster. The 'breaking point' poster, which Nigel Farage was standing in front of. I got so upset about it, so viscerally upset that he had stolen the narrative of who got to be an immigrant and what it meant to immigrate, [away] from immigrants and the children of immigrants. I felt like I was a proud, proud child of an immigrant.

So as I was leaving work, one day, I tweeted a photo of me and my dad, and said something about his journey to the UK. And the hashtag, #proudchildofanimmigrant. I cycled home. Then a couple of other people had done something similar. So I retweeted them, then I did child time and played with my kids. Then sat down to check the news and the hashtag had pretty much gone viral on Twitter.

It was a really, really positive, warm, lovely thing. It's the second time I've had something go viral, because the first time was when we released a video of us sending a lamb chop into space, which was to promote 'Meatspace'. But my timeline was just filled with so much warmth and love and these small, brilliant stories of significant, active citizens of the UK.

For me, that was the moment I really realised what this new novel was about and what question I'd been trying to wrestle with. That really helped with the edit of it. I did quite a significant edit of the book after that. So writing for me isn't a struggle, so much as me wrestling with something, like a question.

Jennifer Croft, translator

It's hard to become a literary translator, but it's also hard to become a writer. I think it does require another day job at first and possibly for a long time. It requires a lot of humility, a lot of dealing with rejection. I've been rejected from absolutely everywhere and absolutely everything. It's good because I've gotten totally used to it.

Terri White, journalist and author

My ambition was born out of desperation and panic. But also, I'd learned at a very young age at school that you could be rewarded for being clever, or you could be rewarded for hard work. That all this negativity at home and all this chaos and violence and awfulness at home, that you could create a space where none of that existed, where actually you were rewarded for all the right things. I carried that through into my work. I thought I could build this other reality where I was able to succeed, and where everything was seen in a positive light, and where I could work hard, and where all of that would be rewarded.

I think that the economic side of it was very, very important to me, which is, my Mum had never been financially independent.

Our family had existed on benefits and she'd relied on her partners. That meant that she didn't have her own car, so she couldn't escape the house and drive away, it meant she couldn't take us and leave somebody because she had no money to be able to take us anywhere, to even pay for a night in a B&B. I saw the consequences of having complete economic dependence on somebody else, or even just complete economic dependence on the state. She had no other options. I was always determined that I would have options, that it would be in my control. That, I think, is what drove my ambition, and my determination to prove that I was good enough, that I was something. When you've had the childhood that I had, you internalise a lot of what you're told, which is, 'You're nothing, you're nobody, you'll never be anything.' Part of your drive becomes a desire to prove that person or those people wrong.

Elif Shafak, novelist

I started writing at a relatively early age – publishing, also, at a relatively early age. There was so much I didn't know about the writing process, the publishing process. It can be very lonely. It is a very solitary task. I think you need to learn, very quickly, not to mind too much what other people might say or what they might think about your work.

It has to come from within, the energy, because we're not doing teamwork and because so much depends on your faith in the story. I think we need to build an inner garden and to learn to retreat into that inner garden. I wish I knew at the very beginning that I would need to nurture an inner garden and how important that was, no matter what's going on outside, that there is this space you can go back to again and again. I think that's where most of my fiction comes from. All I'm trying to say is you need to have faith in your work and that faith has to come from within.

Helen Lewis, journalist and author

I think it's an experience lots of people have in journalism and people don't want to talk about [it]. Moving from there [the *Daily Mail*] to here [the *New Statesman*], I experienced as a huge relief. But I also experienced it as a sense of personal failure that I couldn't hack it. Some part of me thought, 'This was incredible.' Like I'd been on one of those *SAS: Are You Tough Enough?* programmes, and I'd pulled out at the third 15-mile hike. Now I watch those programmes, I'm like, 'Just leave, you're having a terrible time. You've got dysentery and your foot's falling off, just leave.'

But I can understand the impulse that you feel that there's a big challenge that you've been presented with. But now I look at those people and I think, actually, it's a kind of Stockholm Syndrome, particularly when you're paid really, really well. You've got a certain lifestyle that you're used to. There's a lot that you will put up with in terms of workplace culture, in terms of hours, in terms of whatever, because actually, you're scared about what life would be like on the outside.

Linda Grant, novelist and non-fiction writer

How do you write? You write. I think that one of the things which is so little understood is, most writers do draft after draft after draft after draft. You look at your first draft and you think, 'Oh my god, I should not drop dead, so anybody could come into my computer and see this – this is just dreadful.' You get it to a point where you think, 'Okay, there's something here. There's something that's working, there's something that I can make better. There's something that I can live with.'

I think that's quite an important thing: can I live with this for the two years that it takes to write it? Am I interested enough in these characters? I think, every time I sit down, it's like casting off into the unknown. I've no idea what I'm doing. I get kind of suicidal. I think I've lost it, I'll never write another novel. And then, some months later, you think, 'Okay, yeah, I was right to stick with this.'

Lennie Goodings, publisher and author

You have to believe in yourself. I'm sorry, I know that sounds unbelievably clichéd, but the fact is the world in some ways doesn't need more novels, doesn't need more memoirs, doesn't need more non-fiction, because there's hundreds of books published every single year. It's going to be easy to feel like what you have to say is not important; what you have to say is going to be knocked.

You have to have a resilience at the heart of yourself, because once you make the first hurdle, which is getting an editor or getting an agent, rather, or getting a publisher, then you've got the world. The world – I wouldn't say it's exactly hostile, but it's not exactly welcoming to everything creative by any means, and the choices are phenomenal, as we know.

So you have to hold that core of resilience that will be fine when you get a shit review, and you still think: 'That's okay, I know I did the best I could, and I know what I did was right for me.' I know it's a very clichéd thing to hang on to and to say, but actually, if you don't have that, if you're not tough enough to hold that space for yourself, in yourself, you should just not publish. You should not publish publicly – you should just do it for your friends. You've got to have a tremendous resilience and toughness at the core to be an author.

Simon Lancaster, speechwriter and author

Never take other people's advice. Always trust your gut and follow your instincts. I think the very worst speeches are speeches that are written by committee. The worst speeches that I've been involved with have been speeches where I've been a little bit too timid and afraid to push back, so I've tried to incorporate a multitude of different perspectives. As a result, it's a bit like a car where you get five people trying to drive at once: it doesn't really work very well. A speech needs to be a single, good vision.

12

LIFE VS WRITING

'To hold a pen is to be at war.'

– Voltaire

Writing can be deeply rewarding. It can enliven the imagination and deliver stimulation, focus or catharsis. It offers writers the opportunity to bring new facts – or old injustices – to light. Finding the correct words for your thoughts and crafting them in an elegant sentence is satisfying. The relationships you can develop with your peers, sources and editors can be intellectually vivifying.

But a love of writing can also be a challenge to real-life relationships. For some, long stints spent reporting or researching have made family life difficult, even impossible. In the world of journalism, friendship between correspondents may be tempered by a sense of competition. Writing can ultimately feel very lonely.

If you write about living subjects – particularly friends or members of your family – you will probably have to have awkward conversations about the nature of your work and the way they are represented in it. Christina Lamb tells us about the complexity of writing about Benazir Bhutto, then the prime minister of Pakistan, after she had developed an amicable relationship with her. When Toby Young dramatised the sex scandals that took place at the *Spectator* in the early 2000s, Boris Johnson, his friend and editor, was among the farce's targets.

Franz Kafka once wrote that 'writing means revealing oneself to excess'. Memoirists may have to strike a balance between what they reveal of themselves and what they reveal of other figures who appear in their account. Events can be interpreted and remembered differently and for that reason, Kit de Waal conferred with her siblings when working on her memoir, *Without Warning and Only Sometimes*. Terri White chose to avoid talking about her brother and sister in *Coming Undone*.

The pursuit of stories and the truth can be dangerous, too. Patrick Kingsley tells us about working in Egypt for *The Guardian* and attracting the attention of the authorities there. Sebastian Junger, who covered the war in Afghanistan for several years, speaks with candour about the 'psychological fallout' he experienced as a result of his work and Alex Perry, likewise, found reporting from Afghanistan to be traumatic. These writers put themselves at great personal risk and were changed as a result. They're a reminder that far from being a refuge or way of detaching from 'real life', writing frequently requires a deep engagement with all that is most dangerous and raw in human experience.

Lucy Hughes-Hallett, author and biographer

I remember the day that Nicholas [Pearson], my publisher, rang to tell me that I was on the shortlist for [the Samuel Johnson] prize. I was actually at my parents' house. My mother had died; my father was still alive, but in a care home. My brothers and I had decided that we had to sell the house. I was seeing all these removal vans, which were leaving the house – and any house, even if it's not a very big one, has an awful lot of clutter in it. All this stuff, all my parents' possessions, a lot of them just going to the dump – old sofas and mattresses, you know, stuff that nobody's ever going to want. It was incredibly painful. I got the great news that I was shortlisted for this prize, but it remains one of the saddest days of my life. One's book life does go alongside real life.

Another instance of that was when *Cleopatra* came out. I can remember Dan, my husband, coming into the maternity ward – I was in hospital for about two weeks when my twin daughters were born, because the second one was very small and there were worries about her, so I stayed in hospital. I remember Dan coming in with the reviews, and I'd been looking forward all my life to publishing a book and seeing the first reviews of it. When he came in, all I wanted to do was sleep, I didn't want to look at anything. So again, one's personal life and one's literary career are not always in perfect sync.

Oliver Bullough, journalist and author

At the time, my girlfriend (my now-wife) was a doctor here in the UK. She was quite clear that I had to make a choice between being a foreign correspondent and her – she didn't put it exactly like that, but I was made to understand. So I chose her and came back to the UK. I tried to work for Reuters in London for a bit, but it wasn't nearly as much fun writing about the oil-products market as it had been bouncing around Russia reporting on everything that was happening. So I left after six months of unsuccessfully trying to persuade myself that I was interested in being in Canary Wharf. I became a freelancer, which is what I've been doing ever since.

Henry Winter, journalist and author

If you're a football journalist, every day is Christmas Day. We are very fortunate. People come into the profession and they go, 'This is really weird, because your biggest rivals are also your biggest mates.' We go to each other's weddings, some people are godparents to each other's children, and yet you're trying to slit each other's throats with stories and who's got the best interviews, who's got the best intro?

We're really competitive with each other, but we'll go for a drink afterwards. If, say, Ian Ladyman, who writes fantastic interviews for the *Daily Mail*, has got a great read on a Saturday morning – and he often gets them, and there's a certain rivalry over who gets the best interviews on a Saturday morning – I'll send him a text. First thing I said, 'Fantastic. You've done me there. It's an absolutely brilliant interview.' There is that respect.

Colin Thubron, travel writer and novelist

Even when I was earning rather well by writing standards, it'd have been really hard to bring up, say, two children alone, or with no other financial assistance. It would have been difficult [to balance travel writing and having a family]. I think I would have gone on trying, but my output would be very depleted. If I had married as I might have done at the age of 24, 25, it would have been very hard indeed. I think probably I would have ended up in publishing. If I'd married, say, in my mid-30s, that would have been rather different; I'd have been more set on my professional journey and I would have been luckier. But in both cases, [it would have been] a whole lot harder. As it was, I married extremely late and it's all fine.

Stig Abell, journalist and editor

I get abuse on social media about [having worked at] *The Sun*, still, all the time, but I've got loyalty. I took the job. I made the decision to take the job. Although things were done – decisions were made without my knowledge, or that I wasn't party to – I'm slightly loath to say: 'Well, I wouldn't have done that.'

That may be true or may not be true. But it's difficult, because once you work for somewhere, you work for that paper and you've got to be loyal to it. But some things are harder to defend than others, definitely.

Ann Goldstein, translator

I don't know who she [the writer published as 'Elena Ferrante'] is. I haven't met her. I mean, as far as I know, I haven't met her. I do correspond through the publishers . . . Fortunately, since I really don't know who she is, I can honestly say no to anybody who asks me. I think that's a good position to be in.

The other part of the question of being the public face of Ferrante is, of course, it's a very strange position to be in. But since I don't know who she is, and I don't really know anything about her any more than what she writes, I can't really speak for her.

I think that if she wants to not be public, she should be allowed not to be public. I think that this kind of hunting for it, and the speculation, it's unnecessary. I mean, as she herself says, the books are there.

Her first novel, *L'Amore Molesto*, *Troubling Love*, was published in, I think, 1992. You've probably read *Frantumaglia* [a non-fiction book by Ferrante, subtitled *A Writer's Journey*] where there's a letter to the publisher where she says right away, 'I'm not going to do anything for this book. Because it'd be public.' I think in the beginning, she just felt that she wanted her privacy, for whatever reasons. And I think, as time went on, it became somewhat also of a political statement, in the sense of a feeling that the author being marketed was something that she just didn't want to do and didn't believe in. I know other writers have sometimes said, 'I wish I had done that.' But you really can't.

Amanda Craig, novelist

I wrote [A Vicious Circle] when I had two small children, one of whom was very ill. It took almost five years to write. It was very much conceived as being in this Victorian model which I've since taken forward, although I'd already started to repeat characters, reuse characters, even from the first novel, Foreign Bodies.

... I was not an idiot. I knew that some of my jokes [in A Vicious Circle, a satire of London's literary journalists and publishing sector] might be perhaps a bit close to the bone. I actually asked Hamish Hamilton to give me a libel reading. They agreed and, very luckily, Giles Gordon [her agent] came with me to this meeting, which was with the Penguin in-house lawyer. We began to go through the book and to make very small changes. I was completely honest about the people, the real-life people – and there was always more than one who had given me the ideas for particular characters.

Claire Alexander [the editor of the book] was absolutely convinced that the villain of the book – the boyfriend of the Irish waitress, Mary – was modelled on the now-dead Philip Kerr. She wouldn't listen to anything that I said. She interrupted the libel meeting about ten minutes into it – it was literally less than a quarter of an hour – saying, 'This is an absolute waste of my time.

Nobody but a lunatic would wish to claim to be these characters.'
And she flounced out.

Well, the problem with libel is that there always are lunatics
waiting to claim that this character can only be them. The novel
had been due to come out in, I think it was, September. I was on
holiday and this letter arrived from this ex-boyfriend who had
by then become quite a leading critic. I had gone out with him
15 years previously at Cambridge: we'd had a two-year relationship that had ended pretty badly – so badly that I had not seen
him or communicated with him in all that time. But he claimed,
nevertheless, to be the model for this highly unpleasant person in
the literary world.

Penguin, having defended people like Salman Rushdie to
the hilt, just dropped me in it – made no attempt to fight this, to
counter it. They announced that the book was being cancelled . . .
Not only was there no attempt to defend me, but someone who's
employed by Penguin, I was told by several people, went up to
[David] Sexton at a party and told him that if he prosecuted me,
he could win £30,000.

What they didn't reckon on is that I am a really tough
person. I hope I'm a nice person as well, but I will not be bullied.
People my entire life have tried to bully me, for lots of different
reasons. I was in a terrible state. I was also coping with this
very sick baby.

I began to think how I could rescue this book and myself,
because I was absolutely determined I would not be beaten. The
best thing that I did was to ring up the Society of Authors, who
are like the trade union for authors, and they knew all about it.
They immediately suggested that I get in touch with this great libel
lawyer, this man called David Hooper. I had no money and I was
also facing the prospect that, if this did go to court, we would lose

our home that we had struggled for years and years to be able to buy. It was a really awful situation.

He said, 'I'll read this and I'll give you an opinion.' He read it and he couldn't believe that they'd just dropped it. He said, 'This is a ludicrous situation. You can make a few small changes and it's perfectly publishable.' As soon as I heard this, I let my agent know. My agent, who was a very jolly, mischievous, robust man, was slightly treating this as a great story. All the nationals were writing about this because it was such a ludicrous situation. But for me [it was] incredibly serious.

I don't know how aware people are of how the libel laws used to be, but it is the only crime which you are not deemed innocent until proved guilty. You are assumed to be guilty unless you can prove your innocence. That's what was extraordinarily difficult and dangerous for me. I'm one of the people, alongside Simon Singh, who helped to get that changed. It was so dreadful for defendants that it was suppressing not just freedom of speech, but things like scientific inquiry.

Terri White, journalist and author

I'm not in touch with my mum or my dad. I am very close to my brother and sister. My brother read [her memoir, *Coming Undone*] before publication because he had to verify some of the things in the book. He learned a lot of stuff for the first time, especially a lot of the stuff from when I was an adult and how ill I was in New York – when nobody in my family really knew what was going on. He was wonderful about it and understood why I felt the need to write the book, and was incredibly, incredibly supportive. He spoke of feeling guilty that he didn't know and hadn't been able to help me. When you're that ill, if you choose to make that completely invisible to people, you can, and you will, and I did.

My sister was incredibly supportive as well, but neither of them are really mentioned in the book. There's one mention of them when we're walking down a path. I made that choice very deliberately because my story is my story and theirs is theirs. It is not my place to tell theirs. The same really with my mum: I made a choice very early on that I would only include stories about my mum if it was directly relevant to me and the story I was telling.

I would hope that she would think it was fair. I would hope that she would understand why I maybe felt the need to write the book. I don't know if she's read it; she may well have done. I knew that I'd been responsible around the people in the book and I knew that I'd been more than fair, so I didn't in any way – and I thought I might – feel guilty or worried or like I'd screwed anybody over or anything like that. I hope I went out of my way to do the opposite.

Jeremy Gavron, novelist and non-fiction writer

My mother died when I was four years old; she committed suicide. My father really decided that the best way to deal with that was to try and forget about her, so we didn't talk about her, he put away most of her possessions, he gave away or threw away, hid her papers. The things he did keep – a box of photographs – he hid away. The only thing actually, that was kept, was that she'd written a book called *The Captive Wife,* which was an early work of feminist sociology. That was up on a high shelf. Other than that, there was really no sign of her in the house that I grew up in. So [I grew up] not knowing about her, or knowing very little, my grandmother was the one person who would tell me a few stories, but not knowing very much about and not knowing why she killed herself, and never really speaking about her.

He [my father] told me at 16 – the one conversation I had with him between the age of four and in my 40s really. He took me for a drive in his car, so he didn't have to look at me while he told me. He was devastated; he'd adored her, I think he was just utterly devastated by the whole thing. He told me a very basic version of the story of what had happened – that she'd fallen in love with a colleague. She was teaching at Hornsey College of Art at the time, and she'd fallen in love with the colleague who'd rejected her. She'd killed herself. That was all he told me.

I, as children do, bought into the taboo, I didn't talk about her. I remember I was breaking up with a girlfriend at university and I used this story that I'd never told anybody – that my mother had killed herself – as a sort of emotional weapon in the breakup. After that, I was a bit more honest about it. I would tell people very occasionally. But still, as I grew older and I became a journalist, I found little bits more about her in clearing out my grandparents' house. I found some documents, I found a newspaper article telling me about her inquest or a report of her inquest. I found an envelope, which was a suicide note scrawled on a little white envelope. These are in my grandfather's papers. But I still didn't know that much about her. I didn't really make much attempt to find out more about her until my brother, her other son, died suddenly of a heart attack when he was 46. I was 43.

I was utterly thrown by that. Not just by my brother's death, which would have been enough to do so. It was like when an earthquake reveals something long buried. That's what it felt like. I felt a kind of grief welling up from deep inside me, because I'd never been able to grieve for my mother. There was no funeral. We never spoke about her. So for two or three years, I was in a state of limbo, really. I didn't know what to do with myself.

I published my previous novel [*An Acre of Barren Ground*] . . . a week before my brother died. So every time I even thought about writing a novel, I felt sick. The idea that all stories led to one end, it felt like to me, which of course they do. But it felt very present to me in that situation at that time. Slowly, I began to realise that in order to get myself out of this hole that I was in, this emotional psychological hole, I have to address what had put me there. Which was my family situation, my brother, my mother. I began asking questions about my mother for the first time in my life in my 40s.

Kit de Waal, novelist and short-story writer

I'm the custodian of the family history. I don't know why – I've got a really good memory. Even before writing the memoir, my siblings would ring me and say, 'Who was that woman that lived up the road?' and I'd just know, for some reason. So I was the best-placed person, really, to talk about our childhood.

But when I wrote it, because there's some difficult things there, I really wanted to make sure that not only had I got it right, but that my siblings felt okay about it. I'm getting paid – they're not. I'm going to give the potted history of our life – they're not. So when I finished it, and it was about 72,000 words, I sent it to my four siblings. I said, 'Right, here it is. Read it. If you object to anything, just send me the page and the paragraph number or the chapter, and it comes out. No negotiation. I will not try and persuade you that that did happen. Anything you're uncomfortable with, just tell me and it comes out.'

Christina Patterson, journalist and author

The starting point [of her memoir, *Outside, the Sky is Blue*] was my sister's schizophrenia. When she was 14, she had a breakdown and was sent off to the adolescent unit at the mental hospital. She was five years older than me. We were young children and we didn't know what was going on, and our parents didn't really tell us. We knew that she wasn't well, but it was years before it was actually diagnosed as schizophrenia. It had a very big impact on the whole family – most of all on her – but on all of us, in different ways. I wanted to write about the impact of mental illness on a family.

In the 20 years since then, she died, my father died, then my mother died. Then, in 2019, just before the pandemic, my brother died. She and my brother died very suddenly and unexpectedly. So by the time I sat down to write the version of the book I wrote, it was very different from the original book, because it had lots of other thoughts in there, including: what's it like to be the last one left when you don't have children, and neither of your siblings have children?

Cal Flyn, *journalist and author*

[In *Thicker Than Water*] I was writing about someone who we're reasonably distantly related to. It was [Angus McMillan] my great-great-great uncle, so it wasn't somebody that any of us had known within our lifetimes. I think that made it easier, but, at the same time, I was lucky that my family reacted in the way they did, because it didn't occur to me until quite far down the line that this impacted on them as well, that I was writing about someone in our family, not just mine. They've all responded really nicely. But I think I should have had that conversation explicitly at the beginning and said, 'I'm going to write about this – is that okay?'

Maggie Fergusson, *journalist and author*

Michael Morpurgo read the George Mackay Brown book [that she wrote] and then got in touch out of the blue and said, 'Would you like to write something about me?' I was a little bit wary – such a very different subject. He's an incredibly nice man, Michael Morpurgo, very, very nice. I'm very fond of him. But it was a completely different sort of story. It is very different to write about somebody who's still alive.

Really, I would suggest that anyone who's thinking about writing about somebody who's still alive, thinks again. Of course, you have the advantage that your subject is there to answer questions and tell you everything that's happened. But with the best will in the world, if people are still alive, they really don't want you to tell a kind of warts-and-all story. You just can't.

Irvine Welsh, novelist and screenwriter

Sometimes I'm typing away and I look and I think, 'Fuck, where did this come from? Did I just write this? What is all this?' You have that moment like, 'What's my mother going to think about all this? What's my girlfriend going to think about this?'

Then you think, 'These are good feelings to have, they're really good.' That means you're tapping into something, if you're worried about this kind of social embarrassment.

Toby Young, journalist and author

In 2004 there were various sex scandals that beset the *Spectator*. Rod Liddle left his then-wife on their honeymoon and returned to London to run off with the *Spectator*'s receptionist. Boris [Johnson], who was then the editor – turned out to be having an affair with the deputy editor, Petronella Wyatt, even though he initially dismissed this rumour as an 'inverted pyramid of piffle'. And Kimberly Fortier, then the publisher of the magazine – turned out she was having an affair with the blind Home Secretary, David Blunkett.

I was sharing the theatre critic beat at the time with a guy called Lloyd Evans. He still does it, actually. We decided that somebody was bound to write a sex farce set in the *Spectator*'s offices, and it would become this massive West End hit, and we'd kick ourselves for not doing it. We decided to have a crack at it ourselves, and we wrote a sex farce called *Who's the Daddy?* and it was put on at the back of this pub in Islington called the King's Head – not far from where I lived, and not far from where Boris lived.

It was a huge success insofar as a pub show can be a success – it sold out almost overnight. It got four-star reviews in most of the broadsheets and we had three offers to take it into the West End. But [on opening night], Boris, who'd been very good – up until this point, he'd been extremely good about the whole thing, he'd taken it on the chin. I remember he sent Lloyd and me a postcard which said, 'I always knew my life would be turned into a farce and I'm just glad it's been entrusted to such distinguished men of letters.' If he could have used a typeface called irony, he would have done, but that was the extent of his criticism of us. He'd really been very sporting about the whole thing. He hadn't fired us, hadn't tried to dissuade us from putting it on, even though it was ripping the piss out of him in virtually every scene.

He did baulk at the West End transfer. He didn't threaten me or Lloyd with the sack, but he tried to appeal to our better nature, and essentially said, 'You've achieved what you wanted to achieve, you've established your bonafides as playwrights, you can now get another play put on, why take this one into the West End? You'll only be doing it to line your pockets and you'll be doing that at my expense. I've been very good about this until now – we've been friends for 20, 25 years, doesn't that mean anything?' Etc., etc. In the end, we decided not to take it into the West End.

Christina Lamb, journalist and author

At the beginning, when I was in Pakistan, I think [Benazir Bhutto] was in her mid-30s and I was 21, 22. She became prime minister and she would invite me to things at the prime minister's house as a friend, which meant that I had tremendous access. But also, I found it quite difficult: how do you report on somebody who's actually running the country [when] she's inviting you round? I thought, 'Well, the important thing was just doing my job, and I should write exactly what I saw.'

If something bad was happening – in fact, there was tremendous corruption in her first government – I said to her about all these things. I was mostly writing for the *Financial Times*, meeting lots of business people and they were telling me horrendous stories, particularly about her husband, so I was asking her about that. I also felt strongly, as a woman, that she was the first woman prime minister in the Islamic world and in Pakistan, that she should be doing a lot of things for women that needed to be changed. She didn't do that, so I used to have quite heated discussions with her.

I still wrote all these things, whereas she felt: 'You're either with us or you're against us' – and so if I was a friend, I shouldn't be writing these things. We did fall out. But she was actually a very loyal person and she was in exile in London for years, so I used to see her here. We repaired the relationship.

Patrick Kingsley, journalist and author

Neither government liked what I was doing. [Referring to Mohamed Morsi, the former president of Egypt, and Adly Mansour, the interim president.] I basically had the opinion that, if you're a foreign correspondent who doesn't have much cultural knowledge or insight to offer your readers, what you can do – that maybe it's a bit harder if you're a local correspondent, just for safety reasons – is to do big, hard-hitting investigations. That's basically what I saw as my role: to investigate stuff that was less likely to land me in trouble than maybe an Egyptian journalist, although Egyptian journalists did, and do, fantastic investigations.

So I did an investigation into army abuses that made the Muslim Brotherhood government – the government when I first arrived – hate me. They stopped allowing me to come to their press conferences. Then, when they got ousted, I just kept going along that vein, but the government, the new government, was a different government – and they also had a huge problem with me. I don't think either side particularly liked what I was doing.

It was quite a difficult time – it was nothing like what it is for a local journalist – but I was getting followed. Your phones are obviously tapped. They would do news segments about me on TV that said, 'This person is a terrorist.' They wrote editorials about me in the local papers, as they did to other foreign correspondents as well, but certainly I was under quite a lot of pressure. It was difficult.

If you're in the street reporting, you can get picked up by the police – and I was, maybe half a dozen times – and then you're questioned. Most of the time you get out and it's not the end of the world, unlike what it would be if you're an Egyptian, but there was that constant pressure and that constant feeling of knowing that the stuff you write is going to get you into some kind of trouble.

Alex Perry, journalist and author

[Reporting from Afghanistan in 2001] worked out for me. I survived. There was a friend of mine who was shot in the chest, and survived, ten yards from where I'd been sitting. I wrote a story that won several awards and got included in *Best American Something* – Reporting or Writing – some kind of anthology. It established me, really. It still goes on to this day: I get asked to take part in historical documentaries and so on.

I wasn't freelance, I was staff at *Time* magazine – but I had zero training. I didn't have a flak jacket. My [satellite] phone had broken almost as soon as I picked it up. I had no idea what I was doing. Tess, my wife, will tell you that I picked up a decent dose of PTSD from that as well – just being, for three or four days, in very close proximity to people killing each other. It was, at the time, an incredibly adrenalising, electric experience – but it was extremely hard to come down off that for several years.

Sebastian Junger, journalist, author and film-maker

When Tim [Hetherington, a photojournalist and co-director of *Restrepo*] died, I was about to turn 50. I saw what his death did to everyone around him who loved him. All of a sudden, war reporting seemed rather selfish. It didn't seem heroic and noble: it seemed selfish. You're not gambling with your life, you're gambling with the emotional lives of everyone who loves you. That seemed like a selfish choice to make.

I decided to stop war reporting, which in some ways was great, because war reporting is quite easy. It's just inherently dramatic. It is not that hard to write or produce films about war that are attention-getting, because war is attention-getting. When I stopped war reporting, I had this sort of identity crisis of like, 'Well who am I, then?' That forced me into some much richer terrain intellectually and personally and emotionally.

The consequences of war reporting are huge. The consequences of trauma are huge, and you can be traumatised in all kinds of ways: car accidents, deaths of loved ones. Life is painful for everybody, eventually, and war reporting is definitely painful. I had, for years, been struggling with some psychological fallout from war reporting. At first I didn't know – I had no idea what it was. I thought something was wrong with me. I kept having panic attacks and I would get depressed and quite angry. Things that were very out of character. I didn't understand what was happening and finally it was explained to me like, 'This is trauma. You're reacting to trauma.'

Liberia was particularly horrific. That was particularly hard for me and, after Tim was killed, I just had this avalanche of trauma reactions. I wound up breaking up my marriage. I became extremely depressed and angry, and I wouldn't say suicidal, but I could see how people could be. Suddenly I could understand that way of thinking about oneself. I knew I was in trouble when I started thinking, 'Well Tim was the lucky one, he got taken out of here before life turned really painful. I have to go through the whole friggin' thing – he's the lucky one.' When I realised I was thinking that, I realised I really had a problem and my marriage broke up and a lot of things changed in my life.

Max Hastings, journalist and author

I think one of the most important things is that some people should believe in you – even if it's only your parents. I was lucky to have Charles Wintour [the former editor of the *Evening Standard*], who was my great mentor. Charles thought that I had potential to be something good. And it made a huge difference to me.

When I became editor at the *Evening Standard*, somebody stuck on my desk, for fun, my old personnel files. One of the things I found in it was a letter of my mother's, to Charles Wintour, begging him to stop me going to wars, because she thought I was going to get killed sooner or later doing it.

13

SUCCESS

'I think I shall write books, and get rich and famous; that would suit me, so that is my favourite dream.'

– Louisa May Alcott

All writers dream of a huge hit. If they are honest with themselves, many of them also dream of the trappings that a hit can bring – riches, fame, perhaps a villa on the French Riviera. But, as we've discovered by posing nosy questions to authors who have produced world-shaking books, the experience of enormous literary success can bring its own complexities.

For starters, there's no formula. No author we've spoken to has ever been able to conclusively indicate what factor, or combination thereof, led to one book of theirs breaking out when the others did not. 'It's very hard to put your finger on why one book suddenly soars,' Kate Mosse, whose quest novel *Labyrinth* was a slow-burn sensation in the mid-2000s, told us. 'It isn't because it's the best book.' Ian McEwan likewise thought his publishers would struggle to shift 5,000 copies of *Atonement*. In fact, the novel sold over 1.5 million copies in the UK alone. And it's not just authors who find it hard to predict success; if there was a way to determine exactly which books will be bestsellers, publishers would no doubt have seized upon it by now and would no longer be making a loss on thousands of books per year.

Great success brings questions. First among them, often, is whether to quit the day job. Joanne Harris gave up teaching in the aftermath of *Chocolat*, when she found herself being doorstepped by reporters outside her school.

Then there's envy, notoriously the writers' sin. Voltaire once remarked that, 'The only reward to be expected from literature is contempt if one fails and hatred if one succeeds.' Great success can still complicate relations with peers. Orlando Figes felt he was ostracised by the British historical establishment after his breakout success *A People's Tragedy*, his book on late 19th- and early 20th-century Russia, which he published at the tenderish age of 36. Max Hastings wryly unpacked the two-way hostility that exists between journalists and academics: 'Journalists will always envy academics their respectability, and academics will always envy journalists the money.'

Success can buy you creative freedom, the time and space to write. David Nicholls likens his 2009 smash *One Day* to a pension, or the long-running West End hit that theatre directors crave to allow them to do more experimental work elsewhere. But success also begs the question of what comes next. Do you try to repeat the same formula? After *Girl with a Pearl Earring* Tracy Chevalier was bombarded with suggestions of other paintings she could reimagine in novels. She refused all of them, and her publishers backed her.

They don't always. After *Trainspotting*, Irvine Welsh wrote an experimental novel. His publisher was unimpressed by this book idea and told him so straight. Welsh took the advice on board, went back to the drawing board, and produced *Marabou Stork Nightmares*, in his view perhaps his best work.

It can be intoxicating, and we hope inspiring, to read these experiences of great literary success. But as this chapter makes clear, the fulfilment of one dream often marks the beginning of another.

Mark Haddon, novelist

It's quite hard negotiating this. But I spend a lot of time pretending that *Curious Incident* [*of the Dog in the Night-Time*] has never existed. Of course, I am hugely grateful. But it's psychologically a very unhelpful thing. I often describe it as the world's largest gold-plated ball and chain.

That's become even more the case since the stage production happened and then grew and then had many, many afterlives. I mean, at this moment, yesterday, the new West End run was announced. So *Curious Incident* is returning to the West End. It's had a world tour. There's a schools' tour happening now. A little bit of me feels embarrassed about the fact that I keep a distance from this. I hope most of the people involved, particularly the new casts, understand that I can't carry on writing new things if my job remains the person who wrote *Curious Incident*. I could go and see a different show every week. I could go meet every new cast; I could remain intimately involved. I've got to let it go. I mean, I know Michael Morpurgo, for example, has remained quite involved with *War Horse*. As far as I know, he's appeared on stage in it, in the chorus a couple of times. I've been very, very firm about not letting that happen.

In fact, I took a vow about two years ago saying that I don't mind people asking me questions about the book. But if I do any kind of interview or event, it's not primarily about *Curious*. After that point, I officially turned down any requests to do events about *Curious* or interviews about *Curious*. As soon as I'd made that decision, I could feel light and space entering my head again.

Ian McEwan, novelist

I don't think of that time [the late 1990s and 2000s] as different from other times, really, except for *Atonement*, I guess. For most literary writers, you're lucky if you just have one book that breaks out. Maybe for some writers, they might have loads, but my sense is, there's always one that you get associated with.

While I was writing *Atonement*, especially just towards the end, I remember phoning my then-editor Dan Franklin at [Jonathan] Cape, saying, 'Look, I think we're going to have trouble selling this novel, because it's really a novel I've written for other writers. If you can sell 5,000 of them, it'd be great.' He said, 'Well, that's fine. I don't mind that.' Then when he read it, he rang back and said, 'You're kidding. It's got three elements that I know mean we'll be able to sell a lot of copies.' I said, 'What three elements?' He said, as if explaining to a complete moron, 'Second World War, country house, and a love affair.' He said, 'We know that we can do something.'

I realised that's why I'm not a publisher. I wouldn't have guessed that. I thought I'd written a novel about literature – how to represent an experience and how a writer spends a lifetime writing the drafts of an experience, and then produces the final copy, which the reader has just read, but is divergent from the facts. I thought, 'This is not going to go down well, but I think it's full of other writers, from Richardson to Joyce to James, and so on.'

No other book of mine has been anything like as successful. So *Amsterdam* [which won the] Booker Prize, irrelevant in terms of sales, and then [*Atonement* was] helped by a very successful movie by Joe Wright. Extremely well cast as well. That got me a reputation that was even worse than the macabre one [early in his career McEwan was christened 'Ian Macabre' due to his dark subject matter] of being a bestselling writer. It stands alone. Nothing else I've written has ever sold even a fraction of that.

I enjoyed it. I mean, it was great. It's wonderful to be read. I got a taste of why people become John Grishams or whatever. The idea that you've crept into the minds of a few million people instead of a few thousand. It is an extraordinary thing. But that period of my life, *Enduring Love* running through to the group you just mentioned. I don't know. Each one seems so different to me that the experience of them, from *Saturday*, *The Children Act* and so on – I can't really group them together as a time.

Joanne Harris, novelist

It didn't take over. I wrote as a hobby, until it became impossible for me to do two things at once. I would have been totally okay keeping on teaching. I'd been a teacher for 15 years; I was good at it. I had three books published while I was a teacher. I think if there had been no moment at which one of the books was so successful that I actually had to give up teaching, I probably would have stayed a teacher and would have written books as a kind of side-line, the way I had for some years. The business of juggling two jobs becomes difficult if one of them is suddenly and unexpectedly successful.

I think the thing about writing books is that unless you're on a deadline, and I wasn't because I wasn't successful enough to have deadlines, you can write at whatever speed you like, in whatever time is available. So I just did that. I wasn't particularly expecting to be more successful than my first two books had been.

It came as a big surprise when my third book [*Chocolat*, published in 1999] was just unexpectedly popular. That meant that I had to do touring, that I had to do promotion. All sorts of things that I'd never done before. So I had a look at my day job. By then *Chocolat* had been such a success that there were people actually turning up, members of the press, turning up at the school and trying to doorstep me there. I thought, 'Right, this is untenable. You have to quit, at least for a while, to see what happens with this.' So I took a year's sabbatical, fully expecting to go back. Of course I never did – because once you've opened that particular box, then there's no going back into it.

Monica Ali, novelist

What was good about [the success of *Brick Lane*], what was difficult about it? There were lots of good things. I think my first reaction to that question is always well, what's difficult about having a first novel that disappears, unremarked and unlauded and unread? I mean, that's bloody difficult, I imagine. So I'm always very wary about complaining about anything that's difficult about having a successful first novel, because compared to having a novel come out and vanish, it's all upside, right? On the other hand, being honest now and looking back, I mean, I was very blithe about how great everything was.

Even the writing process, people would ask me, 'How did you manage to write with such young children and so on?' I'd go, 'It was fine. I'd fit it into naptime and writing in the night and so on.' But actually, the truth was, I was completely exhausted. It was hard. It was really hard. And the fact that the book was published in a lot of different countries as well, there was a lot of pressure to go and support those publications, do interviews and do publicity. While all that is gratifying, I didn't want to be away from home as

Success

much as I was away from home. I found it really, really hard. But I was in denial about how hard I was finding it.

[But] it also meant that I could carry on writing what I wanted to write, which was also huge . . . Was it difficult writing the second book? I think I was just naive and bull-headed in writing whatever I wanted to write. I knew perfectly well that the smart move commercially would be to parlay *Brick Lane* into a bit of a brand, build a readership. But I'm not a marketing machine. I'm a writer.

Tracy Chevalier, novelist

I think any writer who has one book that stands out from the others that they've written has this. Everybody associates them with that book. When you go on to write the next one, what do you do? Even the one after that, or the one after that. People are always assuming you're going to write something that's similar. I had people saying, 'What painting are you going to do? You're going to do the *Mona Lisa* next' – or give me all kinds of advice about what painting I should do next. 'Or are you going to write a sequel?' I would joke – 'You mean, *The Woman with a Pearl Necklace*? Like her 10 years later, when she's a woman.' I just thought, 'Tracy you can't do that, you've got to go for what your gut tells you you want to write about and the readers will follow if they want.'

So I kind of doggedly have pursued my own path ever since. I'm blessed with publishers who don't tell me what to do. I haven't ever had a publisher say to me, 'Oh, I don't think you should write about fossils. Nobody's going to read that.' Or, 'You're going to write about William Blake? I'm not sure.' Or, 'You're going to write about apples in 19th-century America – what?' No – they just let me do it. They are sensible. They let me get on with it. That has been a great relief to me because I don't want to write a book about a painting all the time. I don't want to get into a rut. I want to do my own thing and I want the readers to trust me that I can tell them a story that they're going to want to read.

Anne Enright, novelist

The Booker [Prize] was a sea change in my financial circumstances. It also was a job in itself for a while. It took me away from the desk for maybe a year, or a year or two. There was a year of getting on planes and stuff. I couldn't turn anything down really, because I'd spent so long, I suppose, before that, not getting on the planes. Again, my husband said, 'Just don't have any regrets.' I suppose the only regret I have is that I don't have any regrets. I should just have stayed at home and written more books. It took me a while to get my head back. But the Booker makes you anomalous to a great degree. When I'm talking to younger writers or to people who might be listening to this podcast, for example, who want to see a way into making their life as writers feasible, I can't just say, 'Well, what you have to do is win the Booker and then it'll be all right.' It is an anomaly in a writer's life to have something like that land.

Howard Jacobson, novelist

That experience of every first-time writer – the book's out, the book's out, today the book's out. You wake up on the morning that your book's out and, do you know, the world doesn't change. Nothing is any different. Sun shines or it doesn't shine. People say hello to you or they don't. Life is the same. You have not changed the world. Being a writer has not made you or anybody else any different. So you get used to that.

[As the years went on] my agent would often get – would send me – letters from the Dutch, the Germans, the French. 'We really love Howard Jacobson. We'd love to publish him, but it's comic and it doesn't translate.' Suddenly, overnight that changed. I mean, my agent had the most extraordinary night, the night of the Booker [Prize]. He couldn't go to bed because his phones were ringing. America, Canada, Brazil – they all wanted to translate *The Finkler Question*. Not on the strength, I mean, it's pathetic, isn't it – not because it was a good novel, not because they liked it, but because it had won the Booker Prize. And because it had won the Booker Prize, they wanted to publish it. So I mean, I've got a shelf, which I proudly [have] downstairs and it's got like 35 different translations of *The Finkler Question*. That was a huge difference. Because although you tell yourself you just want to write your books, and if you've got five readers, that will be enough. What's the Stendhal phrase, not to the happy few? He didn't sell very many novels, Stendhal, he dedicates one of the books to the 'Something few.' [It is in fact 'To the Happy Few'.] I felt that I'm writing for a few people, and that's fine. But also the secret is you want to write for the whole world. You really want to write for the whole world, and you actually want to be the only person that the whole world is reading. You want to be the novelist that takes over from all others. So when I started to be translated everywhere, that soothed my ambition.

Irvine Welsh, novelist and screenwriter

I wrote a really shit book after *Trainspotting*, which was kind of an experimental novel. Whenever you say to your publisher you're writing an experimental novel, you just see the colour drain from their face. They pull away the *à la carte* menu and put the set menu in front of you, basically. They hide the wine list, and all that kind of stuff.

So when you have the success that I had with the first two books you think you can do anything, basically. So I did things like, I photocopied my gas bill 50 times and put that in, these were 50 pages in the book – nonsense like that. I got somebody to write me a poem about something and stick that in the book. It was a mess, basically, it was an incoherent piece of drivel. And Robin [Robertson], who was my editor at the time, he said, 'This is just rubbish. It's nonsense. There's nice bits and pieces in there, interesting bits and pieces in there, but stop showing off, basically. Just find what you want to write about. Think about something you're really passionate about and want to talk about.'

I did. I went back to the drawing board and I wrote *Marabou Stork Nighmares*, which is probably one of my best novels, maybe my best in some ways. But it wouldn't have come out, the lesson for me was – I shouldn't have tried to publish that nonsense. But I was correct to write that nonsense, basically. Because that kind of enabled, and kind of begat that process of writing *Marabou Stork Nightmares*. So I think, as a writer, you have to distinguish between writing and publishing. Sometimes you're writing to find what you're writing about, basically.

Orlando Figes, historian

I think as a young man, I dealt with it very badly. I mean, when you have a book like *A People's Tragedy* at the age of 36, that's really a curse in academia, in British academia. It's really a curse. People hated me, and were envious of me. But the way they dealt with that, or with me, was just to put me down the whole time. So I wasn't promoted. I didn't ever get elected to the British Academy. I didn't get half the number of research awards. I got none, for many, many, many, many years. So, it was just this sense of, yeah, I probably wanted some recognition from the academy that my work was rigorous, as they say. That it was based on scholarship, and it wasn't just pot-boiling for a bestseller list, which is how they presented it. But that doesn't bother me anymore.

Max Hastings, journalist and author

There's always jealousy. Journalists will always envy academics their respectability, and academics will always envy journalists the money. Antony Beevor and I make far, far more money out of our book sales than they will ever dream of. Not surprisingly, some of them are pretty sore about it. I came across, in Anthony Powell's commonplace book the other day, a line which made me laugh. He said, 'One never ceases to be surprised that one's contemporaries will forgive one almost anything, except a moderate degree of success.' But the only thing I can ever say in one's own defence, it was not necessarily bound to be that way. One could have been blown up or shot, as quite a few friends of mine were, in all those innumerable wars. Secondly, I could have easily gone bust, because things didn't work out that way.

. . . the Falklands was the first biggie, and the Falklands book [*The Battle for the Falklands*, co-written with Simon Jenkins, published 1983] sold 130-something thousand in hardback . . .

The next time I broke 100,000 in hardback, would have been with – the other books like *Normandy* and all the rest of it sold well, but they didn't sell . . . but *All Hell Let Loose* [a history of the Second World War, published 2011]. We sold I think 145 [thousand] in hardback. But I start getting a bit shaky on the numbers. And then also you start getting really good foreign sales.

David Nicholls, novelist and screenwriter

I know some theatre directors, and what they always long for is a show in the West End that will run, but will allow them to go off and do other things and take some of the pressure off – the requirement to keep doing work that they don't necessarily love. For me that's *One Day*. It sells enough copies a year for me to carry on. I'm incredibly grateful for that. Even after ten years, it still has these little flurries where someone picks it up and tweets about it, and it has a little push in sales. That's great. So that's my pension. Then I'm very, very, very lucky as a writer to have that because the other areas that I work in, TV and film, are quite precarious. It's very rare for a writer to write successfully, as a screenwriter, for 40 or 50 years. You go through highs and lows, and I'm sure I will. I'm sure that's all ahead of me. But I'm lucky to have the security of at least one big success that will tide me over.

. . . It was horribly difficult [following up *One Day*]. I mean, again, I don't want to feel sorry for myself, because I was busy, I was being asked to do fantastic things and travel the world and go to all these places I'd never dreamed of. It was very easy and pleasant to talk about *One Day*, I could have done it for a lot longer. But there came a point where I had to kind of clear my head and I got all the copies out of the office and actually moved somewhere else to work, a completely bare space, and thought, 'Right, get on with it, do something else.' But I think the worst thing that happens is you become very self-conscious, because you start to ask what people want. Not just what people want in the UK, but what people want in Brazil, what do they want around the world? What do they want to read next?

I think also philosophically – not philosophically, that's a bit high-minded – but you start to think about what kind of writer you are. I don't mind reading writers whose books are all largely the same, who will come back again and again to the same themes, the same situations and characters. John le Carré didn't sit down and think, 'I better not write anything else about disillusioned spies.' It's fine, he's John le Carré. At the same time, I like a lot of artists who are always surprising me, who are always doing completely new things, or adding in new style and new forms about new subjects. What are you going to be, are you going to show your versatility? Or are you going to produce *One Day 2*, but do it really to the best of your abilities and not be embarrassed by it? It's a real dilemma.

Simon Scarrow, novelist

After a while, and it was about five or six books in, I think it was *Centurion* suddenly just zoomed up in the charts for some reason. I don't know why. It was partly because we changed the titling, because up to that point, it had been *The Eagle Something* in every one of the titles. Then some marketing guy said, 'Let's just call it *Centurion*.' I was a little bit, 'I don't know about that.' I don't know how much that had to do with the success or it was just because the thing had reached a natural point where the sales are going to go up. But suddenly, it was a *Sunday Times* bestseller.

At that point, everything was fairly secure. Suddenly, the publisher wants more books, and two books a year and things like this. So I was beginning to get quite a lot of pressure, in a way, because I was teaching and suddenly the publisher wanted two books a year. You can teach and write one book a year relatively easily. But suddenly, when it becomes two books, then you're feeling under the cosh a bit. I was having lunch with a historical novelist and a friend of mine, called Chris Humphreys, who I think is one of the people who should be a massive success. But he's had a bad publisher and that's just the way these things go. I was saying, 'Look, it's a real problem.' He just asked me a very interesting question. He said, 'Look, Simon, how much are you making from teaching?' I told him. He said, 'How much are you making from writing?' That's the point I thought 'Oh, yes, so you can actually become a full-time writer.' That's the point at which I thought I'd take a sabbatical from teaching.

Of course, I've never gone back. I suppose the big gear shift came when another publisher was interested in poaching me. I was coming towards the end of a contract at Headline, and this other publisher came up. Somebody I had known at Headline had gone on to this other publisher. They said, 'Oh, we should do lunch sometime.' Of course, as so often is the case in these things, whenever publishers and agents take you out for lunch, it is never for friendship. There's always another agenda. So then he said, 'Oh, I'm coming up to Norwich sometime on business, do you want to drop in for dinner?' So we had some dinner, did some shooting and stuff. Then he said, 'Well, Simon, I'd really like to build your career with you.' So he came up with this offer. My agent went back to Headline and said, 'Look, we're thinking about moving, because we've had this offer.' It was a really interesting reaction. Headline sent two couriers to me on the same morning. The first one arrived with a letter threatening me with legal action, if I went to this other publisher. The second one arrived with an offer for the next deal that was above the price offered by the second publisher. Things just went a bit bonkers after that. Luckily, the way things tend to work in publishing is, as long as things are going relatively okay, whenever they offer you a certain thing, that becomes this new benchmark from which you negotiate up. So things have worked out quite well. Certainly well enough to pay for one messy divorce and get remarried. So it's working out.

Kate Mosse, novelist

I'll start with *Labyrinth*. It was a book that had been bought at auction. So there was a certain amount of interest about it. Then I spent the next few years writing it. I spent longer than I should have done writing it, because I had a job, this is the thing. I would say that it was not an auspicious publishing, in a way, because *Labyrinth* published on the 7th of July 2005, which is, as many of your slightly older audience will know, the day the bombs went off in London. So I was going up to London for a book that I had been thinking about for 10 years, and today was coming out. I got off. This is, again, before everybody had mobile phones, and you've got alerts, and everybody knew everything straightaway. I got off the train. I started to walk through London. I thought, 'This is really weird. There's so many people out and about.' I mean, it felt oddly crowded. Then I arrived at my publishers, and my publisher said, 'How the hell are you here?' I was like, 'What do you mean?' They said, 'You haven't heard? Four bombs have gone off in London, there's lots of people missing, lots of people dead.' It was, of course, the worst thing for London and for all those families. So book publication is completely irrelevant. I only say this, because what is so interesting is what happened to the book. There was lots of advertising on the underground, obviously, that was all shut. Basically, nothing was going to happen. Rightly so, because we needed to think about the stuff that matters. But booksellers were hand-selling it. For anybody who doesn't know, that means if somebody goes into a bookshop and says, 'Can you recommend a book?' the bookseller says, 'What about this one?'

At the end of the first week on sale, against all the odds and expectations, it went into number ten in the hardback chart. That was beyond my expectation. None of us could quite believe it. I honestly felt that was going to be the biggest moment of my life, actually. My lovely husband actually laminated the *Sunday Times* with me at number ten, because we thought that would be the thing that would go on the wall. It felt amazing. Then just this weird thing happened. Normally what happens is all the sales are at the beginning. You go in at a certain point in a chart, and then you slip down the charts, week after week, unless you're Richard Osman, obviously, and then you're at the top of the chart for all of time. And that's an amazing and wonderful thing. But for me, what happened was, it was at number ten. Then it was at number nine, and then it just worked its way up to the top of the chart – that felt like the most extraordinary thing. I knew that people that I had never met must be reading it. It was absolutely wonderful. We went to Carcassonne [a town in France where Kate Mosse has a house] for the summer. People would send me pictures of the copy they'd bought, and it felt like this unbelievable moment.

Why do I think it happened? It's very hard to put your finger on why one book suddenly soars. It isn't because it's the best book. There's always some alchemy that makes that happen. But I actually think, genuinely, I benefited from another author. That author was Dan Brown with *The Da Vinci Code*. That novel, it was a very transformational moment. It was a great quest novel. Millions of people had read it. They were looking for novels that they felt would connect in the same sort of way. Then I had a review in the newspaper. Now this is not my view of Dan Brown's book, I hasten to add, but I had a review in the newspaper saying, 'This is the Dan Brown for people with A-levels.' It's awful, of course. But my publisher slapped that all over the universe, of course. The algorithms do their job.

So I genuinely think that part of *Labyrinth*'s success can be put down to coming after Dan Brown. One of the most interesting things about what Dan Brown's book did was, so many men were talking about the fact they hadn't read a novel for years, and they were reading him. My books are for anyone who likes my sorts of books, if you like an adventure story, it's for you. I write women's stories. But I write for male and female readers who like that kind of thing. So there was a whole new load of relatively new readers who were looking for more to read. I think I've benefited enormously from that.

Then the final thing that made it the book that topped the overall chart for 2006, and has made it sell over eight million copies now and all of these things, was being picked for Richard and Judy's Book Club, in the days when it was on the television. It's absolutely terrifying when you're on that, because you're not there. They make a film about you, which is lovely, but you don't know what Richard and Judy are going to say about the book and you don't know what their guests are going to say about the book. They might quite like it; they might not like it very much. So I was sitting at home with my children in Bognor Regis, which is where we lived at the time. Five in the afternoon, with a huge glass of wine, shaking, all of us sitting holding hands. We lived in a small place; everybody lives close by or very close. My mum had told absolutely everybody that I was going to be on the television. I was just thinking, 'Oh my god, if it's a terrible review, it'd be awful.' Even in my mum's village, the butcher, of all people – I'm vegetarian – had put up a sign that said, 'Barbara and Richard's daughter on the television tomorrow.' So if it was going to be a catastrophe, we're going down in flames.

Fortunately, they loved it. The day after it was on Richard and Judy, it sold 65,000 copies. It was top of the charts for seven months. Most of us will never have that experience. It was not at all what I'd ever expected to happen to me. I was incredibly lucky to have those things that happened. That just meant that it was that book, that time. I never stopped being grateful for that, because it transformed our lives. We went from being a writer and a teacher and completely normal, needing to do lots of extra work and lots of journalism and lots of things. I had a full-time job and my husband worked part-time, because he was a teacher . . . What it meant was that I could give up doing any other job. I could be a full-time writer. That is the dream for all of us, that you can actually write in the day, you're not writing around your other job and your other responsibilities. It's not what you expect to happen at 45, for your life to change so much. So I still, whenever I see Richard or Judy, I still say thank you. Because it really did change our lives.

ACKNOWLEDGEMENTS

Always Take Notes would not exist without the generosity of its interviewees. Over the past six years, scores of people from across the literary world have been willing to give up their time and share their experiences, wisdom, regrets and triumphs. We'd like to thank each and every guest – whether they're quoted here or not – for speaking to us and handling our probing questions with grace. Your candour is what makes *Always Take Notes* a valuable resource for writers everywhere.

Those insights wouldn't reach listeners without the efforts of our producer, Artemis Irvine. Thank you for your ideas, enthusiasm and efficiency, and for always seeking inventive ways to reach new audiences. (We'll produce a viral Instagram Reel one day, we're sure of it.) Thank you, too, to the previous producers of the show – Katy Lee, Nicola Kean, Olivia Crellin, Ed Kiernan and Elizabeth Davies – for helping us put together this great archive of material. We're grateful to Jessica Dannheisser, who wrote our theme music, and to James Edgar, who designed the podcast's visual identity. Thanks too to Jessica Hudson, Hayden Cooke and Alex Wade for their legal wisdom, and to Zahra Hankir and Eoin Redahan for their work on social media at different times.

We'd like to salute Kassia St Clair, who helped set up *Always Take Notes* back in 2017. She was a thoughtful and fun collaborator, and it has been wonderful to see her tremendous success in the years since. Ellie Halls, who co-hosted from 2018 to 2019, was also an insightful interviewer with a wide-ranging knowledge of the magazine industry. To both of you: thank you for all you did to take the show from strength to strength.

We owe a debt of gratitude to Patrick Walsh, our literary agent, and Rebecca Sandell at PEW Literary for all their help in bringing this project to fruition. Thank you also to our brilliant editor at Ithaka Press, Sarah Braybrooke: this book benefited enormously from her astute feedback. Not only did she help shape the wealth of material into something coherent and compelling, but she also offered patient, wise counsel through various administrative challenges. She has been a great partner for, and champion of, *Always Take Notes*. We're also grateful for the work of Sarah's colleague Leonie Lock, and Francine Brody for her careful copy editing.

Finally, we'd like to thank the audience of the podcast. When we speak to guests we sometimes forget that anyone else is listening, and every time we receive feedback and suggestions from listeners – in particular when we hear someone has found *Always Take Notes* useful – it makes what we do seem worthwhile.

From Simon:
From my side, thanks first to Rachel, the co-host of *Always Take Notes*. Before I started working with her, I was told that: 'If you were trying to invade a country, she's the kind of person you would want as your chief of staff' – and this is entirely true; her formidable powers of organisation continue to impress and on occasion astonish me, not least at certain critical points of bringing this book together. Rachel is also a thoughtful and adroit interviewer,

an extremely straightforward person to work with, and a kind friend. So much of my work is solitary, and I treasure this collaborative and creative part of my life with her.

I'd also like to thank my girlfriend Hyun – who has lived with this podcast for all the time we've been together. Hyun has been as supportive of first the show and later this book as she is of all my literary and creative endeavours, and has also offered insightful suggestions of her own. Not for the first time, thank you Hyun. Also my parents Michael and Margaret, and my brother Thomas.

I'm grateful to all the editors who make my life as a writer possible, in particular Arabella Pike at HarperCollins, Morgan Entrekin at Grove Atlantic, Jonathan Beckman at *The Economist*'s *1843* magazine, Jeremy Keehn at *Businessweek* and David Wolf at *The Guardian* Long Read. Further to our joint note, it's also a pleasure to be working again with Sarah Braybrooke, who proved such a thorough and courageous supporter with my previous book *The Changing of the Guard*. It's satisfying to see your career continue to blossom.

Finally, much of the critical work of pulling this book together was done while I was in the Alps working on *Snowlines*, my new book project. I'd like to thank Michael and Anita Wicky, who made me so welcome in their house in Worb outside Bern during those vital final weeks.

From Rachel:
I've had the privilege of co-hosting *Always Take Notes* since 2020, and I owe that honour entirely to Simon. Thank you for taking a chance on a young journalist with no podcasting experience and for all the guidance you have provided since. Your determination, organisation and kindness have always been evident, but in recent months I have also come to appreciate your ability to see the funny

side of almost any setback. To paraphrase Rudyard Kipling, thank you for keeping a cool head when I was losing mine.

Thank you to my colleagues at *The Economist* – particularly Andy Miller and Imogen White – who have long been supportive of my work on *Always Take Notes*. It still seems miraculous that I am able to work with such talented people and make a living talking about books, TV and film with them. I'm grateful to them both for encouraging me to go after new opportunities and for indulging my (usually unfunny) anecdotes.

My parents, Fiona and Chris, not only nurtured my love of literature in childhood, but urged me to pursue it as an adult – even as my siblings entered more sensible and stable professions. Thank you for everything you have done, and continue to do, for me. I owe my sister, Sophie, a huge thank you for supplying legal and financial advice and for being such an enthusiastic supporter of all my endeavours. My brothers, Matthew and Timothy, have always been sources of intelligence and wit. The physical fights over new editions of *Harry Potter* were character building.

Lastly, I am forever grateful to my fiancé, James. When editing this book, I spent whole weekends hunched over my laptop with my headphones on; he provided sustenance in the form of cups of coffee, sage counsel, silly jokes and words of encouragement. Thank you for being the most patient, most brilliant person I know.

Always Take
Notes hosts

Simon Akam, co-host, 2017–present

Simon Akam (@simonakam) is a British magazine journalist and author. His writing has appeared in publications including the *New Yorker*, the *London Review of Books*, *The Economist*, *The Guardian*, *Outside*, the *New York Times*, and *GQ*. Simon's first book, *The Changing of the Guard – the British Army since 9/11*, was published in 2021 to widespread acclaim. The *Times Literary Supplement*, choosing a book of the year, described it as 'A state-of-the-nation book of resounding power, deep conviction and far-reaching significance.' Simon's second book, *Snowlines*, will be published by HarperCollins in the UK and Grove Atlantic in the US.

Rachel Lloyd, co-host, 2020–present

Rachel Lloyd (@rachelsllloyd) is the deputy culture editor of *The Economist*. As well as writing reviews and essays, she commissions stories on books, television, film, music, architecture and comedy for the weekly print edition and the website. In 2021 she was nominated for Young Journalist of the Year by the Society of Editors for her 'very absorbing' writing and 'excellent coverage of the arts in time of covid crisis'. In 2022 she completed a diploma in Script Development at the National Film and Television School. Prior to joining *The Economist*, Rachel worked at literary agencies in London and New York.

Eleanor Halls, co-host, 2018–2019

Eleanor Halls (@eleanorhalls1) is a culture writer, editor and podcaster. She is the music editor and associate cultural editor at *The Telegraph* and also co-hosts the pop culture podcast *Straight Up* with Kathleen Johnston alongside monthly special guests including Nile Rodgers, Sophie Ellis-Bextor, Pandora Sykes, Zack Snyder, Sean Paul and RAYE. Previously she was senior staff writer at *GQ* magazine, where she interviewed everyone from Stormzy and Jeremy Corbyn to Naomi Campbell and Jeff Bridges. Her media newsletter *PassTheAux*, for which she has written about the toxicity of fan culture, how AI has affected journalism and fiction's gender divide, is available on Substack.

Kassia St Clair, co-host, 2017–2018

Kassia St Clair (@kassiastclair) is Britain's bestselling historian under 40. Her first book, *The Secret Lives of Colour*, a top-ten bestseller, was selected as Radio 4's Book of the Week and has been translated into twenty languages. *The Golden Thread: How Fabric Changed History* was a Radio 4 Book of the Week, a *Sunday Times* Book of the Year and was shortlisted for the Somerset Maugham Award. Her third book, *The Race to the Future*, will be published in the UK in November 2023 and in the US in 2024. Her features, interviews, essays and reviews have appeared in *The Economist*, *The Telegraph*, *Architectural Digest*, the *TLS* and *Wired*.

CONTRIBUTORS'
BIOGRAPHIES

Ferdinand Addis, historian

Ferdinand Addis is the author of *Rome: Eternal City*, a narrative history of Rome which spans 3,000 years over some 650 pages. He has been fascinated by the Italian city since reading Livy as a teenager. He studied classics at university before embarking on a career as a journalist and author. He wrote three short books for the publisher Michael O'Mara before moving on to his epic biography of Rome, which was published in 2018. He is now working on a history of Roman Britain. We interviewed Ferdinand in 2019.

Monica Ali, novelist

Monica Ali is the author of novels including *Brick Lane, Alentejo Blue, In the Kitchen, Untold Story* and *Love Marriage*. *Granta* named her one of their best young British novelists in 2003 ahead of the publication of her first book, *Brick Lane*, which was then adapted into a film in 2007. Monica has been nominated for awards including the Booker Prize, the National Book Critics

Circle Award and the Orwell Prize. *Love Marriage*, her latest work, was an instant *Sunday Times* bestseller; an adaptation is in development at the BBC. We interviewed Monica in 2022.

Jon Lee Anderson, journalist and author

Jon Lee Anderson is a staff writer at the *New Yorker* and the author of several books, including *Guerrillas: Journeys in the Insurgent World*, *Che Guevara: A Revolutionary Life*, *The Fall of Baghdad* and *The Lion's Grave: Dispatches from Afghanistan*. Along with his brother, Scott Anderson, he co-authored *Inside the League* and *War Zones*. He began writing for the *New Yorker* in 1998 and has covered conflicts in Afghanistan, Angola, Lebanon, Libya, Iraq, Somalia and Sudan – to name a few – for the magazine; he has also written extensively about Latin America. We interviewed Jon Lee in 2019.

Leaf Arbuthnot, journalist and novelist

Leaf Arbuthnot is an assistant editor at the *Week* and has written for publications including the *New Statesman*, *the Sunday Times*, *The Times*, *Tatler* and *Vogue*. Her first novel, *Looking for Eliza*, about the unlikely friendship between two lonely women in Oxford, was published in 2020. She has also written *The Birthday Party*, a serialised novel. We interviewed Leaf in 2021.

Jeffrey Archer, novelist

Jeffrey Archer has sold more than 275m copies of his books worldwide. He wrote his first novel aged 34, when a failed business deal left him heavily in debt. His third novel, *Kane and Abel*, sold over 1m copies in its first week of release in 1979. He has now written more than 20 novels, alongside short stories, a play and non-fiction, and is published in 97 countries and more than 33 languages. Archer was deputy chairman of the Conservative party in the 1980s and was made a life peer in 1992. In 1999 he stood as the Conservative candidate for mayor of London. He later withdrew his candidacy, having been charged with perjury and conspiracy to pervert the course of justice. He served two years in prison, and subsequently published a three-volume diary of his time inside. We interviewed Jeffrey in 2019.

James Ashton, journalist and author

James Ashton has been a financial journalist for more than 20 years. He was city editor of the *Sunday Times*, then city editor and executive editor of the *Evening Standard* and *Independent*. He has also written for *Business AM*, the *Daily Mail*, *The Scotsman*, *The Telegraph*, *The Times* and Reuters. He is the author of books including *The Nine Types of Leader* and *FTSE: The Inside Story*. His latest book, *The Everything Blueprint: The Microchip Design That Changed the World*, was published in May 2023. We interviewed James in 2021.

Sara Baume, novelist

Sara Baume featured on *Granta*'s 2023 list of Best Young British Novelists. She is the author of three novels, *Spill Simmer Falter Wither*, *A Line Made by Walking* and *Seven Steeples*, as well as a work of non-fiction, *Handiwork*. *Spill Simmer Falter Wither* was shortlisted for the Costa First Novel Award and longlisted for *The Guardian* First Book Award and the Desmond Elliott Prize. Her work has also won the Davy Byrnes Short Story Award, the Hennessy New Irish Writing Award, the Rooney Prize for Irish Literature and an Irish Book Award for Best Newcomer.

Her fiction and criticism have appeared in publications including *The Irish Times*, *The Guardian* and *Granta* magazine. We interviewed Sara in 2017.

Jonathan Beckman, journalist, editor and author

Jonathan Beckman is the editor of *1843*, *The Economist*'s magazine of long-form storytelling. Before joining *The Economist*, he was senior editor of the *Literary Review*. He is the author of *How to Ruin a Queen: Marie Antoinette, the Stolen Diamonds and the Scandal that Shook the French Throne*, for which he won the Somerset Maugham award and the RSL/Jerwood Award for Non-Fiction. We interviewed Jonathan for our first-ever episode in 2017.

Oliver Bullough, journalist and author

Oliver Bullough is a journalist and author who specialises in writing about corruption and dirty money. After studying history at university Oliver moved to Russia, where he worked first for an English-language magazine in St Petersburg, then for the *Times of Central Asia* in Kyrgyzstan, and subsequently for Reuters, where he covered the war in Chechnya. Oliver's early books – *Let Our Fame Be Great* in 2010 and *The Last Man in Russia* in 2013 – examined respectively the Caucasus and a dissident Orthodox priest. His more recent books have focused on financial crime, with *Moneyland* in 2018 and in 2022 with *Butler to the World*. Oliver's journalism also appears in *The Guardian*, the *Sunday Times*, the *New York Times* and *GQ*. We interviewed Oliver in 2022.

William Boyd, novelist and screenwriter

William Boyd was born in Ghana and grew up there and in Nigeria. His novels, many of which have been bestsellers, include *A Good Man in Africa*, *The New Confessions*, *Any Human Heart*,

Restless and *The Romantic*. He has won the Somerset Maugham Award, the James Tait Black Memorial Prize and the Prix Jean Monnet. His numerous screenwriting credits include adaptations of Evelyn Waugh's *Scoop* (1988) and *Sword of Honour* trilogy (2001), as well as the film *The Trench* in 1999, which he also directed. His collections of short stories include *On the Yankee Station* (1981), *The Destiny of Nathalie 'X'* (1995) and *Fascination* (2004). His work has been translated into 30 languages. We interviewed William in 2021.

Ed Caesar, journalist and author

Ed Caesar is a contributing staff writer to the *New Yorker* and the author of two books. *Two Hours*, published in 2015, followed the world's greatest long-distance runners and their efforts to beat marathon records; the book won a British Sports Book Award. *The Moth and the Mountain*, published in 2020, chronicled Maurice Wilson's attempt to climb Everest in 1934. Before joining the *New Yorker*, Ed's work was published in the *Atlantic*, *Esquire*, the *Independent*, *GQ*, the *New York Times Magazine* and the *Sunday Times Magazine*. He has reported from a wide range of countries, including the Democratic Republic of Congo, Kosovo, Iran and Russia. We interviewed Ed in 2019.

Candice Carty-Williams, novelist

Candice Carty-Williams is a novelist and showrunner for television. Her debut novel, *Queenie*, earned a six-figure advance and, after publication in 2019, became a bestseller and won Blackwell's Debut Book of the Year and Book of the Year at the British Book Awards. The novel is being adapted for television by Channel 4 and Disney. An original TV show written by Candice, *Champion*, will be released on the BBC and Netflix in 2023. Candice formerly worked in publishing and in 2016 created and launched *The Guardian* and 4th Estate BAME Short Story Prize for under-represented writers. We interviewed Candice in 2017.

Tracy Chevalier, novelist

Tracy Chevalier is the author of ten novels, including *Girl with a Pearl Earring*, which has sold more than 5m copies worldwide and been adapted into a film, a play and an opera. Tracy moved to Britain from America in the 1980s and worked in publishing before completing an MA in Creative Writing at the University of East Anglia. Her other novels include *Remarkable Creatures*, about two eccentric 19th-century women searching for fossils on English beaches; *The Last Runaway*, focusing on an English Quaker who emigrates to Ohio in the 1850s and helps runaway slaves; and *A Single Thread*, which features a group of female embroiderers in Winchester in the 1930s. We interviewed Tracy in 2021.

Amanda Craig, novelist

Amanda Craig is the author of novels including *Foreign Bodies*, *A Vicious Circle*, *The Lie of the Land* and *The Golden Rule*. Her new novel, *The Three Graces*, was published in June 2023. At the beginning of her career, after a brief spell in advertising and PR, Amanda became a journalist – writing for the *Sunday Times*, *The Observer*, *The Telegraph* and the *Independent* – and went on to win the Young Journalist of the Year and the Catherine Pakenham Awards. She was the children's critic for the *Independent on Sunday* and continues to review children's fiction for the *New Statesman* and literary fiction for *The Observer*. We interviewed Amanda in 2020.

Jennifer Croft, translator

Jennifer Croft won the Man Booker International Prize in 2018 for her translation of Olga Tokarczuk's Polish novel *Flights*. Jennifer has received a slew of other plaudits for her work, including NEA, Cullman, PEN, Fulbright and MacDowell awards, as well as the inaugural Michael Henry Heim Prize for Translation. Her work has appeared in publications including the *New York Times*, *Granta*, *Vice*, *n+1* and *The Guardian*. We interviewed Jennifer in 2019.

William Dalrymple, historian and travel writer

While still at university in 1986, William set off to follow on foot the outward route of Marco Polo from Jerusalem to Mongolia and wrote a bestselling account of the journey, *In Xanadu*. In 1999, after three other books of travel, he concentrated on writing history. *White Mughals*, published in 2003, won the Wolfson Prize. *The Last Mughal* won the Duff Cooper Memorial Prize. These books have now been combined with two others, *The Return of a King* and *The Anarchy*, to form a quartet on the rise and fall of the East India Company. That quartet itself is now in development to turn into a television drama series. William writes for the *New York Review of Books*, the *New Yorker* and *The Guardian*. In 2020 *Prospect* magazine named him as one of the world's top 50 thinkers. We interviewed William in 2021.

Louise Doughty, novelist

Louise Doughty is the author of ten novels, including *Apple Tree Yard*, a number-one bestseller which was adapted as a four-part series by the BBC. Her sixth novel, *Whatever You Love*, was nominated for the Costa Novel Award and Orange Prize for Fiction; her eighth novel, *Black Water*, was chosen by the

New York Times as one of their Notable Books of the Year. Louise has been nominated for many other awards including the *Sunday Times* Short Story Prize and the Crime Writers' Association Silver Dagger. She also created and wrote the BBC drama *Crossfire* (2022). Her work has been translated into 30 languages and her latest novel, *A Bird in Winter*, was published in August 2023. We interviewed Louise in 2020.

Robert Douglas-Fairhurst, academic and author

Robert Douglas-Fairhurst is a professor of English literature at Oxford University and a fellow of Magdalen College. His books include *Becoming Dickens: The Invention of a Novelist*, which won the Duff Cooper Prize for biography in 2011; *The Story of Alice: Lewis Carroll and the Secret History of Wonderland* (2015), which was shortlisted for the Costa Prize, and most recently the memoir *Metamorphosis: A Life in Pieces* (2023), which details his experience living with multiple sclerosis. After undergraduate studies and a PhD at Cambridge, Robert moved to Oxford in 2002. He has edited editions of Charles Dickens, Charles Kingsley and J.M. Barrie, and contributes to *The Guardian*, the *Literary Review*, the *New Statesman*, *The Spectator*, *The Times* and the *Times Literary Supplement*. He has also served as a judge for the Man Booker and Baillie Gifford prizes. We interviewed Robert in 2022.

Geoff Dyer, novelist and non-fiction writer

Geoff Dyer is a prolific author known for blurring genre boundaries. His many books – which have been published in 24 languages – include the novel *Jeff in Venice, Death in Varanasi*, *But Beautiful* (about jazz), *Yoga For People Who Can't Be Bothered To Do It*, *Zona* (about Andrei Tarkovsky's film *Stalker*) and *Broadsword Calling Danny Boy* (on the film *Where Eagles Dare*). Geoff has also edited selections of essays by John Berger and D.H. Lawrence and his awards include a Somerset Maugham Prize, a National Book Critics Circle Award, and the Windham Campbell Prize in Non-Fiction. We interviewed Geoff in 2020.

Sophie Elmhirst, journalist

Sophie Elmhirst writes regularly for *The Guardian* Long Read, the *Gentlewoman* and *The Economist*'s *1843* magazine, among other publications. In 2020 she won the British Press Award for Feature Writer of the Year and a Foreign Press Award for Finance and Economics Story of the Year. In 2021 she was longlisted for the Orwell Prize for Journalism for pieces about Tampax, a hospital cleaner's life during the pandemic and the battle over how women give birth. Her first book, *Maurice and Maralyn*, about a British couple shipwrecked in the Pacific Ocean in 1973, will be published in 2024. We interviewed Sophie in 2020.

Merve Emre, author, academic and literary critic

Merve Emre is a contributing writer for the *New Yorker*, the Shapiro-Silverberg Professor of Creative Writing and Criticism at Wesleyan University and the Director of the Shapiro Centre for Creative Writing and Criticism. After a stint as a management consultant, Merve completed a PhD and has taught English literature at McGill University in Canada and Oxford University. Alongside her academic work, Merve has written books including *Paraliterary: The Making of Bad Readers in Postwar America* and *The Personality Brokers* (published in Britain as *What's Your Type?*), about the Myers-Briggs personality test. As well as the *New Yorker*, her essays have been published in the *New York Review of Books*, the *New York Times Magazine*, the *Atlantic* and the *London Review of Books*. We interviewed Merve in 2022.

Anne Enright, novelist

Anne Enright is the author of novels including *The Gathering*, *The Forgotten Waltz*, *The Green Road* and *Actress*, as well as a book of non-fiction, *Making Babies*, and several short stories. *The Gathering*, which was published in 2007, won the Booker Prize; Anne has also received the Andrew Carnegie Medal for Excellence in Fiction and the Kerry Group Irish Fiction Award. In 2015 she was appointed the first Laureate for Irish Fiction and in 2018 she received the Irish PEN Award for Outstanding Contribution to Irish Literature. In 2022 she was given the Lifetime Achievement Award by the Irish Book Awards. We interviewed Anne in 2020.

Niall Ferguson, historian

Niall Ferguson, the author of 16 books, is the Milbank Family Senior Fellow at the Hoover Institution, Stanford University, and a senior faculty fellow of the Belfer Centre for Science and International Affairs at Harvard. His books include *The Pity of War: Explaining World War One* (1998), *Empire: How Britain Made the Modern World* (2003), and a life of Henry Kissinger, the first volume of which was published in 2015 as *Kissinger, 1923–1968: The Idealist*. His most recent book is *Doom: The Politics of Catastrophe* (2021). Niall's awards include the Benjamin Franklin Prize for Public Service (2010), the Hayek Prize for Lifetime Achievement (2012), the Ludwig Erhard Prize for Economic Journalism (2013) and Columnist of the Year at the 2018 British Press Awards. We interviewed Niall in 2018.

Maggie Fergusson, journalist and author

After studying history at university, Maggie Fergusson briefly worked in finance before joining *Harper's & Queen* magazine (now known as *Harper's Bazaar.*) As a freelance writer, she was sent by *The Times* to interview the Scottish poet George Mackay Brown in 1992, and it proved the beginning of a friendship that would culminate with a prizewinning biography, published in 2006. *George Mackay Brown: The Life* won the Saltire First Book Prize, the Marsh Biography Award, the Yorkshire Post Book of the Year Award and the Scottish Arts Council Biography Award. Maggie has also written a biography of children's author Michael Morpurgo, subtitled *War Child to War Horse*, which was published in 2012. She became Secretary of the Royal Society of Literature in 1989; she continues to work at the RSL as the Literary Advisor and edits their annual magazine. We interviewed Maggie in 2022.

Orlando Figes, historian

Orlando Figes is author of nine books on Russian and European history, which have been translated into more than 30 languages. Born in London, he studied history at Cambridge University and, as a graduate student, completed archival research in the Soviet Union in the 1980s. He rose to prominence in 1996 with his second book, *A People's Tragedy: The Russian Revolution 1891–1924*, which the *Times Literary Supplement* later named as one of its '100 most influential books since the war'. His subsequent works include *Natasha's Dance: A Cultural History of Russia*, *Crimea: The Last Crusade* and *The Europeans*, and until recently he was a professor of history at Birkbeck College, University of London. His debut play, *The Oyster Problem*, which grew out of

The Europeans and focuses on Gustave Flaubert, premiered in 2023. We interviewed Orlando in 2023.

Cal Flyn, journalist and author

Cal Flyn worked as an investigative reporter for the *Sunday Times* and data reporter at *The Telegraph* before turning to literary non-fiction. Her first book, *Thicker Than Water*, which dealt with colonialism in Australia and intergenerational guilt, was published in 2016 and selected by *The Times* as one of the best books of the year. Her second book, *Islands of Abandonment*, about abandoned places, was published in 2021. The book was a *Sunday Times* bestseller and was shortlisted for the Baillie Gifford Prize, the Royal Society of Literature's Ondaatje Prize and the Wainwright Prize, among other awards. We interviewed Cal in 2018.

Aminatta Forna, novelist and non-fiction writer

Aminatta Forna is the author of a memoir, *The Devil that Danced on the Water*, about her father – a dissident who was executed in Sierra Leone – as well as several award-winning novels, including *Happiness*, *The Hired Man*, *The Memory of Love* and *Ancestor Stones*. She has also published *The Window Seat*, a collection of essays. The recipient of a Windham Campbell Award from Yale University, Aminatta has won the Commonwealth Writers' Prize Best Book Award and been a finalist for the Neustadt Prize for Literature, the Baillie Gifford Prize, the Women's Prize for Fiction and the IMPAC Award. Her work has been translated into more than 20 languages. Currently Aminatta is the director of the Lannan Centre at Georgetown University and is a Professor of Creative Writing at Bath Spa University. We interviewed Aminatta in 2021.

Oliver Franklin-Wallis, journalist and author

Oliver Franklin-Wallis is a magazine journalist and features editor of British *GQ*. His own work has appeared in *Wired*, British *GQ*, *The Guardian*, the *New York Times*, the *Times Magazine*, the *Sunday Times Magazine* and *The Economist's 1843* magazine, among other publications. In 2017 he was named Print Writer of The Year by the British Society of Magazine Editors and in 2021 he won Freelance Writer of the Year at the Freelance Writing Awards. His first book, *Wasteland: The Dirty Truth About What We Throw Away, Where It Goes, and Why It Matters*, was published in June 2023. We interviewed Oliver in 2017.

Hadley Freeman, journalist and author

Hadley Freeman was a staff writer at *The Guardian* from 2000 to 2022, working in London and the US on the fashion desk, as a features writer and as a columnist. She now writes for the *Sunday Times* and has also contributed to other publications including the British and American editions of *Vogue*. She has written several books: *The Meaning of Sunglasses* was published by Penguin in 2009, *Be Awesome: Modern Life for Modern Ladies* and *Life Moves Pretty Fast: The Lessons We Learned from 80s Movies*, were published by 4th Estate in 2014 and 2016 respectively. Hadley's bestselling family memoir, *House of Glass: The Story and Secrets of a Twentieth-Century Jewish Family*, was published in 2020 and the paperback was Waterstone's Book of the Month in March 2021. Most recently, HarperCollins published *Good Girls: A Story and Study of Anorexia* in 2023. We interviewed Hadley in 2020.

Jeremy Gavron, novelist and non-fiction writer

Jeremy Gavron is the author of novels including *Moon, The Book of Israel* (winner of the Encore Award for best second novel) and

An Acre of Barren Ground. In 2015 he published *A Woman on the Edge of Time*, a non-fiction book about his mother, an academic who committed suicide in 1965, when Jeremy was four years old; the book was shortlisted for the Gordon Burn Prize. *Felix Culpa*, released in 2018, was a novel pieced together from lines from more than eighty other books. We interviewed Jeremy in 2018.

Ann Goldstein, translator

Ann Goldstein is an editor and translator. She joined the *New Yorker* in 1974 and rose to become the head of the copy department in the 1980s. During her time at the American magazine she began studying Italian and translating works into English. Since then she has translated fiction by Alba de Céspedes, Primo Levi and Pier Paolo Pasolini. Ann is perhaps best known for her translations of Elena Ferrante's phenomenally successful *Neapolitan Quartet*; the books have sold more than 10m copies in 40 countries. Ann has won the PEN Renato Poggioli prize and an award from the Italian Ministry of Foreign Affairs, among other accolades. We interviewed Ann in 2019.

Lennie Goodings, publisher and author

Lennie Goodings is the chair of Virago Press. Born in Canada, Lennie came to Britain in the 1970s and joined Virago as a publicist in 1978. In subsequent roles – first in marketing, then as publisher – Lennie worked with authors including Maya Angelou, Margaret Atwood and Sarah Waters. She won the Bookseller's Industry Award for Editor and Imprint of the Year in 2010, a Lifetime's Achievement Award at the Women of the World festival in 2018 and was elected as an Honorary Fellow of the Royal Society of Literature in 2020. Her book, *A Bite of the Apple*, a memoir-cum-history of Virago, was published in 2020. We interviewed Lennie in 2021.

James Graham, playwright and screenwriter

James Graham is one of Britain's best-known contemporary playwrights and has also written widely for film and television. James's first award was the Pearson Playwriting Bursary in 2006. His big break came when his 2012 play, *This House*, written for the National Theatre and set in the British parliament in the 1970s, enjoyed a sell-out run and garnered widespread critical acclaim. His subsequent work includes the 2017 play *Ink*, about the early days of Rupert Murdoch's career, *Brexit: An Uncivil War* (2019), which was broadcast on Channel 4 and HBO and starred Benedict Cumberbatch, and *Dear England* (2023) about the renaissance of the English football team under manager Gareth Southgate. His work has won several Olivier Awards and been nominated for a BAFTA, an Emmy and several Tony Awards. We interviewed James in 2019.

Linda Grant, novelist and non-fiction writer

Linda Grant began her career as a journalist, writing for *The Guardian* and the *Independent on Sunday*, before publishing *The Cast Iron Shore*, her first novel, in 1996. Her subsequent books include a family memoir about her mother's dementia, *Remind Me Who I Am, Again* (1998), the novels *When I Lived in Modern Times* (2000), *Still Here* (2002), *The Clothes on their Backs* (2008) and *Stranger City* (2019), and a non-fiction book on Israel, *The People on the Street* (2005). She won the Orange Prize for Fiction in 2000 and the Lettre Ulysses Prize for Literary Reportage in

2005, and was shortlisted for the Man Booker Prize in 2008. We interviewed Linda in 2020.

Mark Haddon, novelist

Mark Haddon's bestselling novel, *The Curious Incident of the Dog in the Night-Time* (2003), won 17 literary prizes, including the Whitbread Award, and has sold over 10m copies worldwide. It was the first book to be published simultaneously in two imprints, one for children, one for adults. In 2012 the National Theatre produced a stage adaptation that went on to win seven Olivier Awards in 2013 and the 2015 Tony Award for Best Play. Mark's other novels include *A Spot of Bother* (2006), which was short-listed for the Costa Novel Award, *The Red House* (2012) and *The Porpoise* (2019). He has worked as an illustrator for publications including the *New Statesman*, *Private Eye* and *The Guardian*, written and illustrated numerous children's books, produced a book of poetry, and won awards for both his radio dramas and his screenplays. We interviewed Mark in 2019.

Tessa Hadley, novelist and short-story writer

Tessa Hadley is the author of eight novels. Her first, *Accidents in the Home* (2002), was published when she was 46 and was longlisted for the Guardian First Book Award. *The Past* (2015), about tensions running beneath a family holiday in an inherited house, won a Windham-Campbell Literature Prize. Her most recent novel, *Free Love*, detailing a married woman's affair with a younger man in the 1960s, appeared in 2022. Tessa regularly publishes short stories in the *New Yorker* and a new collection of her short fiction, *After the Funeral*, was published in 2023. She taught literature and creative writing at Bath Spa University. We interviewed Tessa in 2023.

Andrew Hankinson, journalist and author

Andrew Hankinson is the author of two books. His debut, *You Could Do Something Amazing with Your Life* [*You Are Raoul Moat*], was a work of narrative non-fiction published in 2016; it told the true story of Raoul Moat, who went on a shooting spree in the north of England in 2010, from the murderer's perspective. His second book, *Don't Applaud. Either Laugh or Don't.*, was about the Comedy Cellar in New York. Elsewhere, he has written for the *FT Weekend Magazine*, *The Guardian*, the *New Statesman*, the *New Yorker*, *The Observer* and *The Spectator*. He also hosts *Logroll*, a podcast about non-fiction books. We interviewed Andrew in 2019.

Joanne Harris, novelist

Joanne Harris worked as a teacher for 15 years, during which time she published three novels, including *Chocolat* (1999), which was made into an Oscar-nominated film starring Juliette Binoche. The success of *Chocolat* allowed her to become a full-time writer, and since then she has written 19 more novels, plus novellas, short stories, game scripts, the libretti for two short operas, several screenplays, a stage musical and three cookbooks. Her books are now published in over 50 countries and have won a number of British and international awards. She has been a judge for the Whitbread Prize, the Orange Prize, the Desmond Elliott Prize, the Betty Trask Award, the Prima Donna Prize and the Royal Society Winton Prize for Science. She is currently the chair of the Society of Authors and a member of the Board of the Authors' Licensing and Collecting Society. We interviewed Joanne in 2018.

Max Hastings, journalist and author

Max Hastings is the author of 30 books, including *Bomber Command* (which won the Somerset Maugham Prize), *The Battle* for the *Falklands*, *Overlord*, *Armageddon* and *Vietnam: An Epic Tragedy, 1945–1975*. He began his career as a foreign correspondent for the BBC and the *Evening Standard*; he went on to become editor-in-chief of the *Daily Telegraph* and the *Evening Standard*. Max was named Journalist of The Year and Reporter of the Year in the 1982 British Press Awards, and Editor of The Year in 1988. He reflected on his journalistic career in two memoirs, *Going to the Wars* and *Editor*, and continues to contribute to *Bloomberg*, *The Times* and the *Sunday Times*. We interviewed Max in 2018.

Giles Hattersley, journalist

Giles Hattersley is the features director at British *Vogue*. He studied English at Warwick University and completed an MA in fashion journalism before joining the *Sunday Times* in 2003. Working his way up from an intern on the Style section, he joined the News Review later that year and went on to become the paper's youngest-ever chief interviewer, aged 25, writing profiles of everyone from Beyoncé to Richard Dawkins. In 2007, he briefly became editor-in-chief of *Arena* magazine, before returning to the *Sunday Times*. In 2017, he was hired by Edward Enninful as features director of British *Vogue*, where he oversees the magazine's arts, politics, celebrity, lifestyle and social trend coverage. We interviewed Giles in 2020.

Lucy Hughes-Hallett, author and biographer

Lucy Hughes-Hallett is the author of books including *Cleopatra: Histories, Dreams and Distortions* and *Heroes: Saviours, Traitors and Supermen*. *The Pike*, a biography of Italian rake Gabriele d'Annunzio, won all three of Britain's most prestigious prizes for non-fiction in 2013: the Duff Cooper Prize, the Samuel Johnson

Prize and the Costa Biography of the Year award. She has also written a novel, *Peculiar Ground*, and a collection of short stories, *Fabulous*. At the beginning of her career, Lucy won the Catherine Pakenham Award for Young Female Journalists. She has written for publications including *The Guardian*, the *Evening Standard* and the *Sunday Times*. We interviewed Lucy in 2018.

Howard Jacobson, novelist

Howard Jacobson has written 16 novels and several works of non-fiction. In 2010 he won the Booker Prize for *The Finkler Question* (he was also shortlisted in 2014 for *J.*) Born in Manchester, Howard spent his early career as an academic; during the 1970s he taught at Wolverhampton Polytechnic in the West Midlands, an experience which provided the material for his first novel, *Coming from Behind*, published in 1983. Other novels include *Kalooki Nights* (2006), *The Act of Love* (2008), and *Live a Little* (2019). His memoir *Mother's Boy – A Writer's Beginnings* was published in 2022. We interviewed Howard in 2021.

Marlon James, novelist

Born in Jamaica in 1970, Marlon James's novel *A Brief History of Seven Killings*, which explores the attempted assassination of Bob Marley in 1976, won the Booker Prize in 2015. It was also a finalist for the National Book Critics Circle Award in the United States and a *New York Times* Notable Book. Marlon is now working on a trilogy of African fantasy novels, which began with *Black Leopard, Red Wolf*, a finalist for the US National Book Award for fiction in 2019, followed by *Moon Witch, Spider King* in 2022. His earlier novels include *The Book of Night Women*, which won the Dayton Literary Peace Prize in 2010, and *John Crow's Devil*, his debut in 2005. He teaches at Macalester College in Minnesota. We interviewed Marlon in 2022.

May Jeong, journalist

May Jeong is a contributing editor at *Vanity Fair*. She has spent many years reporting on Afghanistan and a months-long investigation into the bombing of the Médecins Sans Frontières hospital in Kunduz for the *Intercept* won several plaudits. Her work has also appeared in publications including *Harper's*, the *London Review of Books* and the *New York Times*. We interviewed May in 2019.

Dylan Jones, journalist, editor and author

Dylan Jones was the editor of British *GQ* between 1999 and 2021. He began his career in journalism at *i-D*, before moving to *The Face* and then *Arena*. He has also written for *The Guardian*, the *Independent*, *The Observer* and the *Sunday Times*. Alongside his journalism, Dylan has written or edited more than 25 books, including *Jim Morrison: Dark Star*, *David Bowie: A Life* and *Faster Than a Cannonball: 1995 and All That*. In 2012 he was awarded an OBE for services to publishing. We interviewed Dylan in 2018.

Ben Judah, journalist and author

Ben Judah has reported from across Europe and his writing on politics and society has appeared in a broad range of publications, including the *Sunday Times*, the *Financial Times*, *Politico*, the *New York Times* and *Foreign Policy*. He has interviewed and profiled French President Emmanuel Macron, Pakistan's former Prime Minister Imran Khan, and Rishi Sunak when he was UK chancellor. Ben's first book, *Fragile Empire: How Russia Fell In and Out of Love with Vladimir Putin*, was published by Yale University Press in 2013. His second book, *This is London: Life and Death in the World City*, published by Picador, was shortlisted for the Baillie Gifford Prize in 2016 and for the Ryszard Kapuscinski Award for Literary Reportage in 2019. His most recent book, *This is Europe: The Way We Live Now* was published in 2023. We interviewed Ben in 2018.

Sebastian Junger, journalist and author

Sebastian Junger is the *New York Times* bestselling author of *The Perfect Storm, Fire, A Death in Belmont, Wire, Tribe* and *Freedom*. Attracted since childhood to 'extreme situations and people at the edges of things', Sebastian grew up in New England and worked as a high-climber for tree removal companies. After a chainsaw injury, he decided to focus on journalism, primarily writing about people with dangerous jobs. That led to his debut book in 1997, *The Perfect Storm*, an account of the loss of a fishing boat, which went on to sell over 5m copies. Sebastian has reported on conflict in Afghanistan, the Balkans and West Africa. As a contributing editor at *Vanity Fair*, he established a partnership with photographer Tim Hetherington, with whom he collaborated on the documentary *Restrepo* in 2010. The film was nominated for an Oscar before Hetherington's death in Libya in 2011. We interviewed Sebastian in 2022.

Alex Kay-Jelski, journalist and editor

Alex Kay-Jelski is the editor-in-chief of *The Athletic UK*, a subscription-based sports website. Previously sports editor of *The Times* and the *Daily Mail*, Alex set up the British operations for *The Athletic* in 2019, hiring well-known names from other publications (and new young journalists) in a move that shook up the sportswriting scene. In January 2022 the *New York Times* acquired *The Athletic* for $550m. As of May 2023, it had 3.3m subscribers. We interviewed Alex in 2022.

Patrick Kingsley, journalist and author

Patrick Kingsley is the Jerusalem bureau chief for the *New York Times*. He joined the newspaper in 2017, first as Turkey bureau chief, and then as a roving writer, reporting from places including the Czech Republic, Finland, Germany, Greece, Hungary, Malta, Moldova, Spain, Switzerland, South Africa and Zimbabwe. Patrick previously worked for *The Guardian*, reporting from across the Middle East; in 2015 he was named its first-ever migration correspondent and won Foreign Affairs Journalist of the Year at the British Journalism Awards. His first book, *How to Be Danish* (2012), was an exploration of contemporary Danish society. His second book, *The New Odyssey* (2016), chronicled the European refugee crisis. We interviewed Patrick in 2018.

Sam Knight, journalist and author

Sam Knight has been a staff writer at the *New Yorker* since 2018. He has written profiles of snooker player Ronnie O'Sullivan, former Labour leader Jeremy Corbyn, and Prime Minister Theresa May. His first book, *The Premonitions Bureau*, was published in 2022 and became a *Sunday Times* bestseller. Previously, Sam's work for the Long Read section of *The Guardian* became influential and widely shared. 'London Bridge is Down', his article on plans for the Queen's death, published in 2017, was viewed almost 4m times and remains the most popular *Guardian* Long Read ever published. He has won two Foreign Press Association Awards and was shortlisted for the 2018 Orwell Prize for political writing. We interviewed Sam in 2017.

Christina Lamb, journalist and author

Christina Lamb is the *Sunday Times*'s chief foreign correspondent. She started her reporting career in 1987, when she was in her early 20s; her coverage of Afghan mujahideen fighting with Soviet forces earned her the Young Journalist of the Year award at the British Press Awards. Since then she has worked all over the world and won a slew of awards, including Europe's top war reporting prize, the Prix Bayeux. Alongside her journalism, Christina has written ten books, including *The Africa House*, *I Am Malala* (with Malala Yousafzai), *Farewell Kabul* and *Our Bodies, Their Battlefield*. We interviewed Christina in 2019.

Simon Lancaster, speechwriter and author

Simon Lancaster started writing speeches for members of Tony Blair's cabinet in the late 1990s and now runs Bespoke Speechwriting Services. He has written speeches for top politicians and the CEOs of some of the biggest companies in the world, including Unilever, Rio Tinto, HSBC and Nestlé. Simon is the author of *Speechwriting: The Expert Guide* (2009); *Winning Minds: Secrets from the Language of Leadership* (2015); *You Are Not Human: How Words Kill* (2018) and *Connect! How to Inspire, Influence and Energise Anyone, Anywhere, Anytime* (2022). He is a fellow at Henley Business School, lectures at Cambridge and Oxford Universities, and regularly appears as a media pundit on oratory. His TEDx 'Speak Like a Leader' talk has received more than 4m views on YouTube. We interviewed Simon in 2020.

Helen Lewis, journalist and author

Helen Lewis is a staff writer at the *Atlantic*, where she covers the politics of culture. She started her career on the training programme for sub-editors at the *Daily Mail* and worked at the tabloid newspaper for several years. In 2010 she joined the *New Statesman* and became deputy editor there. In 2020 Helen published *Difficult Women: A History of Feminism in 11 Fights*, which was named a BBC Radio 4 Book of the Week. She has also appeared on radio and television; in 2022 Helen hosted *The New Gurus*, an eight-part podcast. We interviewed Helen in 2018.

Alexander McCall Smith, novelist

Alexander McCall Smith is the creator of *The No. 1 Ladies' Detective Agency* series of novels, which have sold over 20m copies in English alone. He was a professor of medical law before turning his hand to writing fiction, and his first book, *The White Hippo*, a children's title, was published in 1980. The first novel in the *No. 1 Ladies' Detective Agency* series appeared in 1998. His other series include the *44 Scotland Street* novels, the *Isabel Dalhousie* books and the *Ulf Varg* series of 'Scandi blanc' set in Sweden. Alexander's work has been translated into 46 languages and in 2007 he received a CBE for services to literature. In 2015 he received the Bollinger Everyman Wodehouse Prize for Comic Fiction and in 2017 The National Arts Club (of America) Medal of Honour for Achievement in Literature. We interviewed Alexander in 2020.

Colum McCann, novelist

Colum McCann is the author of seven novels, three collections of stories and two works of non-fiction. His novel *TransAtlantic* was longlisted for the Booker Prize in 2013, and his previous novel,

Let the Great World Spin, won the National Book Award, the International IMPAC Dublin Literary Award and was a *New York Times* bestseller. His most recent novel, *Apeirogon* (2020) became another *New York Times* bestseller and was again longlisted for the Booker. His first major non-fiction book, *American Mother*, will be published in 2024. His work has been published in over 40 languages and he teaches on the MFA programme at Hunter College in New York. Colum is also the president and co-founder of the non-profit global story exchange organisation, Narrative 4. We interviewed Colum in 2020.

Ian McEwan, novelist

Ian McEwan is the critically acclaimed author of 17 novels and two short-story collections. He was the first-ever student on the University of East Anglia's celebrated creative-writing course, and his earliest published work, a collection of short stories, *First Love, Last Rites*, won the Somerset Maugham Award in 1976. Ian's novels include *The Child in Time*, which won the Whitbread Novel of the Year Award in 1987; *The Cement Garden*; *Enduring Love*; *Amsterdam*, which won the Booker Prize in 1998; *Atonement*, which won the National Book Critics' Circle Fiction Award in 2003; *Saturday*; *On Chesil Beach*; *Solar*; *Sweet Tooth*; *The Children Act*; *Nutshell*; and *Machines Like Me*, which was a number-one bestseller. *Atonement, Enduring Love, The Children Act* and *On Chesil Beach* have all been adapted into films. We interviewed Ian in 2023.

Hollie McNish, poet

Hollie McNish is an award-winning poet, writer and performer. After initially rising to prominence online, she has published four collections of poetry: *Papers, Cherry Pie, Why I Ride* and *Plum. Nobody Told Me*, a collection of prose and poetry about parenthood taken from Hollie's diaries, was additionally published in 2016 and won the Ted Hughes award for New Work in Poetry. In 2021 she released *Slug: and other things I've been told to hate*, a bestselling memoir that again mixes poetry and prose. She has also recorded an album of poetry and music, co-written a play about the history of women's football in Britain, and completed a reimagining of *Antigone*. We interviewed Hollie in 2021.

Rebecca Mead, journalist and author

Rebecca Mead is a staff writer at the *New Yorker* and the author of three books. *One Perfect Day*, published in 2007, explored the wedding industry. *My Life in Middlemarch*, a mix of biography, literary criticism and memoir, was published in 2014; it was a *New York Times* bestseller and named a book of the year by several newspapers. *Home/Land*, published in 2022, reflected on leaving New York (where she had lived for 30 years) to return to Britain. At the *New Yorker* she has profiled individuals ranging from Margaret Atwood to Lin-Manuel Miranda. In 2020 she was a recipient of a Guggenheim Fellowship. We interviewed Rebecca in 2019.

Sian Meades-Williams, journalist and author

Sian Meades-Williams is a writer and the creator and editor of *Freelance Writing Jobs*, a weekly media-industry newsletter. She has written for publications including *The Guardian*, the *Independent*, *The Times* and the *New York Times*. In 2021 she launched the Freelance Writing Awards. In 2022 she published *The Pyjama Myth*, a guide to 'the highs, lows and in-betweens of life in the competitive world of freelance writing'; later that year *Belville*, her novel-in-progress, won the Yeovil Literary Prize. We interviewed Sian in 2022.

Jed Mercurio, screenwriter and novelist

Jed Mercurio is a television writer, producer, director and novelist. A former hospital doctor and Royal Air Force officer, Jed made his entry into television after he answered an advert in the *British Medical Journal* seeking advisors for a hospital drama; he was soon scripting the BBC series *Cardiac Arrest*. Jed's subsequent television credits include *Bodies*, *Bodyguard*, *Lady Chatterley's Lover* and *Line of Duty*. Jed's screenwriting work has achieved award wins or nominations at the BAFTAs, Emmys and Golden Globes and he has also published several novels, including *Ascent* (2007) which focuses on a Soviet fighter-pilot-turned-cosmonaut. We interviewed Jed in 2023.

Kiran Millwood Hargrave, poet and novelist

Kiran Millwood Hargrave is best known for her award-winning children's fiction. She started writing poetry in her final year at university, producing three poetry books and a play before turning to children's stories. Her bestselling debut, *The Girl of Ink & Stars*, about a mapmaker's daughter who must save her island, won the Waterstones Children's Book Prize in 2017 and the British Book Awards Children's Book of the Year. Her second standalone story, *The Island at the End of Everything*, was short-listed for the Blue Peter Book Award and the Costa Children's Book Award. Her third book, *The Way Past Winter*, was the Blackwell's Children's Book of the Year in 2018. Her first book for adults, *The Mercies*, debuted at number one on *The Times* bestseller chart. It was named a *New York Times* Notable Book of the Year and won a Betty Trask Award. We interviewed Kiran in 2017.

David Mitchell, novelist

David Mitchell is the author of nine novels, including *Cloud Atlas*, *The Thousand Autumns of Jacob de Zoet* and, most recently, *Utopia Avenue*. He featured as one of *Granta*'s Best Young British Novelists in 2003 and has been nominated for the Booker Prize five times. His work has appeared in over 30 languages, and in 2007 *Time* magazine named him one of the 100 most influential people in the world. David's novel *The Bone Clocks* (2014) won the World Fantasy Book Award and his screenwriting credits include *Matrix: Resurrections*. With KA Yoshida, David has also translated from the Japanese the internationally bestselling memoir *The Reason I Jump*. We interviewed David in 2022.

Peter Moffat, playwright and screenwriter

A barrister-turned-writer, Peter Moffat started out with plays – his first, *Fine and Private Place* was broadcast on BBC Radio – before going on to create several television dramas, including *Criminal Justice*, *Silk* and *North Square*, for which he won the Broadcasting Press Guild Writer's Award. He was awarded two BAFTAs for *Criminal Justice*, which was the basis for HBO's Emmy-winning series *The Night Of*, starring Riz Ahmed. Other credits include the mini-series *Cambridge Spies*, the television film *Einstein and Eddington*, and the series *The Last Post*, which was inspired by his father's role in the Royal Military Police. His American series for Showtime, *Your Honor*, stars Bryan Cranston and he also created *61st Street* with Michael B. Jordan as an executive producer. We interviewed Peter in 2018.

Charles Moore, journalist and author

Charles Moore was selected by Margaret Thatcher to write her authorised biography, which appeared in three volumes – *Not for Turning, Everything She Wants* and *Herself Alone* between 2013 and 2019. He joined the staff of the *Daily Telegraph* in 1979, and as a political columnist in the 1980s covered several years of Mrs Thatcher's first and second governments. He was editor of the *Spectator* 1984–1990; editor of the *Sunday Telegraph* 1992–1995; and editor of the *Daily Telegraph* 1995–2003, for which he is still a regular columnist. The first volume of his biography of Margaret Thatcher won the Elizabeth Longford Prize for Historical Biography, the H.W. Fisher Best First Biography Prize and Political Book of the Year at the Paddy Power Political Book Awards. We interviewed Charles in 2019.

Kate Mosse, novelist

Kate Mosse is the author of ten novels and short-story collections, as well as four plays and four works of non-fiction. She is also the founder and director of the Women's Prize for Fiction, the largest annual celebration of women's writing in the world. Kate's books, which have been translated into 38 languages, have sold over 5m copies and are published in more than 40 countries. *Labyrinth*, the first volume in her hit *Languedoc Trilogy*, was the bestselling title in Britain in 2006. *Sepulchre* (2007) and *Citadel* (2011) followed. Another series, *The Joubert Family Chronicles*, comprises *The Burning Chambers* (2018), *The City of Tears* (2020) and *The Ghost Ship* (2023). Kate's non-fiction includes *An Extra Pair of Hands*, a memoir about caring, and *Warrior Queens & Quiet Revolutionaries: How Women (Also) Built the World*. We interviewed Kate in 2021.

Fraser Nelson, journalist and editor

Fraser Nelson is the editor-in-chief of the *Spectator*, a role he has held since 2009. Previously a financial journalist with *The Times* and political editor of *The Scotsman*, during his tenure at *The Spectator* Fraser has overseen a near doubling of the magazine's sales. He is also a columnist with the *Daily Telegraph*, sits on the board of the Centre for Social Justice, a centre-right think tank, and has presented two Channel 4 documentaries on the subject of inequality. We interviewed Fraser in 2023.

David Nicholls, novelist and screenwriter

In 2009 David's novel *One Day* was a global bestseller, published in 40 languages, and he is also the author of *Sweet Sorrow*, *Us*, *The Understudy* and *Starter for Ten*. On screen, David has written adaptations of *Far From the Madding Crowd* and *When Did You Last See Your Father?*, as well as turning his own novels *Starter for Ten* and *One Day* into feature films. His adaptation of Edward St Aubyn's *Patrick Melrose*, starring Benedict Cumberbatch, was nominated for an Emmy and won a BAFTA for Best Writer. Other works for TV include episodes of *Cold Feet*, *Tess of the d'Urbervilles* and two-part love story *The 7.39*. We interviewed David in 2022.

Rosie Nixon, editor and novelist

Rosie Nixon is the creative brand ambassador of *HELLO!* magazine and the author of three novels (*The Stylist*, *Amber Green takes Manhattan* and *Just Between Friends*) as well as a work of non-fiction, *Be Kind*. She has worked in the magazine industry for more than 20 years and previously held senior roles at *Grazia*, *Glamour* and *Red*. In 2017 Rosie was named Editor of the Year by the British Society of Magazine Editors in the entertainment and celebrity category. From 2016 to 2023 she was the editor-in-chief of *HELLO!* We interviewed Rosie in 2021.

Ruth Ozeki, novelist

Ruth Ozeki is a novelist, film-maker and Zen Buddhist priest. In the 1980s Ruth worked in film, first as an art director and production designer for low-budget horror films, then as a writer, producer and director of independent films. *Halving the Bones* (1995), a documentary about bringing her grandmother's remains over from Japan, was nominated for the Grand Jury Prize at the Sundance Film Festival. Her first novel, *My Year of Meats*, was published in 1998 and *All Over Creation* followed in 2003. In 2010 Ruth was ordained as a Soto Zen Buddhist priest. *A Tale for the Time Being*, published in 2013, was shortlisted for the Booker Prize. Ruth won the Women's Prize for her most recent novel, *The Book of Form and Emptiness* (2021). We interviewed Ruth in 2022.

George Packer, journalist and author

A staff writer for the *Atlantic* and a former staff writer for the *New Yorker*, George Packer is the author of *The Unwinding: Thirty Years of American Decline*, which was a *New York Times* bestseller and won a National Book Award in 2013. His other non-fiction books include *The Assassins' Gate: America in Iraq*, *Blood of the Liberals*, which won the Robert F. Kennedy Book Award in 2001, *Our Man: Richard Holbrooke and the End of the American Century* and *Last Best Hope: America in Crisis and Renewal*. He has also written two novels, *The Half Man* and *Central Square*. George's writing has appeared in the *New York*

Times Magazine, *Mother Jones*, *Harper's* and other publications. We interviewed George in 2022.

Christina Patterson, journalist and author

Christina Patterson is a writer, broadcaster and consultant. She began her career in publishing and worked as a literary programmer for the Southbank Centre; from 2000 to 2003 she was director of the Poetry Society. She joined the *Independent* and wrote columns and interview pieces as well as investigations into nursing, for which she was shortlisted for the Orwell Prize in 2013. Christina published her first memoir, *The Art of Not Falling Apart* in 2018, and *Outside, the Sky is Blue: A Family Memoir*, in 2022. She continues to write for the *Sunday Times* and *The Guardian* and frequently appears on radio and television. We interviewed Christina in 2022.

Alex Perry, journalist and author

Alex Perry is a journalist, author and writer for film and television. His books include *Falling Off the Edge*, *Lifeblood* and *The Rift*. *The Good Mothers*, a book about the women who exposed the true might of the Calabrian mafia, was excerpted in the *New Yorker* in 2018 and adapted into a television mini-series in 2023; the show was screened at the Berlin International Film Festival where it won the inaugural Series Award. His journalism has won several awards and has appeared in *The Guardian*, *Harper's*, *Newsweek*, the *Sunday Times Magazine* and *Time*, among other publications. We interviewed Alex in 2019.

Patrick Radden Keefe, journalist and author

Patrick Radden Keefe is an award-winning staff writer at the *New Yorker* magazine and author of the *New York Times* bestsellers

Empire of Pain – about the Sackler family's role in the opioid crisis in America – and *Say Nothing*, which investigates a murder in Northern Ireland during the Troubles. His earlier non-fiction books, *The Snakehead* and *Chatter*, examined Chinatown crime and the shadowy world of signals intelligence respectively. Patrick started contributing to the *New Yorker* in 2006. He received the National Magazine Award for Feature Writing in 2014. *Say Nothing* received the National Book Critics Circle Award for Non-Fiction as well as the Orwell Prize for Political Writing. *Empire of Pain* was awarded the Baillie Gifford Prize for Non-Fiction. We interviewed Patrick in 2020.

Ian Rankin, novelist

Ian Rankin is the multi-million-copy bestseller of over 30 novels and the creator of Detective John Rebus. Ian's books have been translated into 36 languages and adapted for radio, the stage and the screen. He is the recipient of four Crime Writers' Association Dagger Awards, including the Diamond Dagger, the UK's most prestigious award for crime fiction. He has also won America's Edgar Award, Denmark's Palle Rosenkrantz prize, the French Grand Prix du Roman Noir and Germany's Deutscher Krimipreis. After graduating from the University of Edinburgh in 1982 and before success with his Rebus novels, Ian held several jobs including working as a grape-picker, a swineherd, a journalist for a hi-fi magazine, and a taxman. His first published novel, *The Flood*, appeared in 1986, and the first Rebus novel, *Knots & Crosses*, emerged the following year. We interviewed Ian in 2018.

Jay Rayner, journalist and author

Jay Rayner is *The Observer*'s restaurant critic. After studying politics at Leeds University, where he edited the student newspaper,

Jay entered national newspaper journalism, winning Young Journalist of the Year at the British Press Awards in 1992. The restaurant critic of *The Observer* since 1999, Jay has also worked extensively in television, including as a judge on *MasterChef.* In 2018 he was named Restaurant Writer of the Year in the Fortnum and Mason Food and Drink Awards. He has written several books, including *The Ten (Food) Commandments, Wasted Calories and Ruined Nights, My Last Supper* and *Chewing the Fat.* We interviewed Jay in 2020.

Tim Rice, lyricist

Tim Rice has worked in music, theatre and films since 1965. After initially considering a legal career, he began collaborating with composer Andrew Lloyd Webber, writing song lyrics for the hit musicals *Joseph and the Amazing Technicolor Dreamcoat* (first performed in 1968), *Jesus Christ Superstar* (1971) and *Evita* (1978). Tim has since worked with other distinguished popular composers such as Elton John (*The Lion King, Aida*) and Alan Menken (*Aladdin, Beauty and the Beast*). His awards include three Oscars, four Tonys, five Grammys and one Emmy. In recognition of his work in film and theatre, Tim was inducted as a Disney Legend in 2002. In 2008 he received a star on the Hollywood Walk of Fame. Tim was knighted by Queen Elizabeth II in 1994. We interviewed Tim in 2020.

Simon Scarrow, novelist

Simon Scarrow has sold over 5m books and his work has been translated into 24 languages. He worked as a schoolteacher before becoming a full-time writer, and his Roman-era *Eagles of the Empire* series, featuring soldier-heroes Cato and Macro, debuted in 2000 with *Under the Eagle.* Subsequent titles in the *Eagles* series include *Centurion, Praetorian* and *The Blood Crows*. Simon's other work includes a quartet of novels about the lives of the Duke of Wellington and Napoleon Bonaparte; *Sword and Scimitar*, a novel about the 1565 Siege of Malta; *Playing with Death*, a contemporary thriller written with Lee Francis; and a new series set in Berlin during the early months of the Second World War. We interviewed Simon in 2021.

Samira Shackle, journalist and author

Samira Shackle writes long-form features about a range of subjects, including inequality, gender, politics and terrorism, for publications including *Al-Jazeera, The Guardian* and *Prospect*. Her work has also appeared in a range of other outlets, including the *Independent, The Times, Monocle* and *Vice*. Her first book, *Karachi Vice: Life and Death in a Contested City*, published in 2021, is a modern history of Pakistan's largest city through the testimony of five ordinary citizens. It was chosen as a Radio 4 Book of the Week. We interviewed Samira in 2021.

Elif Shafak, novelist

Elif Shafak is the author of 12 novels and 7 works of non-fiction; her work has been translated into 56 languages. *The Forty Rules of Love* (2009) was chosen by the BBC as one of 100 novels that have shaped the world; *10 Minutes 38 Seconds in This Strange World* was shortlisted for the Booker Prize and the RSL Ondaatje Prize in 2019. Her latest novel, *The Island of Missing Trees*, was shortlisted for the Costa Book Awards in 2021 and chosen for Reese Witherspoon's influential book club. Elif holds a PhD in political science, and she has taught at various universities in America, Britain and Turkey, including St Anne's College, Oxford, where she is an honorary fellow. We interviewed Elif in 2022.

Jonathan Shainin, journalist and editor

Jonathan Shainin is the head of special projects at *The Guardian*. He started his career as a fact-checker at the *New Yorker* before moving to Abu Dhabi in 2007 to work on the *National*, an English-language newspaper. Between 2010 and 2013 he was a senior editor at the *Caravan*, India's first magazine of long-form journalism, before returning to the *New Yorker* as news editor. In 2014 he joined *The Guardian* and launched the paper's Long Read section. We interviewed Jonathan in 2018.

Nikesh Shukla, author

Nikesh Shukla is an author and screenwriter whose writing focuses on race, racism, identity and immigration. He edited the bestselling essay collection *The Good Immigrant* (2016), which featured 21 writers' reflections on race in Britain, including contributions from Riz Ahmed, Musa Okwonga, Bim Adewunmi, and Reni Eddo-Lodge. *The Good Immigrant* won the reader's choice at the Books Are My Bag Awards. Nikesh's debut novel, *Coconut Unlimited*, was shortlisted for the Costa First Novel Award in 2010. Other work includes the further adult novels *Meatspace* and *The One Who Wrote Destiny* and the young-adult title *Run, Riot*. Nikesh has written for *The Guardian*, *Esquire*, *Buzzfeed* and *Vice*. He was one of *Foreign Policy* magazine's 100 Global Thinkers in 2016 and was named one of the *Bookseller*'s 100 most influential people in publishing in 2016 and 2017. We interviewed Nikesh in 2018.

Rory Stewart, author

Rory Stewart has worked as an academic, diplomat, author, broadcaster, soldier and politician. After a brief period in the

British Army he joined the Diplomatic Service, serving overseas in Jakarta, Montenegro and as the coalition Deputy-Governor of two provinces in southern Iraq following the 2003 invasion. On leave from the Foreign Office he walked for 21 months, crossing Iran, Afghanistan, Pakistan, India and Nepal. That trip led to his first book, *The Places in Between* (2004), which was a *New York Times* bestseller. Other books include *The Marches* (2016), *Can Intervention Work?* (co-authored with Gerald Knaus in 2011) and *Politics on the Edge* (2023). Rory spent almost a decade in the British parliament, serving as Sceretary of State for International Development, Minister of the Environment and Minister of State for Justice. We interviewed Rory in 2018.

Samanth Subramanian, journalist and author

Samanth is a senior writer at *Quartz* and a contributing writer for *The Guardian* Long Read. His writing has also appeared in *Granta*, *Harper's*, the *New Yorker*, the *New York Times* and *The Economist*'s *1843* magazine, among other publications. He is the author of three books, *Following Fish: Travels Around the Indian Coast* (which won the Shakti Bhatt First Book Prize in 2010), *This Divided Island: Stories from the Sri Lankan War* (shortlisted for the Samuel Johnson Non-Fiction Prize and the Royal Society of Literature's Ondaatje Prize) and *A Dominant Character: The Radical Science and Restless Politics of J. B. S. Haldane*, published in 2020 (shortlisted for the Duff Cooper Prize). We interviewed Samanth in 2020.

Jack Thorne, playwright and screenwriter

Jack Thorne is a writer of film, television and theatre. He has won five BAFTAs for his television work on *The Fades*, *This is England*

'88, *Don't Take My Baby*, *This is England '90* and *National Treasure*; he also helmed the BBC's and HBO's adaptation of Philip Pullman's *His Dark Materials*. In film, his credits include *Wonder*, *The Swimmers* and *Enola Holmes*. In theatre, a play he co-wrote, *Harry Potter and the Cursed Child*, won multiple Olivier and Tony Awards. He debuted two new plays, *The Motive and the Cue* and *When Winston Went to War with the Wireless*, in 2023. We interviewed Jack in 2021.

Colin Thubron, travel writer and novelist

Colin Thubron worked in publishing in London and New York before writing his first travel book, *Mirror to Damascus*, in 1967. Other early books continued to focus on the Middle East, but later he was drawn towards the Soviet Union and Communist China. In 1982 Colin travelled by car into the Soviet Union, a journey described in *Among the Russians*. His best-known travel books include *Behind the Wall* (winner of the Hawthornden Prize and the Thomas Cook Travel Award), *In Siberia* (which won the Prix Bouvier), *Shadow of the Silk Road*, and most recently *The Amur River* (2021). Colin has also published eight novels, including *The God in the Mountain* (1977), *Turning Back the Sun* (1991) and *Night of Fire* (2016). Between 2008 and 2017 he served as president of the Royal Society of Literature. We interviewed Colin in 2022.

Kit de Waal, novelist and short-story writer

Born in Birmingham to an Irish mother and a Caribbean father, Kit de Waal worked for several years in criminal and family law, sitting on adoption panels and writing manuals on foster care. Her experience in this field informed her debut novel, *My Name is Leon*, which was published in 2016 (when she was in her 50s) following a six-way auction. It was later adapted into a television film in 2022. Her other work includes the novel *The Trick to Time, Becoming Dinah* (a young-adult title) and the memoir *Without Warning and Only Sometimes*. Kit has also worked to increase diversity in publishing, using some of her advance from *My Name is Leon* to fund a creative-writing scholarship and editing *Common People: An Anthology of Working-Class Writers* in 2019. We interviewed Kit in 2022.

Irvine Welsh, novelist and screenwriter

Irvine Welsh's first novel, *Trainspotting*, sold over 1m copies in Britain. He has written 12 further novels, four books of shorter fiction and numerous plays and screenplays. Born in the Leith area of Edinburgh, Irvine moved to London in 1978 where he immersed himself in the punk scene. In his early 20s he also spent 18 months addicted to heroin. After returning to Edinburgh he studied for an MBA and worked in the local council's housing department. *Trainspotting*, an account of Scottish heroin addicts written in a thick Leith dialect, was published in 1993. It became a cult success, helped by a film adaptation in 1996 directed by Danny Boyle. Irvine subsequently wrote two sequels and a prequel to *Trainspotting*, as well as a number of standalone novels, including *Glue* (2001) and *The Blade Artist* (2016). We interviewed Irvine in 2022.

Terri White, journalist and author

Terri White is a writer, broadcaster and the former editor-in-chief of *Empire* magazine. She began her journalism career working on titles including *Woman & Home* and *Marie Claire* before joining the launch team of *Nuts* in 2003. In 2010, aged 29, Terri became the editor of *ShortList*, a men's lifestyle magazine, and moved to New York in 2014 to run *Time Out New York*. During that time, Terri's mental health deteriorated and she ended up in a psychiatric ward – an experience she chronicled in her acclaimed memoir, *Coming Undone*. Now a freelance writer, she contributes to publications including *The Guardian*, the *New Statesman* and the *Sunday Times*. We interviewed Terri in 2021.

Henry Winter, journalist and author

Henry Winter is chief football writer at *The Times*. He has been writing about football for 35 years, covered England since 1994 and attended nine World Cups. He joined the *Independent* at its launch in 1986, moved to the *Daily Telegraph* in 1994 and joined *The Times* in 2015. Alongside his newspaper journalism, Henry ghost-wrote the autobiographies of Liverpool players Kenny Dalglish, John Barnes and Steven Gerrard, and co-wrote *FA Confidential* with former FA Chief Executive David Davies. He is also the author of *Fifty Years of Hurt: The Story of England Football and Why We Never Stop Believing*. We interviewed Henry in 2021.

Toby Young, journalist and author

Toby Young has written for *The Times*, *The Sun on Sunday*, the *Daily Mail*, the *Daily Telegraph* and has been a columnist at the *Spectator* since 1998. His book, *How to Lose Friends & Alienate People*, about his stint at *Vanity Fair*, was published in 2001. It became a bestseller and was adapted into a film in 2008 starring Simon Pegg and Kirsten Dunst. In 2006 he co-wrote a play called *Who's the Daddy?*; it won Best New Comedy at the Theatregoers' Choice Awards (now the WhatsOnStage Awards). Toby co-founded the West London Free School and is the general secretary of the Free Speech Union. We interviewed Toby in 2020.

Gary Younge, journalist and author

Gary is an author, broadcaster and a professor of sociology at the University of Manchester. He has written books including *Another Day in the Death of America*, *Stranger in a Strange Land* and *No Place Like Home*. Gary joined *The Guardian* in 1993, and after reporting from all over Europe, Africa, North America and the Caribbean, he was appointed *The Guardian*'s US correspondent in 2003. In 2015 he returned to London, where he became an editor-at-large; in 2020 he left the newspaper. *Dispatches from the Diaspora*, a collection of Gary's journalism, was published in 2022 and in 2023 he won the Orwell Prize for Journalism. We interviewed Gary in 2021.

INDEX

'One piece of advice that I wish I had had at the beginning of my career is not to just do whatever anybody asks you to do.' • 'It's very, very rare that you're going to have the time to sit down and write 2,000 words uninterrupted. So look at your diary, figure out where the times are and gun it when you have the time.' • *The great thing is just to begin - just to begin, not to be too overcome with fear at the task that faces you, the scale of the challenge. None of us is equal to the projects we take on, but we have to approach it like ants, a little bit at a time. It's amazing what gets done in the end.* • 'I've been rejected from absolutely everywhere and absolutely everything. It's good because I've gotten totally used to it.' • *'End each writing day at a point that you are not completely out of creative juice and you're pretty certain about what is going to happen next, because that makes it so much easier to pick it up the next morning.'* • 'You need to have faith in your work and that faith has to come from within.' • *Find out what you want to write and then work on that, pursue that. Don't be too mindful of what others say you should be doing. If you're doing it out of that, you're not going to learn to write and you're not going to write well: it has to come from within.'* • 'Never take other people's advice.'